LIFE, LETTERS AND SPEECHES

AMERICAN INDIAN LIVES

# LIFE, LETTERS & SPEECHES

GEORGE COPWAY
(Kahgegagahbowh)

Edited by
A. LaVonne Brown Ruoff
and Donald B. Smith

University of Nebraska Press
Lincoln and London

George Copway's work was originally published as *The Life, Letters and Speeches of Kah-ge-ga-gah-bowh or, G. Copway, Chief Ojibway Nation* (New York: S. W. Benedict, 1850). Acknowledgments for the use of previously published material also appear on p. ix.

⊖ The paper in this book meets the minimum requirements of American National Standard for Information Sciences – Permanence of Paper for Printed Library Materials, ANSI Z39.48-1984.

Library of Congress Cataloging-in-Publication Data
Copway, George, 1818–1863?
Life, letters and speeches / George Copway (Kahge-gagahbowh); edited by A. LaVonne Brown Ruoff and Donald B. Smith. p.   cm. – (American Indian lives)
Includes bibliographical references and index.
ISBN 0-8032-1470-7 (cloth: alk. paper)
1. Copway, George, 1818–1863? 2 Ojibwa Indians –
Biography. 3. Ojibwa Indians. I. Ruoff, A. LaVonne
Brown. II. Smith, Donald B. III. Title. IV. Series.
E99.c6c8 1997 973'.04973–dc20 [B] 96-35888 CIP

ISBN-13: 978-0-8032-6463-2 (paper: alk. paper)
ISBN-10: 0-8032-6463-1 (paper: alk. paper)

# Contents

# Preface

The text of this edition is from George Copway's *Life, Letters and Speeches of Kah-ge-ga-gah-bowh or, G. Copway, Chief Ojibway Nation* (New York: S. W. Benedict, 1850), which the editors selected because it contains letters and speeches not present in *The Life, History and Travels of Kah-ge-ga-gah-bowh* . . . (Albany NY: Weed and Parsons, 1847; Philadelphia: Harmstead, 1847).

Obvious errors in Copway's text that might lead to confusion, such as some misspellings, omitted punctuation marks, or duplicated words, have been corrected. In annotating the text, the editors have identified all individuals, events, places, and quotations they could find. Many of Copway's quotations from hymns and poetry are so obscure they do not appear in standard collections, concordances, or quotation lists. A. LaVonne Brown Ruoff annotated Copway's allusions pertaining to the United States and Donald B. Smith, those to Canada. The bibliography contains full references to published works; full bibliographic information on archival sources and city directories is included in the notes. Throughout the essays and annotations by Ruoff and Smith, tribal names are spelled according to current usage: *Ojibwe* rather than *Ojibwa* or *Ojibway*, *Pequot* rather than *Pequod*.

# Acknowledgments

A. LaVonne Brown Ruoff's research for this edition was done under grants from the Research and Fellowship Divisions, NEH, and the Institute for Humanities, University of Illinois at Chicago. Portions of her essay have appeared in her article "Three Nineteenth-Century American Indian Autobiographers," *Redefining American Literary History*, ed. A. LaVonne Brown Ruoff and Jerry W. Ward Jr. (New York: Modern Language Association, 1990); they are reprinted with permission of the Modern Language Association of America. She is grateful for the assistance of John Aubrey and other staff members at the Newberry Library, Chicago; this edition would not have been possible without access to its collections. Also invaluable were the assistance of David Himrod and the collections at the Union Library, Seabury-Western Theological Seminary and Garrett-Evangelical Theological Seminary, Evanston, Illinois. Daniel F. Littlefield Jr. also provided important information about Nicholas Cusick.

Donald B. Smith's essay was adapted from a paper presented at a conference on the Native in Literature: Canadian and Comparative Perspectives, the University of Lethbridge, Alberta, 14 March 1985; it later appeared as "The Life of George Copway or Kah-ge-ga-gah-bowh (1818–1869)—and a Review of His Writings," in the *Journal of Canadian Studies* 23.3 (1988): 5–38. He is extremely grateful to the Social Sciences and Humanities Research Council of Canada for a grant, awarded in 1993, for further research on the lives of six nineteenth-century Mississauga converts to Methodism, one being George Copway.

Both editors are especially grateful to Thomas King, who first introduced them at the Native in Literature Conference, University of Lethbridge, Alberta, in 1985. The present edition grew out of discussions begun at that conference.

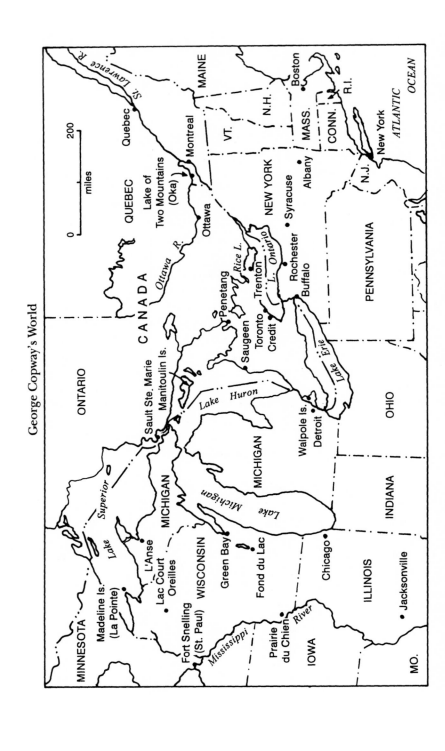

George Copway's World

# The Literary and Methodist Contexts of George Copway's *Life, Letters and Speeches*

A. LaVonne Brown Ruoff

## Background

*Life, Letters and Speeches* by George Copway (Ojibwe, 1818–69) is the first full-life autobiography written by a Native American reared within his traditional tribal culture.[1] As a Methodist convert, Copway created a life history that combines Western European forms of spiritual autobiography and missionary reminiscence with Native American oral traditions and ethnohistory. It is a rousing tale of growing up Ojibwe, conversion to Christianity, devotion to missionary duty, and perilous adventures in Indian country. His autobiography offers vivid insights into the author's transformation from a traditional Ojibwe into an acculturated missionary. It is also a valuable account of Ojibwe life and the missionary movement among Indians in Canada and the upper-midwestern United States in the early nineteenth century.

Since that time, American Indians have written personal narratives and autobiographies more consistently than any other form of prose. The full-length confessions or autobiographies of Western European literature are not part of Indian oral tradition. Barre Toelken comments that in many tribes "one is not to speak of himself in any full way until after he has become someone—such as having had many children or an illustrious life" (29–30).[2] Nevertheless, as H. David Brumble III concludes, there were at least six forms of American Indian preliterate autobiographical narratives: coup tales, which described feats of bravery; less formal and usually more detailed tales of warfare and hunting; self-examinations, such as confessions required for participation in rituals or accounts of misfortunes and illnesses; self-vindications; educational narratives; and tales of the acquisition of powers.[3] Although some Indian authors of

1

personal narratives consciously adopted literary forms popular among non-Indian readers, they often blended these with tribal narratives in which personal history was expressed within the contexts of the myths, stories, and histories of their tribes or bands, clans, and families. These narratives also incorporated forceful commentary on non-Indians' treatment of Indians.

When Native American authors first began to write personal narratives, the word *autobiography* was not in general use. Coined by Robert Southey in 1809, the term did not appear in the titles of books published in the United States until the 1830s. During the first half of the century, American Indian authors were more influenced in their choice of autobiographical form by spiritual confessions, which describe the subject's private or inner life, than by memoirs, which chronicle the subject's public career. As Christian converts, early Native American autobiographers such as William Apess (Pequot, b. 1798) and Copway consciously modeled their works on religious narratives, especially on spiritual confessions and missionary reminiscences.[4] Barry O'Connell notes that oral or written accounts of one's spiritual experience had been "mandatory for generations in most Protestant churches" (1–2). Among the literary models that helped shape conventional patterns for such testimony were John Bunyan's *Grace Abounding* (1666) and *Pilgrim's Progress* (1678 and 1684). Even homes with few books owned *Pilgrim's Progress* and the Bible. O'Connell stresses that those who could not read would have known these writings because they were often read aloud (1–2).

Spiritual confessions, which also influenced slave narratives, were logical models for both religious and ideological reasons. They linked Indian autobiographers to Protestant literary traditions and identified the authors as civilized Christians whose experiences were as legitimate subjects of written analysis as were those of other Christians. As G. A. Starr points out, writing any kind of autobiography assumes both one's own importance and the appropriateness of writing about one's experiences. Implicit in these assumptions is the Protestant principle that only an individual's exertions can influence his or her soul. Consequently each person must examine carefully the events in the development of the soul. Also implicit is the belief that because spiritual life varies little from person to person, individuals can measure their own spiritual state by that of others (Starr 4–5, 14).

The double value of spiritual autobiographies was that while they chronicled the author's spiritual development, they also enabled readers to repeat the process by identifying with the writers' spiritual pilgrimages (Starr 19, 27). Roy Pascal comments that the autobiographer relates experiences —the interaction of a person and events— rather than facts (16). Starr stresses that spiritual autobiographies placed little emphasis on the actual recording of experience. Undertaken as religious exercises, these works used facts purely as grounds for reflection (27). According to Daniel B. Shea Jr., the autobiographical act in the spiritual autobiographies of early America is reduced to testifying that one has conformed to certain patterns of feeling and behavior (9). This pattern is also reflected in slave narratives, which, as Francis Smith Foster points out, did not include positive information unless it could be used to contrast directly with a negative experience or to document slave customs: "Courtships and marriages, for example, occur between the lines or are briefly and impersonally mentioned" (112). These principles inform the structure of Copway's life history.

The task of achieving credibility for their personal narratives was as formidable to American Indians as it was to former slaves.[5] On the one hand, Native American autobiographers had to convince their readers that they were members of the human race whose experiences were legitimate subjects of autobiography and whose accounts of these experiences were accurate. On the other hand, they had the moral obligation to portray the harsh injustices they and their fellows suffered at the hands of white Christians. While chronicling their struggles either to achieve or to maintain a sense of individual identity, these narrators had to avoid antagonizing their white audiences. They also had the dual task of describing experiences common to slaves or Indians and those unique to themselves. However, these narrators were not typical of the groups they characterized because they could read and write. In addition, fugitive slaves who wrote differed from other slaves by having escaped bondage and Christian Indians differed from traditionals by having rejected Native for non-Native religion (Butterfield 15–18; Foster, *Witnessing Slavery* 67–70).

When the first personal narratives by American Indians were published, in the late 1820s, the tide of popular taste and of Indian-white relations ensured a ready audience for Indian authors. During this decade, increased literacy and cheaper methods of book production resulted in an expanded market for all kinds of books. Religious, slave, and captivity narratives as well as works about the West were popular during the 1820s and 1830s. The image of the Indians as "unfeeling savages" in captivity narratives competed with their representation as the "noble-but-doomed red men" in James Fenimore Cooper's Leatherstocking tales, widely read during this period (Pearce, 196–236; Berkhofer 86–95). The success of these narratives and the public's continuing interest in Indians stimulated Native Americans to publish their own autobiographies.

Indian-white relations also influenced the content and popularity of Indian autobiographies. The death knell for Indian hopes for retaining tribal lands east of the Mississippi was sounded in 1830 with the passage of the Indian Removal Act, which authorized the U.S. government to resettle Indians from these areas to Indian Territory, now Oklahoma, and other locations deemed suitable. As the Indian presence became less threatening, whites increasingly wanted to read about vanished "red men" or assimilated Indian converts to Christianity.

The first published, full-life history written by a Native American is William Apess's *Son of the Forest* (1829), which appeared in a revised and expanded edition in 1831.[6] Apess gives a shorter account of his life in *The Experiences of Five Christian Indians of the Pequod Tribe* (1833, rev. and repub. 1837). Barry O'Connell concludes that this shorter account was probably written before the publication of *A Son of the Forest* (1). When he was approximately four years old, Apess was taken from his alcoholic grandparents, who had abused him; from the age of five he was bound out to a series of white families. He later ran off to join the army during the War of 1812 and became a Methodist preacher. His life history focuses on growing up as an Indian among non-Indians and on his journey toward conversion, fall from grace, commitment to religion, and experiences as a Methodist minister.

Not until 1847, when Copway's *Life* appeared, was another full autobiography published by an Indian writer. Educated Indians had little leisure to write personal narratives, because they devoted their energies to helping their people retain tribal lands, obtain just compensation for land cessions, or gain civil rights. No sooner was removal implemented than whites violated it by migrating westward into Indian territories. What began as a stream of settlers in the 1830s became a flood by the 1850s. During removal, non-Indian authors lamented the passing of the "noble savage," doomed to extinction by the necessity of "Manifest Destiny." Cooper's Leatherstocking tales vividly portray this stereotype, as do the narratives about famous Indians and their tribes. In 1833 the narrated Indian oral autobiography, a major literary form in the late nineteenth and twentieth centuries, was introduced with the publication of *The Life of Ma-ka-tai-me-she-kia-kiak, or Black Hawk.* Narrated by Black Hawk (Sauk, 1767–1838) to translator Antoine Le Claire and revised for publication by John B. Patterson, this popular book went through five editions by 1847. Biographical dictionaries of famous Indians, such as Samuel Drake's *Indian Biography* (1832, repub. as *Biography and History of the Indians of North America*) and B. B. Thatcher's *Indian Biography* (1832), based on Drake's work, also were printed during this period (Berkhofer 88–89; Pearce 118; Krupat, *For Those Who Come After* 34–35, 45–47).

Paralleling the interest in the "noble-but-doomed" Indian were scientific studies of the Indian published in the late 1830s (Bieder 309–12). One of the most influential was Henry Rowe Schoolcraft's *Algic Researches* (1839), a study of Ojibwe and Ottawa cultures. The success in the 1830s of books about Indians created a literary climate favorable to the appearance of Copway's works. To a U.S. public imbued with the belief that the noble red man must assimilate or perish, this Ojibwe convert to Methodism from the woodlands of Canada seemed to represent what the Indian must become in order to survive—the embodiment of both the noble virtues of the savage past and the Western European culture of the civilized present. The public eagerly embraced Copway, who cast himself in this image in his *Life, History and Travels of Kah-ge-ga-gah-bowh (George Copway)* (1847). Letters and notices praising the book were appended to the second edition issued by James Harmstead. Enthusiasm for this autobiography was so great that it went through seven printings by 1848. A slightly revised edition, to which Copway added speeches and published letters, appeared in 1850 under two different titles: *The Life, Letters and Speeches of Kah-ge-ga-gah-bowh or, G. Copway, Chief Ojibway Nation* (New York) and *Recollections of a Forest Life: or, the Life and Travels of Kah-ge-ga-gah-bowh, or George Copway, Chief of the Ojibwey Nation* (London).

5

Copway's life history incorporates traditions from earlier written personal histories and from American Indian oral narratives. It is also a multi-voiced narrative of the self. Arnold Krupat argues that Native American autobiography consists of individually written autobiographies by Indians and compositely produced Indian autobiographies. Krupat distinguishes between these two forms as follows: "In Native American autobiography, the self is most typically not constituted by the achievement of a distinctive, special voice that separates it from others, but, rather, by the achievement of a particular placement in relation to the many voices without which it could not exist." Representing the encounter between a narrator and an editor (and sometimes translator) and between two cultures, these autobiographical texts are dialogic rather than monologic (*Voice in the Margin* 133). David Murray concludes that American Indian autobiographies have either required the ability of a particular Indian to comply "closely enough with the standards of written English and the conventions of literary marketing to be published or, much more commonly, the collaboration of several people" (67). Although Copway's *Life* is written rather than narrated to an editor or translator, nevertheless it is a multivoiced text that includes the voices of both Copway and his wife Elizabeth. It also contains the author's own multiple voices that express bi-cultural and conflicting points of view: the Ojibwe traditionalist versus the Native American assimilationist, the defender of Ojibwe religion and cultural traditions versus the champion of Christianity and American education, and the angry Indian protester versus the humble, pious missionary.

Copway's use of authenticating devices reflects one aspect of multivoiced discourse. Like the slave narrators, Copway incorporates documentation to prove that he is an educated man capable of writing an autobiography. In a prefatory "Word to the Reader," Copway humbly acknowledges that he has had only three years of school and has spoken English for only a few years.[7] However, he assures his readers that although a friend (probably his wife, Elizabeth) corrected all serious grammatical errors, Copway himself both planned and wrote the volume. To substantiate his literacy, he buttresses his volume with quotations from the Bible, hymns, and literature. No doubt Elizabeth, a writer and poet, supplied many of the literary references. The long letter he quotes from Rev. William J. Rutledge, his schoolmate at Ebenezer Manual Labor School in Jacksonville, Illinois; his numerous references to those he met on his travels; and the addition of his speeches and published letters in the revised edition—all substantiate his stature in the dominant society. Copway also uses documents to answer his critics. To counteract charges that he was not an *"authorized agent* to forward the interests of my poor people," Copway inserts Chief Joseph Sawyer's letter dated 4 July 1845, appointing him as agent for a proposed Canadian Manual Labor School, as well as his own letter pertaining to this role (Copway's emphasis).

Because Copway incorporates Ojibwe ethnohistory and oral traditions as well as the conventions of the spiritual confession and missionary reminiscence, his *Life* is far more complex in its structure than Apess's *Son of the Forest* or the slave narratives of the period. The first section is an ethnographic account of Ojibwe culture, in which Copway balances general descriptions with specific examples from personal experience. The second is devoted to the conversions of his band, family, and himself; the third, to his role as missionary and as mediator between Indians and whites; and the fourth, to a history of Ojibwe-white relations in the recent past.

Copway's blending of myth, history, and contemporary events, and his combining of tribal ethnohistory and personal experience, creates a structure of personal narrative that later American Indian autobiographers used as well. This mixed form, which differs from the more linear personal confession or life history found in non-Indian autobiographies, was congenial to Indian narrators accustomed to viewing their lives within the history of their tribe or band, clan, and family. Julie Cruikshank distinguishes between Native and non-Native concepts of autobiography. As Cruikshank compiled the personal narratives of three Athabaskan women from the Yukon, she discovered that they responded to her questions about secular events by telling traditional stories. Each explained that "these narratives were important to record as part of her life story." According to Cruikshank, the women's accounts included not only reminiscences of the kind we associate with autobiography but also detailed narratives on mythological themes. Cruikshank also notes that these women embedded songs in their chronicles, which they framed with genealogies and with long lists of personal and place names that appear to have both metaphoric and mnemonic value: the women "talk

7

about their lives using an oral tradition grounded in local idiom and a mutually shared body of knowledge" (2).

Copway's autobiography reflects this perspective of narrating one's life within a tribal context, as do numerous other American Indian oral and written personal histories. Copway, like the Athabaskan women whom Cruikshank interviewed, incorporates myths, stories, and songs into his personal narrative. In his *Traditional History* (1850), Copway emphasizes the importance of storytelling to him and his people: "There is not a lake or mountain that has not connected with it some story of delight or wonder, and nearly every beast and bird is the subject of the story-teller, being said to have transformed itself at some prior time into some mysterious formation—of men going to live in the stars, and of imaginary beings in the air, whose rushing passage roars in the distant whirlwinds" (95–96). Copway also stresses that the chiefs are the "repositories of the history of their ancestors." He delineates the rules that determine whether these traditions are true or false and that govern his own research: to inquire into the "leading points of every tradition narrated" and "to notice whether the traditions are approved by the oldest chiefs and wise men" (19).

Copway's goal is not to give an exhaustive account of his life and thoughts but rather to present himself as a typical Indian who, after conversion, exemplifies the ability of individuals in his tribe to become worthy members of mainstream society. Reticence to discuss one's personal life is characteristic of spiritual confessions and slave narratives as well as many American Indian personal histories. This is particularly evident in Copway's guarded discussion of his wife. He suddenly announces his marriage to Elizabeth Howell in 1840, without giving any details about how they met or their courtship. He describes her as "a help meet indeed," who shared his woes, trials, and privations, "faithfully labored to instruct and assist the poor Indians," and astonished him with her endurance. His characterization reflects the highly generalized depictions of missionaries' wives in most such reminiscences. The closest he comes to expressing his affection is his comment that he was distressed to see her ill from fever when they traveled near Prairie Du Chien, Wisconsin. One of the few instances in which he reveals her individual character is his description of how she and her sister tumbled stone Indian "deities" into the Mississippi River. He is equally reticent about his children.

The birth of his son, whose name is not given, on 9 April 1842 is an occasion for thanksgiving and an opportunity to remind readers of the dangers he and his family faced: "We thanked God for his goodness and mercy in preserving all our lives in the desert." The depth of his love for his son is clear from his vivid account of risking his own life to save the three-year-old from drowning, after the boy fell off a schooner. The birth of other children and the death of a child while he was traveling in Wisconsin are not mentioned (see D. Smith, this volume).

By beginning his narrative with the description of his life as an Ojibwe, Copway demonstrates his strong identification with his tribal culture.[8] Copway and other Christian Indian writers, like the African-slave writers, undertook the dual task of demonstrating to their audiences the virtues of traditional tribal life and the capacity of their race to adapt to white civilization after conversion and education in Western European traditions (Foster, *Witnessing Slavery* 11–13, 44–47). In the ethnographic sections on Ojibwe life, Copway adopts an overwhelmingly romantic and nostalgic tone. He unabashedly appeals to American affection for the stereotype of the Native American as a child of nature at the same time that he uses himself as an example of the Indian's adaptability to white civilization. He speaks in the double voice of the "noble savage" and the "pious convert" in this comment in chapter 1: "I loved the woods, and the chase. I had the nature for it, and gloried in nothing else. The mind for letters was in me, *but was asleep*, till the dawn of Christianity arose, and awoke the slumbers of the soul into energy and action" (Copway's emphasis). Throughout, Copway stresses that the differences between Natives and non-Natives consist of language and custom rather than humanity. Copway uses his own experiences to personalize his generalizations about tribal world-views and customs. The ethnographic sections are designed to persuade his audience of the value of tribal culture and the essential humanity of Indian people, goals of later Indian autobiographers as well. At the same time, he distances himself from these beliefs. In a passage added at the beginning of chapter 4 of the British edition of his *Life*, Copway begins his discussion of the Ojibwe religion by emphasizing the universality of "superstition": "Laugh as we may at another's simplicity and folly, the civilised and uncivilised have always had their notions of ghost-spirits." In his overview of Ojibwe world-

9

views, he emphasizes the spirituality of his people, their belief in "Ke-sha-mon-e-doo," the Great Spirit who made the world, and "Mah-he-mah-ne-doo," the Bad Spirit. His description of the Grand Medicine Lodge, one of the Ojibwe's most sacred rituals, is much briefer than the detailed version in *Traditional History*, where he also narrates the myth of its origin.

Copway stresses that the Ojibwe moral code, which embodies universal human values, links Native and non-Native cultures. Quoting maxims that emphasize kindness, generosity, and respect for parents, the aged, and the indigent, the author concludes that adherence to these precepts brought Indians peace and happiness until they were weaned away by the settlers' whiskey. He suggests a common ground between Native and non-Native cultures with his descriptions of visions and dreams, which played an important role in the Christian conversion literature of the period and were included in Indian oral autobiographies.

Copway documents his inside knowledge of Ojibwe culture by including information about such topics as tribal oral history, clan systems, government, building wigwams, rules that govern hunting grounds, hunting techniques, war songs, and dances. The extracts about Ojibwe life and status from the Report of the Board of Commissioners to the Canadian Provincial Parliament, completed in 1844, further authenticate his narrative. Through the portrayals of his family, the author gives us a sense of Ojibwe heritage and everyday life. Although Copway comments that he "cannot boast of an exalted parentage, nor trace the past history to some renowned warrior in days of yore," nevertheless his descriptions of his family's background demonstrate his pride in his "fathers" who "endured much." Copway proudly proclaims that his great-grandfather, a member of the Crane clan, was the first to settle at Rice Lake after the Ojibwes defeated the Hurons: "He must have been a daring adventurer—*a warrior*—for no one would have ventured to go and settle down on the land from which they had just driven the Hurons . . . unless he was a great hero" (Copway's emphasis).

The author also depicts his father, a medicine man in the early part of his life, as a heroic warrior in the episode in which he bravely confronts seven Mohawks, taking away their guns and the beaver skins they trapped on his hunting ground. Copway adds dimension to this character sketch by portraying his father as "ever kind and affectionate" to him and as a patient teacher. The incidents in which the father instructs the son about basic laws of Ojibwe life, the significance of the author's boyhood vision, and the descriptions of hunting techniques exemplify tribal education and the power of the oral tradition. Copway further emphasizes that his father had always been friendly to non-Indians, a detail clearly designed to capture his readers' sympathy. The author includes less information about his mother, a member of the Eagle clan, describing her as "kind and affectionate," happy "when she saw us enjoying ourselves," and a good hunter. He counteracts the stereotypical myths about Indian mothers not loving their children by describing how she went hungry in order to feed her youngsters. His emphasis on how hard his parents worked to provide for their family undercuts the stereotype of "lazy, improvident Indians."

One of the most moving episodes is his depiction of how his family almost starved after being imprisoned in their birch-bark wigwam for eleven days by heavy snow, with only boiled birch bark, beaver skins, and old moccasins for food. By the tenth day, most of the family was too weak to walk: "Oh how distressing to see the starving Indians lying about the wigwam with hungry and eager looks; the children would cry for something to eat. My poor mother would heave *bitter sighs of despair*, the tears falling from her cheeks profusely as she kissed us" (Copway's emphasis). The poignancy of such hardships tempers the idyllic scenes of Indian life amid the gentle beauty of nature.

At the same time that he strives to educate his readers about traditional Ojibwe culture, Copway distances himself from that culture through his consistent references to the difference in his behavior before and after conversion to Christianity. Like Samson Occom (Mohegan, 1723–92), Copway often adopts the humble voice of the "poor savage" who recognizes the superiority of the religion and culture of the dominant society, as he makes clear in his preface: "I am an Indian, and am well aware of the difficulties I have to encounter to win the favorable notice of the white man" (see Occom, "A Short Narrative" and *A Sermon* 959). In his "Word to the Reader," Copway emphasizes that he has just been brought out of a "wild and savage state"; he is a "stranger in a strange land!" Later he disassociates himself from such customs as the hunter's dance, which the unchristianized Ojibwes used to perform in "the days of our ignorance."

Shuddering to think of those "days of our darkness," Copway thanks "God that those days will never return." Copway feels that as a Native he is unworthy to become a minister. Although conversion and missionary narratives typically contain such statements of humility, Copway expresses his sense of inferiority in racial terms: God was "too great to listen to the words of a poor Indian boy." The voice of God soothes this "unlearned and feeble Red man—a mere worm of the dust."

Another major theme in the book is the progress of Christianity among the Ojibwe, including Copway's own conversion and his missionary training. In demonstrating why the Ojibwes needed Christianity, Copway speaks in the voice of the convert repelled by Native warfare: "Unchristianized Indians are often like greedy lions after their prey; yes, at times, they are indeed cruel and blood thirsty." He describes how warriors would cut open the breasts of their dead enemies and drink the blood: "and all this was out of mere *revenge*" (Copway's emphasis). The appeal of Christianity is the same as it was for Occom and Apess as well as for the slaves—equality with whites.[9] As Copway reminds his audience, "the Great Spirit is no respecter of persons; He had made of one blood all the nations of the earth; He loves all his children alike; and his highest attributes are love, mercy, and justice. If this be so,—and who dare doubt it?—will He not stretch out his hand and help them, and avenge their wrongs?"

Copway powerfully recreates the scene in which his tribespeople converted to Christianity during a camp meeting. Happy of heart, his father utters his first prayer for his son while "the Indians lay about me like dead men." He further demonstrates the power of religion to change his family's life by describing the conversion of his mother two years before her death. The description of one's conversion was an important part of the evangelical tradition in which the penitent is "saved" and "born again." The conversion experiences of Copway, his family, and other Ojibwes link Native American experience to that of non-Native Christian converts because they emphasize the equality of all those "saved," regardless of race. Copway's detailed account of his own spiritual awakening follows the literary conventions of spiritual confessions, in which often a penitent is converted after hearing a powerful sermon or experiencing some traumatic event that arouses in the hearer a deep depression or intense guilt. This reaction is frequently followed by a dream in which a storm, blackness, or a vision of hell gives way to blinding illumination and rebirth. Copway's conversion came while attending a church service to hear a powerful preacher: "The small brilliant light came near to me, and fell upon my head, and then ran all over and through me. . . . I arose; and O! how happy I was! I felt light as a feather. I clapped my hands, and exclaimed in English, 'Glory to Jesus.'" In the British edition of his *Life*, Copway greatly condensed his description of the religious ecstasy he experienced during his conversion, perhaps because he felt the original description was more appropriate for American than British readers.

The dramatic episode marks not only Copway's conversion to Christianity but also his first major step away from his traditional Ojibwe culture into that of the dominant society. That Copway adopts the voice and persona of the pious Christian evangelical is clear from his account of how in 1834 he wrestled with the question of whether he should leave his family behind to join other Ojibwe Christian converts going to aid Rev. John Clark in the Lake Superior missions, in what is now the northern peninsula of Michigan and northern Wisconsin. Copway's transformation from a traditional Ojibwe to an acculturated missionary occurred while he studied at Ebenezer Seminary, near Jacksonville in central Illinois. In describing the two years he spent there, Copway adopts the voice of the stranger who has entered Paradise: "It was here that I learned to read the word of God, and often, for hours together, upon my knees, in the groves, have I been thus engaged." His Ebenezer friends and colleagues substituted for the Ojibwe family he had left behind, and the larger Christian and Methodist community embraced him during his trip east in 1839. His travels through central Illinois and in the east introduced him also to the size, industrialization, and complexities of the United States.

In describing his experiences in Illinois and the east, Copway casts himself as the naive observer, commenting on the wonders and anomalies of the dominant society. Touring the east, he is so awed by the prosperity he sees that tears fill his eyes: "Happy art thou, O Israel, who is like unto thee, *O people saved by the Lord!*" (Copway's emphasis). This awe is tempered by grief over the cost to Native people. He demonstrates his increasing awareness of the difference between what non-Indians preach and what they practice, a common theme in Indian autobiographies. Unlike the converted Indians, who spend Christmas and New Year's in sober reflection, non-Indian Americans gad "about from house to house, . . . indulging in luxuries to excess." Further, many of these professors of Christianity entertain their visitors with "*fire-water* or *devil's spittle*" (Copway's emphasis). Copway's recognition of the extent to which he has separated himself from his people is clear in his description of returning to Rice Lake in 1839, after an absence of five years, only to learn that many of his family and friends had died. Fellowship in Christ, rather than kinship in Ojibwe tradition, now link him to his family and community.

The segments that describe his experiences among the Indians in Canada and the Great Lakes move the narrative from the genre of spiritual confession into that of missionary reminiscence. Copway's descriptions of his missionary work replace the conventional fall from grace and subsequent recapture of faith found in confessional narratives. Leaving the safety of his home, Copway journeys into the wilds of the Great Lakes region, where his spiritual and physical courage is tested. His harrowing adventures among the Lake Superior Ojibwes and the Dakota Sioux of Minnesota appealed to his audience's taste for the sensational and are comparable to those in the Indian captivity, slave, and missionary narratives of the period. In recounting his missionary experiences, Copway depicts himself as a devout minister convinced that the Ojibwes cannot achieve the peace and prosperity he has seen in the non-Indian world unless they abandon their traditional religion. What Copway emphasizes is the joy the converts obtain, not their loss of culture: they are "the happiest of beings; their very souls were like an escaped bird, whose glad wings had saved it from danger and death."

Converting the Ojibwes was not an easy task. During Copway's service in Wisconsin in 1835, Spear Maker threatened to tomahawk the missionaries if they came into his wigwam. When the Copways were in Minnesota, Chief Hole-in-the sky (more commonly called "Hole-in-the-Day") told the missionary that he would convert only after one more battle with the Sioux. Describing his missionary experiences in Minnesota, Copway speaks in the voice of both the dedicated minister and the warrior for Christ willing to endure severe hardships to carry out his mission. Especially powerful is his account of how he walked 240 miles in four days to return to his family after learning that the Sioux had sworn to kill every Ojibwe they could find: "I trusted in the God of battles, and with his aid I was confident that I could prevent these merciless and blood-thirsty warriors from imbruing their hands in the blood of my nation." His harsh language expresses clearly his desire to make apparent the difference between him, as an acculturated missionary, and the unconverted, ancient enemies of his people, who reminded Copway of "his Satanic and fiendish majesty, rejoicing over a damned spirit entering hell."

Copway also takes on the persona of warrior in his discussions of Indian–non-Indian relations and his account of the injustices his people endured, a major focus of the autobiography. He strongly criticizes non-Indians for introducing alcohol, taking Indian land, and failing to send missionaries to the Indians. Like Occom and Apess, Copway emphasizes how destructive alcohol was to Indian culture: "O! that acursed thing. O! why did the white man give it to my poor fathers? None but fiends in human shape could have introduced it among us." Once an unconquered nation, his people have now "fallen a prey to the withering influence of intemperance. . . . They are hemmed in, bound, and maltreated, by both the American and British governments."[10] Copway credits Christianity with leading his father and the Ojibwes away from alcoholism. He castigates the "savage" behavior of Natives when drunk: "Poor untutored red men! you were deluded, and made drunk by white men, and then in your hellish and drunken passions, you turned around and imbrued your hands in the blood of your own relatives and brethren." Copway primarily blames Indian alcoholism on the traders, rather than on the settlers as a whole.

Copway combines the persona of the fearless warrior fighting for justice for his people with that of the wise teacher, educating non-Indians about the current state of Native people. He attributes the decline in Indian population to five causes: the introduction of "King Alcohol," diseases transmitted by whites, inability to live a healthful life after abandoning their wigwams, broken spirits, and "gloomy and cheerless" prospects that break down the "noblest of spirits." For Copway, the Gospel and education were the only hopes for Native Americans. His proposal to improve the lot of Native people is very general: establish more missions and schools, ensure that they have rights equal to those of non-Natives (once Native people are sufficiently educated), and allow them self-government in a territory assigned to them and land ownership.

In *Life*, Copway uses a variety of styles, which often reflect the personas he adopts. He utilizes a plain, journalistic style to describe adventures, such as his boyhood encounter with a bear: "he came like a hogshead rolling down hill; there were no signs of stopping; when a few feet from me, I jumped aside, and cried *Yah*! (an exclamation of fear.) I fired my gun without taking sight; in turning suddenly to avoid me, he threw up the earth and leaves. . . . I dropped my gun and fell backwards, while the bear lay sprawling just by me. Having recovered, I took up my gun and went a few feet from where I fell, and loaded my gun in a hurry." Such passages as this, in chapter 2, and his account in chapter 15 of jumping into a river to save his drowning son reveal his ability as a compelling storyteller.

Far more sophisticated is the style he uses in discussing government policy in chapter 16. Here he uses irony, rhetorical questions, and an emotional oratorical style to demonstrate what Indians have suffered:

> But are not these sufficient of themselves to crush and exterminate even any *white* race, if not protected and defended by friends and wholesome laws? Our people have been driven from their homes, and have been cajoled out of the few sacred spots where the bones of their ancestors and children lie; and where they themselves expected to lie, when released from the trials and troubles of life. Were it possible to reverse the order of things, by placing the whites in the same condition, how long would it be endured? There is not a white man, who deserves the name of *man*, that would not rather die than be deprived of his home, and driven from the graves of his relatives. (Copway's emphasis)

Such passages demonstrate how effective Copway must have been as a preacher and platform speaker.

Less effective is the style in the philosophical sections, where Copway's use of a rhapsodic tone and artificial poetic diction undercut the realism of the autobiography. The plain style used in the narrative sections and in Copway's personal letters suggests that such passages may reflect the influence of Elizabeth Copway, who wrote poetry. They also reflect popular taste of the period. Similar tone and diction were commonly used in evangelical sermons, spiritual confessions, missionary reminiscences, and sentimental fiction. This tendency is especially evident in the following passage from chapter 1: "I was born in *nature's wide domain!* The trees were all that sheltered my infant limbs—the blue heavens all that covered me. I am one of Nature's children; . . . she shall be my glory; her features— her robes, and the wreath about her brow—the seasons—her stately oaks, and the evergreen—her hair—ringlets over the earth, all contribute to my enduring love of her; and wherever I see her, emotions of pleasure roll in my breast, and swell and burst like waves on the shores of the ocean, in prayer and praise to Him who has placed me in her hand."

Throughout the autobiography Copway interweaves quotations from the Bible, hymns, and literature, designed to demonstrate his commitment to religion and his learning as an assimilated Ojibwe. Including numerous religious quotations was traditional in evangelical sermons, spiritual confessions, and missionary reminiscences. Most of the quotations from hymns are taken from *Collection of Hymns for the Use of Native Christians or the Iroquois, to Which Are Added a Few Hymns in the Chippeway Tongue* (1827), translated by Copway's mentor, Peter Jones (Ojibwe). Copway's quotations from such classics as Shakespeare's *Macbeth*, Milton's *Paradise Lost*, and Pope's *Essay on Man* may well have been supplied by his wife. Many of the quotations are so esoteric that they cannot be found in standard reference books and concordances.

## Copway, Methodism, and the Indian Mission Movement

Methodist missionary efforts among the North American Indians probably began when Rev. John Wesley came to Georgia in 1736. In addition to ministering to the colonists, Wesley wanted to convert the Indians. In 1815 Rev. John Stewart, a free-born mulatto who was part Indian, established the first sustained mission among the Wyandottes in Ohio. Reports of the work of this mission were carried in the 1820s to the Wyandottes near Ford Malden, Canada. By 1829 there were nine missionary stations in Upper Canada. The next year a mission was established in Michigan among the Wyandottes and Shawnees on the Huron River; it was later called the Huron Mission. In 1819 the Missionary Society of the Methodist Church was organized at the initiative of Rev. Nathan Bangs. The passage of the "Civilization Bill" of 1819, which made funds available for church-operated Indian schools, spurred the churches to increase their missions among the Indians. During the 1820s the Methodist Episcopal

Church established numerous missions in the west, north, and northwest of the United States. The first Methodist mission of some permanence was established by Rev. John Clark near Detroit in 1833. Two years later Rev. Alfred Brunson was appointed superintendent and missionary to the upper Mississippi Indians. In Canada, Indian missions were entrusted to the Canada Conference in 1828 and placed by the conference under the care of the Wesleyan Missionary Society in 1833. One year later twelve hundred Indians, primarily Ojibwe, were church members. Two Ojibwe missionaries, John Sunday and Peter Jones, were sent to England in 1837 to stimulate interest there in the work. In 1839 missions opened in the territory of the Hudson Bay Company in Canada. By 1854 the society reported over two thousand members in Upper Canada and the Hudson Bay Territory (Vernon 1210–13).

When Copway arrived in Jacksonville in the fall of 1837, Methodism in Illinois was burgeoning. During the first quarter of the nineteenth century, Illinois was under the Western, Tennessee, and Missouri Conferences and was served by circuit-riding preachers. The Illinois Conference, which initially included Indiana, was established in 1824. Eight years later this conference was divided into the Indiana and Illinois Conferences. The latter included all of Illinois, parts of western Indiana, and the Northwestern Territory.

Copway's account of his years at Ebenezer Manual Labor School, which focuses on his religious experiences, acquaintances, and attendance at conference meetings, gives no hint of the emerging conflict over slavery within the Illinois Conference. This controversy erupted during the 1837 annual meeting of the conference, held between 27 September and 5 October at Jacksonville. Most of the settlers in the area were affluent Kentuckians who supported slavery. A conference speaker barely escaped being mobbed for his expression of abolition sentiments. News of this incident must have been disconcerting to the newly arrived Copway. He would also have encountered supporters of slavery in many towns he visited in central and southern Illinois, where settlers had moved from Tennessee, Kentucky, and Indiana. Slavery became an issue again at the 1839 conference at Bloomington, Illinois, held 11–21 September. Copway attended this convention, at which members unanimously refused to concur with the anti-slavery resolution that the New England Conference wished to present to the General Methodist Conference.[11] As Wade Crawford Barclay points out, the history of the relation of Methodism to slavery vitally affected the total life and work of the church. In 1844 the General Conference approved a Plan of Separation to be implemented if the slave-holding states united in "a distinct ecclesiastical connection." Separation occured in 1845, when the plan was ratified by the Louisville Convention, which consisted of delegates from southern conferences (Barclay 357–58).

In 1840 the Illinois Conference was divided into the Southern Illinois and the Rock River, which covered northern Illinois and the territories of Wisconsin and Iowa (Evers 103). Copway served in the Rock River Conference from 1840 to 1842. He attended its first conference, held at Mt. Morris, Illinois, in August 1840, at which he was retained on trial on 28 August. Copway also attended the second at Plattsburg, Wisconsin, in August 1841. He was ordained as a deacon at that convention on 30 August.[12] By late 1842 Copway was back in Canada and no longer under the jurisdiction of the Illinois conferences.

*Life, Letters and Speeches* is Copway's best book. Although his *Traditional History* contains some well-crafted descriptions of his experiences and more information about Ojibwe religion and oral traditions, it also contains lengthy quotations from printed sources, which detract from its originality. Nevertheless, *Traditional History* is a valuable and often-cited resource and its emphasis on the significance of oral tradition as a reliable resource for Native American history is an important contribution. Less successful is his *Running Sketches of Men and Places, in England, France, Germany, Belgium, and Scotland* (1851), the first full-length travel book by an Indian. Although it contains interesting character sketches of London celebrities, it is primarily a collection of quotations from local guidebooks. None of Copway's later books equaled the narrative power of his autobiography. Though long out of print, *Life, Letters and Speeches* remains a vivid and moving account of Ojibwe culture in the early nineteenth century, the dangers faced by Indian missionaries, and the author's journey from being a traditional Ojibwe to becoming an acculturated Native minister and lecturer.

### NOTES

1. Portions of this essay appeared in Ruoff, "Three Nineteenth-Century Autobiographers."

2. Toelken emphasizes that Indian students at the University of Oregon who held such an attitude toward the self simply would not write autobiographical theme assignments.

3. *American Indian Autobiography* 22–23. For bibliographic information about American Indian autobiographies, see Brumble's *Annotated Bibliography* and "The Autobiographies," appended to *American Indian Autobiography*.

4. Although Apess spelled his name as *Apes* in the two editions of *A Son of the Forest*, the first edition of *Experiences of Five Christian Indians* (1833), and other works, he subsequently changed it to *Apess* in the second edition of the *Eulogy on King Philip* (1837) and in the revised edition of *Experience of Five Christian Indians* (1837). See O'Connell xiv n.2.

5. For a discussion of the methods slaves used to authenticate their autobiographies, see Stepto chapter 1. Foster notes that antebellum slave narratives usually begin with what is known about the former slave's birth and childhood (*Witnessing Slavery* 55).

6. The first autobiographical narrative written by a Native American to be published is Hendric Aupaumut's (Mohegan) *A Narrative of an Embassy to the Western Indians* (1827). However, it is a journal rather than a full-life narrative. In 1791 Aupaumut recorded his experiences as he traveled for eleven months among the Miamis, Senecas, Ottawas, Shawnees, Onondagas, Wyandots, and others. See Brumble, "Autobiographies," *American Indian Autobiography* 214–15.

7. See D. Smith's discussion of Copway's various descriptions of his education, this volume.

8. See also Foster, *Witnessing Slavery* 11–13, 44–47. In its nostalgia for the tribal past, Copway's autobiography bears a stronger relationship to the narratives published by African slaves in the late eighteenth century than to those by African American slaves in the nineteenth. For example, *The Interesting Narrative of the Life of Olaudah Equiano, or Gustavus Vassa, the African* (1789) begins with accounts of the geography and culture of the author's native land, Benin (now part of Nigeria), his family, and his childhood (Foster 47). Like the Africans captured on their native continent and transported to North America, Copway and most of the nineteenth-century Native American writers who followed him retained vivid memories of the free tribal life.

9. Cf. William Apess's eloquent description of his own conversion experience in *A Son of the Forest*, reprinted in O'Connell 19–21. Christ appeared before Apess during his vision: "I felt convinced that Christ died for all mankind—that age, sect, color, country, or situation made no difference. I felt an assurance that I was included in the plan of redemption with all my brethren" (19).

10. Cf. the comments on the destructiveness of alcohol to Indian communities in Occom's remarks to "My poor Kindred," in *A Sermon* 960–62, and

by Apess in *A Son of the Forest* and "An Indian's Looking-Glass for the White Man," in O'Connell 6–7, 155.

11. Evers 90, 97, 100–101; Melton 18, 21. Typescripts of the journals of the sessions of the Illinois Conference of the Methodist Episcopal Church and of the Minutes of the Illinois Missionary Society are in Union Library, Seabury-Western Theological Seminary and Garrett-Evangelical Theological Seminary, Evanston IL.

12. Pennewell 90; transcript, "Minutes of the Rock River Annual Conference of the Methodist Episcopal Church, 1840–52," 8, 34, Union Library, Seabury-Western Theological Seminary and Garrett-Evangelical Theological Seminary, Evanston, IL.

# Kahgegagahbowh:
# Canada's First Literary Celebrity
# in the United States

Donald B. Smith

Virtually overnight, George Copway, or Kahgegagahbowh, rose from obscurity to celebrity status in the United States. From 1847 to 1851 the Ojibwe from Rice Lake, Upper Canada (today's Ontario), completed four books and briefly edited his own weekly newspaper in New York City.[1] He spoke to large audiences in cities along the Atlantic seaboard on Native American culture and history and on temperance themes. A biographical study of this writer and lecturer reveals an unusual nineteenth-century Indian who gained, and subsequently lost, access to America's highest political and social circles.

In *Life, Letters and Speeches*, his autobiography, Kahgegagahbowh (pronounced "Kah-ge-ga-gah-bowh") provides an exciting account of his boyhood, in which he identifies himself as "one of nature's children . . . born in *nature's wide domain!* The trees were all that sheltered my infant limbs—the blue heavens all that covered me." He is our only source of information on his life to the age of sixteen.[2]

Kahgegagahbowh describes his Ojibwe childhood as difficult and demanding. Once, for example, he and his family nearly starved. The snow that winter had fallen for a full five days, to such a depth that they could not shoot or trap any game. By the seventh day they had exhausted their provisions, which forced them to eat their parched beaver skins and old moccasins. Only on the tenth day did they, before they became too weak to move, miraculously kill two beaver. Yet, despite the hardships, he added, "I loved the woods, and the chase. I had the nature for it, and gloried in nothing else."

Born in 1818 near the mouth of the Trent River (present-day Trenton, Ontario), Kahgegagahbowh ("Standing Firm") belonged to the Ojibwe, or Mississauga, Indian band who lived near Rice Lake just north of Cobourg on Lake Ontario.[3] His great-grandfather was one of the first Ojibwe, or Anishinabeg ("human beings," as they call themselves), who around 1700 migrated southward into present-day southern Ontario, driving out the Iroquois. The settlers who arrived in the late eighteenth century called the Anishinabeg on the north shore of Lake Ontario "Mississauga." They were a hearty people whose warriors could walk sixty miles a day on a rough forest path.[4]

Copway's parents educated him in the Ojibwe tradition. His father, a veteran of the War of 1812 (he fought for the British at the Battle of Lundy's Lane in 1814), was also a man of power. He introduced Kahgegagahbowh to the Ojibwe's religious beliefs. The Anishinabeg felt that everything around them had a force that could be directed for their benefit. In his youth a young man should go on vision quests, blackening his face and fasting alone in an isolated spot, to seek a non-human spiritual guardian. If he was blessed, an animal or bird or object might appear in a dream and promise its powers at a time of great need. Every man, Copway's father advised him, needed supernatural help, and through this religious search he might secure it.[5]

Agricultural settlement had begun in the Rice Lake area in 1825 with the arrival of over two thousand Irish immigrants (Corkery 150). Every year the entry of large numbers of immigrants reduced the Indian trapping and fishing grounds. The Mississauga resented the intrusion; in Kahgegagahbowh's words the newcomers "hedged in, bound and mal-treated" them.

In the mid-1820s the first Native Christian missionaries, led by Peter Jones, the bilingual and bicultural preacher from the Credit River just twelve miles west of Toronto, reached Rice Lake. Jones, the son of a Mississauga Indian woman and a Canadian government surveyor, had accepted Methodism in 1823. Two years later, at the age of twenty-three, he dedicated his life to mission work among his mother's people. Denied access to much of their former lands and fisheries, the Credit River Mississauga had lost their economic independence. Within a generation disease had also reduced the Mississauga at the western end of the lake, from a population of five hundred in the 1780s to barely two hundred in the mid-1820s. The Mississauga were overwhelmed by these losses, and alcohol abuse became endemic.

Peter Jones generated hope and excitement among the Mississauga along the north shore of Lake Ontario. Already hundreds had followed him into the Methodist Church. The common human values shared by the two faiths, the Christian Indians' adjustment to farming, and the Methodists' abstention from "ardent spirits" all attracted John Copway, as Kahgegagahbowh's father now became known in English. He and his wife both became firm Christians.[6]

Kahgegagahbowh converted to Christianity shortly before his mother's death in 1830. In his words, she "advised us [her children] to be good Christians, to love Jesus, and meet her in heaven." Then the dying woman sang her favorite hymn, one translated by Peter Jones: "Jesus ish pe ming kah e hod. Jesus, my all, to heaven is gone" (see *Collection of Hymns* 38–39). At a Methodist camp meeting that summer, the fourteen-year-old Mississauga boy accepted Christianity. He clapped his hands, yelled out in English, "Glory to Jesus," and threw himself into his father's arms.

In 1828 the Methodists, with funds made available by the New England Company, a private English organization, built a log-cabin village for the 220 Rice Lake people, modeling it on the Credit River Mission. The Methodists also started a school at Rice Lake. James Evans, a remarkable English immigrant who later, at Norway House in present-day northern Manitoba, invented the Cree syllabics, taught there from 1828 to 1831. Young George Copway, as Kahgegagahbowh now became known in English, admired Evans immensely. In the late 1820s 40–50 Rice Lake Indian children attended his school.[7]

The young Mississauga convert disliked his teacher's constant references to the superiority of British institutions and society. At home he learned otherwise. In his autobiography he wrote of Britain's purchase of the Rice Lake area in 1818 for an annual payment of £740: "Much of the back country still remains unsold, and I hope the scales will be removed from the eyes of my poor countrymen, that they may see the robberies perpetrated upon them, before they surrender another foot of territory."[8] Still, the power and influence of the newcomers attracted Copway, and he worked to win the missionaries' approval.

During these years a settler lived with the Copways. The Upper Canadian frontier included a few Europeans who had crossed into Native society, one being an elderly ex-sailor who had strayed into the Rice Lake area around 1830. The man, named Lewis, apparently stayed with the Copways—George, his father, and George's older sister and younger brother (his mother died 27 February 1830)—for three or four years. Lewis learned Ojibwe and regaled them with tales of faraway places and strange beings, "of a monstrous great fish, no doubt the whale and of sharks, sea-bears and mermaids" (Copway, *Running Sketches* 22). The young Indian boy wanted to join the settlers, acquire their powers, and share their opportunities.

In the late twentieth century George Copway might have found an outlet for his extraordinary energy in politics or the law, but Indians in Canada in the 1830s could not vote or even sit on juries (Jones, *History* 217–18). Their own administration lay largely in the government's hands. To lead a useful and meaningful life among the newcomers, Copway really had only one option: his church. When his chance came he took it.

Rev. John Clark, superintendent of the Lake Superior Mission of the American Methodist Church, requested four Native workers from Rice Lake. In 1834 Rev. Daniel McMullen, James Evans's successor, recommended John Cahbeach, a man of about thirty; John Taunchey, Copway's uncle, a man of about thirty-five; Copway's cousin Enmegahbowh (John Johnson), in his mid-twenties; and Copway himself, age sixteen.[9] From this point on information about Copway becomes available from sources other than Copway himself.

Copway remembered twelve years later the exact date of his departure for the northwest: 16 July 1834. Now he entered a new and exceedingly strange world. Why did he accept the call, leaving his father, his family, his band, perhaps forever? No doubt he went because, like Peter Jones, he genuinely believed in Christianity and in the value of European "civilization." His Christian mother's early death also contributed; she would have approved. Moreover, as a Methodist church worker, he could join the settlers' world.

Jones, the Methodists' leading Ojibwe convert, accompanied the missionary party to Penetanguishene on Lake Huron to see them off. At this stage the Christian Mississaugas' leader saw only the devout religious motives of the young convert: "George Kahhooway is an Indian youth of deep piety raised at the Rice Lake Mission School, who went out with the Miss'y John Clark to the far west as an Interpreter."[10]

The young man spent his first winter away from home, 1834–35, at Keweenaw Mission on the southeastern shore of the lake. The second winter Copway and his cousin Johnson were posted at La Pointe, on Madeline Island, about 185 miles further west. By the end of his first year Copway, anxious to do well, had so impressed the missionaries with his earnestness and his ability that they promoted him from interpreter and teacher to preacher.[11]

George stayed at La Pointe with Rev. Sherman Hall, a missionary employed by the American Board of Commissioners for Foreign Missions in Boston. The Presbyterian minister came to know his guest quite well, as that winter they translated together the Gospel of St. Luke and the Acts of the Apostles from English into Ojibwe (Hall 164). One of Copway's character traits, however, alarmed Hall. A few years later he noted that the young Indian believed "his judgment in missionary matters among his own nation, was at least worth as much as that of his superiors." The Presbyterian minister added that now that he was recognized as a preacher, "Copway would not be happy, if he felt that his movements were to be directed by others."[12]

During the winter of 1836–37 Copway, his cousin Johnson, and Peter Marksman, another Ojibwe convert, served in the Christian missionaries' front lines. They established a Methodist mission at Lac Court Oreille, or Ottawa Lake, situated at the head of one of the principal branches of the Chippewa River. It lay about midway between Lake Superior and the Mississippi River—in the war zone between the Ojibwe and the eastern Dakota, or Santee Sioux, the Ojibwes' hereditary enemies (Hall 161, 178). For two decades the Lake Superior Ojibwe had fought the powerful Mdewakonton Dakota (or Sioux), gradually pushing them further westward. One day while Copway was walking with Chief Moose Tail by the Chippewa River, the chief identified the "numerous battle-grounds of days past." Presumably this is the same chief who, pointing to a certain spot, told Copway, "There I killed two Sioux, about thirteen winters ago; I cut open one of them; and when I reflected that the Sioux had cut up my own cousin, but a year before, I took out his heart, cut a piece from it, and swallowed it whole" (Copway, *History* 57, 113).

Despite the threat of a Sioux attack, Copway and Johnson persevered at their remote mission post. They stayed probably because of Superintendent Clark's vow: "If they would be faithful the present year, they should have the opportunity of attending school the two years following." At the Illinois Conference Annual Missionary Society Meeting in the fall of 1836, the missionary superintendent raised fourteen hundred dollars for this purpose.[13] Eager to take up the offer, the young men canoed the following summer to Fort Snelling (present-day St. Paul, Minnesota) on the Mississippi.[14] That fall Copway, Johnson, and Marksman obtained their reward, entrance into the Ebenezer Manual Labor School located about four miles from Jacksonville, Illinois.[15]

An American Methodist who met Copway in Jacksonville later recorded his impressions, giving us another glimpse of the ambitious Native church worker. The young man's address in the church, the onlooker recalled, "though somewhat broken in manner was sensible and forcible." To those who said that the Indians would secure an education only to return and pillage the settlements, Copway immediately replied, "It was education which would cause them to lay down their arms of rebellion—when they knew Jesus Christ and learned to read the Bible, they would love as who loved Jesus Christ, and be our brethren."[16] He won the meeting over. The local Methodists in Jacksonville, then a large town in southern Illinois with a population of two thousand, raised enough money to send three non-Native students, all intending to become missionaries, to join the three Indians.

The earliest surviving letter written by Copway dates back to his entrance to Ebenezer. Determined to secure as good an education as his hosts, to become their full equal, Copway had requested the Jacksonville Methodists to place three Americans in the Indians' class at the school. That first year at the school, however, the teachers did not give the Indians any schoolbooks. This led Copway to write the Methodist book steward on 26 May 1838: "I found it to be poor business in pursuing only [to] the Path up to the Hill of Science."[17]

Upon his graduation in late 1839, Copway decided to visit his family at Rice Lake. Andrew Jackson (after whom Jacksonville was named), the previous U.S. president, had begun the removal of all eastern Indians to new reservations west of the Mississippi (see Wallace). At a time when tens of thousands of American Indians were migrating westward, some at gunpoint, Copway traveled in the opposite direction. En route he visited the major cities of the northeastern states: Chicago, Detroit, Buffalo, Rochester, Albany, New York, Boston, and Syracuse. The young Indian stated his goal in his autobiography: "I was very anxious to see the great cities of which I had read so much at school. I resolved to go through thick and thin for the sake of seeing New York."

Copway's mother, his teacher James Evans, and the sailor Lewis all, in their own way, had contributed to his decision to live in the newcomers' world. A young English woman would strengthen this resolve even further. Upon his return to Upper Canada Copway met Elizabeth, the daughter of Captain Henry Howell, who farmed at Scarborough, eight miles east of Toronto.[18]

One observer later described Elizabeth as "an interesting and genteel woman, one that would appear with grace in any of our drawing rooms"; another called her "a woman of very exceptional character."[19] Five months after their first meeting at Peter Jones's home at the Credit Mission, Copway married the "Female White Flower," the name given her in Ojibwe. Jones performed the ceremony. Elizabeth braved her family's opposition to marry the man she loved, for no members of her large family acted as witnesses at the wedding.[20]

Before the Copways' marriage, Jones and Eliza, his English-born wife, had counseled them on what they might encounter in racially conscious Upper Canada. Many settlers expected educated Indians to conform to their society, but then, still regarding them as inferiors, refused to accept them as equals. When Peter and Eliza married in 1833, several Upper Canadian newspapers denounced the union. The Kingston *Chronicle and Gazette* (21 September 1833) termed it "improper and revolting": "We believe that the Creator of the Universe distinguished his creatures by different colours, that they might be kept separate from each other, and we know of nothing in what we consider religion, to warrant any violation of his evident arrangement." In St. Catharines, the *British Colonial Argus* (28 September 1833) agreed. It argued that the respectable, well-educated English woman had brought "disgrace" upon her family.

Copway looked upon Peter Jones, almost two decades his senior, as his spiritual father. The day after the wedding, the groom personally thanked the Mississauga preacher for everything that he had done for him, "for every *comfort*, for every *gift*, and for every *advice* which you have given me."[21] Before leaving the Credit Mission, Elizabeth Howell Copway penned a note to her friend Eliza Jones. The message indicates the intensity of her Christian faith:

ON THE DECLINE OF LIFE

Soon shall I leave this earthly scene
And be as I have never been
Gentle and slow be my delay
Calm as the evening of a day

When I must resign this breath
And sink within the arms of death
Lord suffer not my faith to fail
nor let the enemy prevail.

Remember me Sister Jones at the Throne of Grace

*Credit June 2nd 1840, Mrs. E. Copway.*[22]

Ironically, Elizabeth Howell Copway, then twenty-four, would live to the age of eighty-seven. But was it social rather than physical death that concerned her? By marrying an Indian did she fear that she had separated herself forever from her own society?

The new Mrs. George Copway wrote very well. Her obituary (she died in 1904) mentioned that she had contributed "numerous articles in Canada and the United States, which displayed great talent."[23] Her three surviving letters show that she had an easy and agreeable writing style. At one point in her life Elizabeth considered becoming a contributor to the *Christian Advocate*, a newspaper in Buffalo, New York.[24] Lacking a good command of written English himself, George likely depended on her for writing assistance and advice.[25] Possibly, for instance, she suggested the quotations from Shakespeare and Pope found in his *Traditional History* (123, 140) and his autobiography, as well as the lengthy passage from Byron in *Running Sketches* (204–6), his account of his European tour.

The Copways spent two years in Minnesota, trying to explain Christianity, the professed religion of the settler, to the Indians. The task proved difficult, as the upper Mississippi Ojibwe, in one missionary's words, "believed that the whites were very wise, very strong, but very deceitful and dishonest, great liars, and ought not to be trusted by the Indians."[26] Placed in the war zone between the Dakota Mdewakonton Sioux and the Ojibwe, the Copways had to move their mission several times, eventually settling at Fond du Lac, at the head of Lake Superior, away from the battlefields.

Copway had few friends at his posting. Apparently he got on very poorly with his non-Native missionary colleagues. Rev. William Boutwell, for instance, found him full of "vanity, self-confidence, and [a] disposition to be headstrong."[27] Furthermore, he was separated from Johnson and Marksman, now both at other, distant mission stations. At the same time the Indians themselves in the Lake Superior and upper Mississippi region regarded Copway as culturally alien. For example, when he, Johnson, and Marksman met some Sioux near Fort Snelling in 1837, one Sioux perceived these men dressed in European clothes to be "Frenchmen," persons of European culture who incidentally happened to be Indian. Alfred Brunson, a Methodist missionary, later recorded the encounter: "While at the mission this time we cut logs and built a school-house and an addition to the dwelling-house. These Chippewas could handle an ax with skill, and could carry up the corners of a log house in raising equal to white men. As they were doing this, one day, the Sioux standing by and looking on, without knowing how or offering to help . . . one of them called out to my interpreter, 'Jim, them ain't Ojibbewas, they are Frenchmen; Ojibbewas can't work so.'"[28]

His Upper Canadian Ojibwe origins did not make Copway a Lake Superior Ojibwe. As William Warren, the son of Lyman Warren, a Lake Superior trader, and his Native wife, noted in his *History of the Ojibway Nation*, written in 1852: "There are several villages of Indians in Upper Canada, who are sometimes denominated as Ojibways. . . . The connection existing between these and the Lake Superior and Mississippi Ojibways, is not very close, though they speak the same language, and call one another relatives" (368).

Eager to return to Canada, George and Elizabeth did so in late 1842. Jones was one of the three ministers who invited them. Initially all went well. The Upper Canadian Methodists recognized the Indian preacher as "an exceedingly clever man and good speaker, both in Indian and English" (Carroll 4: 372). Early in 1843 they sent him on a three-month missionary fund-raising tour of Upper Canada, or Canada West (as it was also termed after the Union of Upper and Lower Canada in 1841), with Rev. William Ryerson. A year later Copway accompanied Jones and Chief Joseph Sawyer of the Credit Mission on a visit to the governor-general, Sir Charles Metcalfe, in Montreal.[29] They went to request that Metcalfe establish an Indian manual labor school. It was quite an honor for the young man, almost twenty years younger than Jones and over thirty years younger than Sawyer, to be included in the delegation.

Yet Jones now came to identify a disturbing weakness in his young colleague: too impulsive, too headstrong. On 1 August 1845 the senior Native Methodist missionary stated, "he has not judgment to carry out any great undertaking. He is too hasty, and withal neglects to seek the advice of those who have older and wiser heads than his own."[30]

Copway's behavior on a missionary tour the next year to the Ojibwe Indians on Walpole Island on Lake St. Clair confirmed Jones's assessment. There, in his enthusiasm, Copway apparently told the assembled Indians that the governor-general wanted them to become Methodists. Word reached Metcalfe of Copway's remarks. Through his secretary he severely reprimanded the Native missionary, advising him that he had never stated that the Methodist faith "was altogether superior to that of the Church of England . . . that he liked the Methodists better than any other body of Christians and that he wished to see all the Indians belonging to that denomination."[31]

Copway's avoidance of his Ojibwe elders entangled him in much greater difficulties than his clash with the governor-general. The American Methodists had noted that he was "not as economical in his expenses as he might be."[32] When he served at the Saugeen Mission on Lake Huron in 1845, the Grand Council of the Methodist Ojibwe of Canada West elected him as their vice president or deputy speaker for the meeting. Once in office he quickly spent beyond the council's appropriations. When he failed to account to the Saugeen people for over £125 taken without the council's approval, they accused him of embezzlement. The charge of theft also arose against Copway at Rice Lake. Because he could write in English his home community had entrusted him with some of their band's business affairs. There, as at Saugeen, he offended the chiefs and leading band members. In May 1846 Chief George Paudash, John Crow, and Copway's own uncle, John Taunchey, who had gone west with him in 1834, reported to the Indian Department that George had drawn out twenty-five pounds of the band's money without the council's authorization.[33]

Although Copway later confessed that he had been "improvident," he remained bitter: "I have found nothing but ingratitude among our People."[34] Unable to pay his creditors, the Indian minister, on the complaint of his own band and that of the Saugeen, entered the prison at Toronto. For several weeks the Indian Department considered laying charges against him but decided not "to incur legal expenses as in all probability nothing can be recovered from Mr. Copway."[35] The Canadian Conference of the Wesleyan Methodist Church expelled him.[36] Understandably, in his subsequent lectures and books he never mentioned his days in jail or his expulsion from his church.

Upon his release from prison Copway formulated two different plans, neither of which involved a return to his band. He traveled, first to Boston to visit David Greene, the secretary of the Presbyterian- and Congregationist-sponsored American Board of Commissioners for Foreign Missions. Could he rejoin the Lake Superior Mission as a missionary to the Lake Superior Ojibwe? A few months later, on 8 December 1846, Greene contacted Sherman Hall at La Pointe. An excerpt from Greene's letter clearly shows how his Ojibwe visitor freely mixed fact and fantasy, stating "that he was dissatisfied with the Methodists; & that his post as govt. agent for some portion of his tribe in Canada did not give him so much opportunity as he desired to labor for their spiritual good; and that he was undecided what course to take." Greene added in his letter to Hall, "He has been, as I infer from having heard of him in various places, rather unsettled, going from place to place, without much of steady employment, for 6 or 8 months, & perhaps more."[37]

As it happened Copway would not need the missionary post, for his second plan succeeded. The defrocked minister had an acute market sense—he took advantage of his Christianized Indian identity and, at the age of twenty-nine, wrote his life story for an American audience. By a strange coincidence, on 9 December 1846 (the very day after Greene wrote Hall), 150 miles west of Boston in Albany, Copway entered the clerk's office of the District Court of the Northern District of the State of New York, and there registered for copyright purposes *The Life, History, and Travels, of Kah-ge-ga-gah-bowh (George Copway), A Young Indian Chief of the Ojebwa Nation, A Convert to the Christian Faith, and a Missionary to His People for Twelve Years.*[38]

The story of the "pagan savage" turned "civilized Christian Indian Chief" proved extremely successful. By the end of 1848 the young Ojibwe's autobiography went through seven printings, and he had become a popular lecturer.[39] It is extraordinary that he had successfully written his book in the summer and fall of 1846, while "going from place to place, without much of steady employment, for 6 or 8 months, & perhaps more" (to quote Greene's earlier letter). Throughout this time period Elizabeth Copway was pregnant. In early 1847 she gave birth to a baby girl, whom she and George named Pocahontas.[40]

The fact that he chose to write his life story marks yet another departure from the culture of his people, for as Brian Swann and Arnold Krupat have noted, "Although the tribes, like people the world over, kept material as well as mental records of collective and personal experience, the notion of telling the whole of any one individual's life or taking merely personal experience as of particular significance was, in the most literal way, foreign to them, if not also repugnant" (ix).

Copway acknowledged the assistance of a "friend" to whom he submitted his manuscript, who then "kindly corrected all serious grammatical errors, leaving the unimportant ones wholly untouched. . . . The language (except in a few short sentences), the plan, and the arrangement are all my own." Curiously, his interesting volume that reviews his life from birth to the time of publication resembles contemporary works of spiritual confessions (see Ruoff, this volume).

Evidence in the manuscript indicates that he himself supplied the information. He definitely, for instance, contributed the section on the wars of the Ojibwe with the Iroquois. Here Copway terms the Ojibwes' opponents *Hurons*, when in English he should have used the word *Iroquois*. In English different designations are used for the two Iroquoian-speaking confederacies, but he was thinking in Ojibwe and made the wrong translation. In Ojibwe the word used for both the Iroquois and the Hurons is *Nahdooways* (Jones, *History* 32, 111; here I follow Jones's spelling of *Nahdooway*).

Certainly Copway provided the references to the Mississaugas' hunting territories in the early nineteenth century: "The Ojebwas each claimed, and claim to this day, hunting grounds, rivers, lakes, and whole districts of country. No one hunted on each other's ground." Without being so absolute, Jones confirms the statement: "Each tribe or body of Indians has its own range of country, and sometimes each family has its own hunting grounds, marked out by certain natural divisions, such as rivers, lakes, mountains, or ridges"

(Jones, *History* 71). Many other stories in the book, however, cannot be verified.

Without question, Copway had worked hastily on the text. For example, it contains a reference to the "Chippewas of Rama," copied from the Canadian Bagot Commission Report of 1845. The excerpt includes the statement that a band of five hundred Potawatomis from Drummond Island (southeast of Sault Ste. Marie) had settled in 1830 between Lake Simcoe and Georgian Bay. This is a printing error in the original; the word *Potawatomi* (the name of a nation distinct from the Ojibwe) should read *Potaganasee*, the name of the Indian Drummond Islanders, who were Ojibwe. From his youth in Upper Canada and his two years of ministry at the Saugeen Copway knew that these Drummond Islanders were Ojibwe, not Potawatomi, yet he did not correct the error, which he includes in his survey "A Geographical Sketch of the Ojebwa, or Chippeway Nation."[41]

Copway's approach to American audiences is revealed in a diary entry of Alexander Winchell. On 19 September 1847 the Indian writer visited the Pennington Methodist Seminary in New Jersey. He badly needed money, as Winchell states he presented himself as a Methodist minister raising funds for a future Indian school near Rice Lake. Winchell, then an instructor at the seminary, commented, "He is a British Wesleyan missionary to his own people & is now in these parts with the object of raising funds for an Institution of learning to be situated on the north of Lake Ontario about midway between Toronto and Kingston in the immediate neighborhood of several small lakes which he showed on the map [Rice Lake]. . . . He is a smart man about 30 I should think . . . coming boldly & with self reliance before a congregation of white people. . . . he sold several books here containing his biography I have also obtained his *autograph*."[42]

Throughout late 1847 and 1848 Copway spoke along the Atlantic seaboard on Indian and temperance themes. In late October 1847 he addressed the Grand Division of the Sons, Cadets, and Daughters of Temperance, at the E Street Baptist Church in Washington. The Washington correspondent of the *Baltimore Clipper* reported on the "extraordinary" impact of "George Copway, a young chief of the Ojibwa nation of Indians, and a Son of Temperance. His voice was strong, clear, and full, with nothing whatever disagreeable in enunciation. With a fine commanding figure, and suitable gestures, and a thorough acquaintance with his subject, he appeared and spoke to great advantage. To be sure he did not evidence a knowledge of the strict rules which govern the English language, but the deficiency in this particular, was more than compensated by his figures of rhetoric and his thrilling incidents."[43]

His phenomenal success as a writer and lecturer, as the noble Indian Christian convert, prompted new ambitions. He dropped his appeal for funds for an Indian manual labor school and, in early April 1848, announced at Philadelphia his plan for "Kahgega," an Indian territory in the American northwest. "Kahgega," the name he selected, reveals his vanity. It duplicated the first half of his Indian name and means "Ever-to-be."[44]

Although American proposals in the 1830s and early 1840s might have influenced him, an earlier Ojibwe plan for an Indian territory in Upper Canada also contributed. In the summer of 1836 four recently converted chiefs from the St. Clair River region had proposed an Indian territory in the Saugeen area, between Lake Huron and Georgian Bay. There, on the last fertile tract remaining to them in Upper Canada, the Ojibwe could "all settle together, separate from the whites, have our own schools, stores, mills, and other requisites in a settlement, all under our own management." In the Saugeen district they need not "associate with the white people any further than might be for mutual benefit." However, Francis Bond Head, the lieutenant-governor of Upper Canada, turned down the idea and instead tried, unsuccessfully, to remove them to Manitoulin Island on the north shore of Lake Huron. The Ojibwe, in council at Saugeen in 1845 (Copway served as the council's vice president), tried again, unsuccessfully, to create a small Indian territory on the northern portion of the Saugeen tract.[45]

The idea of a Christian Indian territory in Upper Canada, run by the converts and legally recognized as theirs in perpetuity, would have remained fresh in Copway's mind in 1848. He also, no doubt, remembered from his missionary days in the American northwest an earlier American plan, one associated with the politician James Duane Doty in 1841. Recently named governor of Wisconsin Territory, Doty endorsed the plan for the establishment of an Indian territory in the present-day Dakotas, whereby the northern Indians could begin farms, develop their own form of government, and perhaps eventually become a separate state in the United States. Copway likely knew of Doty's plan and its subsequent defeat. In August 1842 the U.S. Senate rejected the proposal by a vote of twenty-six to two.[46] Copway now brought forward a variant of Doty's proposal.

In addresses delivered from South Carolina to Massachusetts, Copway, who presented himself as a "chief" and as a Christian missionary, advocated the establishment of a territory of more than eighteen thousand square miles. It would be located in present-day central and southeastern South Dakota (roughly one-third of the state), right in the remaining hunting grounds of the Sioux. His proposal suspiciously resembled Doty's. On the east bank of the Missouri River he hoped one hundred thousand Indians could be exposed to "the cause of Education and Christianity." His plan would replace the federal government's haphazard removal program, which had caused thousands of deaths, giving the land with a secure title to the Ojibwe and their fellow Great Lake Algonquians.[47] Under a non-Native governor and an Indian lieutenant-governor, the "well educated" Indians would administer the territory in the place of the "elder Indians," whose "prejudicial views have ever unfitted them to become a fit medium of instruction to their people." (How far he had come from the teachings of his father, who had told him as a boy, "If you reverence the aged, many will be glad to hear of your name.")[48] One day, Copway predicted, Washington would grant Kahgega statehood.

A number of important literary figures in New York and Boston responded to Copway's appeal. As the Native American of the frontier period became a distant memory in the eastern United States, a more sympathetic view of Indians emerged. Washington Irving had helped to lead the way. In his *Knickerbocker's History of New York*, published in 1809 and revised five times, most extensively in 1812 and 1848, Irving championed the Indians' right to survive, emphasizing those traits that he felt made the Indians superior to European Americans (Syersted 14, 27). When Copway began his newspaper, *Copway's American Indian*, in the summer of 1851, Irving himself sent a congratulatory letter, as did William Cullen Bryant, James Fenimore Cooper, and other men of letters (*Copway's American Indian* 10 July 1851).

The young Indian from Upper Canada became a good friend of two soon-to-be giants of late-nineteenth-century American literature. After the young historian Francis Parkman met Copway in Boston in March 1849, he noted in a letter to a friend, "I liked him much and wanted to see more of him" (Parkman 1: 59). Henry Wadsworth Longfellow had befriended "Kah-ge-ga-gah-bowh" the month before in neighboring Cambridge. The poet wrote in his diary on 26 February, "Kah-ge-ga-gah-bowh an Ojibway preacher and poet came to see us. The Indian is a good-looking young man, He left me a book of his, an autobiography" (S. Longfellow 2: 135). (Exactly six years later Longfellow would publish *The Song of Hiawatha*. Apparently George Copway was the only Ojibwe Longfellow ever met before he wrote his famous poem based on the Lake Superior Ojibwe).

It is interesting to compare Copway's and Jones's public behavior. Recently M. T. Kelly, a novelist and student of North American Indian life, wrote of Jones, "In spite of being an effective preacher and leader Jones seems to have returned to that kind of stillness, almost withdrawal, that many Indians think of as a proper public presentation of self" (Kelly 62). In contrast, Copway had the directness of an aggressive American promoter. To gain support for "Kahgega," he directly appealed to many prominent individuals who, ashamed of their country's callous treatment of the Indian, encouraged him: Governors Briggs of Massachusetts, Ramsey of Minnesota, and Manly of North Carolina; Mayor Havemeyer of New York; Robert Charles Winthrop, Speaker of the Thirtieth Congress (1847–49); Amos Laurence, a wealthy New England philanthropist (to whom Copway would later dedicate his *Traditional History*); and Edward Everett, a former governor of Massachusetts and then president of Harvard University. To obtain the government's support for his Indian statehood plan, Copway even wrote President Zachary Taylor.[49]

Copway visited the Indians in the area of "Kahgega" in the summer of 1849.[50] In a letter Copway mentioned that he intended to take "a literary gentleman" with him.[51] It remains unknown how many Indians he met and where he actually went.

He went armed with letters of introduction, one from John F. A. Sanford, formerly of St. Louis and then of New York. Sanford made a fortune in the fur trade and married a daughter of Pierre Chouteau, the American fur trader and one of the leading financiers of the day. In 1849 Sanford, then engaged in the financing of western railways, had met Copway in New York. In a note dated 28 July 1849, Sanford assured Henry H. Sibley, an American fur trader in Minnesota (later the first governor of the state in the late 1850s), "Mr. C. has been engaged for some time past in some praiseworthy & philanthropic labour for the benefit and improvement of the Indian tribes. If you can be useful to him in any manner, I shall feel obliged. Mr. C. is well & highly spoken of by all who know him & of his good efforts in the present cause, (he) has met the approbations of all with whom he has conversed.[52]

Julius Taylor Clark, a former Indian agent, later claimed that he gave Copway a copy of his epic poem, *The Ojibue Conquest*. With the author's permission Copway published the poem in his own name, in Clark's words, to permit him to "raise funds to aid him in his work among his people."[53] The Indian lecturer simply added to Clark's manuscript an altered introduction; a short poem of his own to his wife, Elizabeth; and revised endnotes. Anxious for his friends' approval, the Indian lecturer, as early as 29 November 1849, wrote Henry Longfellow to announce, "I am about publishing a 'Short History of Ojibway Nation' traditional and I think will be published by the Harpers." He also mentioned, "I have a poem which I about Publishing called the 'Conquest of the Ojibways.'" In June the following year he presented copies of "his" poem to Henry Longfellow and Francis Parkman.[54]

Copway relished the respect and the deference Americans now paid him. He continually twisted facts to place himself in the best possible light. In 1848, for example, he told George Squier, the archaeologist, that he knew the Lenni Lenape's (Delaware) language as well as their system of sign writing and could translate it (Squier 17). As he never lived, worked, or apparently even visited members of this nation in Canada or the United States, his claim seems unlikely. At the same time, Copway constantly promoted "Kahgega," in which he, the namesake of the proposed territory, would obtain a position of power.

Removal seemed imminent in 1850. Copway had witnessed two U.S. treaties, the first in July 1837 at Fort Snelling, by which the Ojibwe sold to the United States the pine lands of interior Wisconsin and a smaller tract in Minnesota. Just before he left Lake Superior in October 1842 Copway also witnessed the treaty signed at La Pointe, when the Ojibwe surrendered their last territory, most valuable for fishing, in northern Wisconsin and in the upper peninsula of Michigan. He knew that the Indian commissioner, William Medill, in the summer of 1847, had already sent officials to the south shore of Lake Superior to arrange for the Ojibwes' removal west of the Mississippi. On 6 February 1850, just four months before his death, President Zachary Taylor ordered the Ojibwe living on ceded land to prepare for removal that summer.[55]

Indian Commissioner Medill, however, himself spoke against Copway's plan for a permanent Northern Indian territory.[56] As Doty's proposal, so similar in detail, had failed, so, in turn, did Copway's. Despite letters of support from prominent individuals, "Kahgega" lacked enough congressional backing. The U.S. Congress, to which he had submitted a formal proposal, never even discussed it.

The U.S. government's neglect of his "Kahgega" scheme did not lead the Indian promoter to renounce American society and return to live in an Ojibwe community. His role model was Pocahontas, the young Indian Christian convert who in 1614 had married John Rolfe, a Virginian settler. More attached to the English at the Jamestown colony than to her own nation, she chose to live with the colonist. Copway wrote in July 1849, "I admire her character [and] think her name merits a place among the great of earth." Without giving the precise meaning of the word in English he did add, revealingly, that "Pah-ka-on-tis," her Algonquian name, "indicates that her nation looked on her with some suspicion" (letter 5, this volume).

Copway now devoted his time to writing. In 1850 he published his *Traditional History*, the first tribal history in English by a North American Indian from Canada.[57] Writing in a discursive but interesting fashion, he reviewed Ojibwe life, legends, customs, language, and history. His section on the Ojibwe's oral traditions of their defeat of the Iroquois around 1700 (traditions that are corroborated by a number of French and English documentary sources) stands as particularly useful. The *Huron* of his autobiography now became *Iroquois*, and the events of the Ojibwe's victorious campaign against them received exact dates (87–91). Following contemporary practice the work is not annotated, nor are the author's sources of information always identified.

The hand of an outside helper is more evident here than in his earlier autobiography. Did sophisticated statements such as the following on Indian government really come from Copway's own pen?

"These young rulers are apt to be more cautious in the exercise of their governing power than those who possess more mature age with its more mature vanities" (140–41). Are these an experienced writer's additions? As Copway himself noted three years earlier, in his autobiography, "It would be presumptuous in one, who has but recently been brought out of a wild and savage state; and who has since received but three years' schooling, to undertake, without any assistance, to publish to the world a work of any kind."

A finer gloss—evidence of outside collaboration—appears in this second volume; at least one story, the story of his first bear hunt, returns from his *Life*, elaborated on in much greater detail (*History* 31–34; *Life* chap. 2). To give the book a fuller text Copway, like many of his contemporary writers, included verbatim excerpts from other published sources, totaling nearly 100 pages in the 298-page book. He reprinted and acknowledged passages from: General Lewis Cass (15–18), the Native historian William Warren (59–67), the report of the Bagot Commission of 1844 on the Indians of the Canadas (180–95), the work of historian Rev. Edward D. Neill (205–52), newspaper clippings, and an unidentified author (36–41, 284–98). In the end, however, the book does not completely succeed, lacking as it does the unity and the content of William Warren's later *History of the Ojibway Nation*; Peter Jones's *History of the Ojebway Indians*, published posthumously in 1861; and even Copway's own autobiography.[58]

Critic George Harvey Genzmer has termed Copway's writing style "an amalgam of Washington Irving, St. Luke, and elements derived from Methodist exhorters" (433). Elemire Zolla, another commentator, finds that his *Life*, "though quite chaotic on the surface, becomes coherent, carefully elaborated to demonstrate, without openly saying so, the superiority of the natives" (238).

In August 1850 Copway traveled to the World Peace Conference at Frankfurt, Germany. That same year S. W. Benedict in New York brought out a new edition of his autobiography under the title *The Life, Letters and Speeches of Kah-ge-ga-gah-bowh*, the edition that is reprinted in this volume. C. Gilpin in London published a British edition, entitled *Recollections of a Forest Life: or, the Life and Travels of Kah-ge-ga-gah-bowh, or, George Copway, Chief of the Ojibway Nation*, in 1851.

Copway went to Europe in 1850 at the invitation of Elihu Burritt, the leading figure in the U.S. peace movement, who encouraged forty Americans, including the "Indian Chief," to attend.[59] The following year Copway began his weekly newspaper and also published *Running Sketches*, his account of his British and European travels. Elizabeth, who accompanied her husband on the British section of his journey, possibly helped to transcribe the spelling of the German and French words that appear in the travelog and to select many of its lengthy extracts from British guidebooks and newspapers (*Running Sketches* 282–83). The book reviewer in the *New York Daily Tribune* enjoyed the book but expressed some reservations: "The latest production of the enterprising Ojibway, recording his experience during a recent European tour, in which he was feted and flattered beyond measure as a specimen of a live North American Indian. Several of his descriptions are very clever, and as naive confessions of the effect of European life on a native of the forest, may be read with interest. There is too much book-making in the volume, even for a Yankee compiler, to say nothing of an Indian chief, and a great portion of the extracts from common-place sources would have been better omitted."[60]

By late 1850 a number of those who had initially befriended him lost interest. His deficiencies as a lecturer in English became apparent to those who listened to several of his talks. He repeated the same material. The novelty he represented could not be sustained. Burritt himself became disillusioned. He commented in his diary after hearing Copway at the Frankfurt Conference, "the Indian Chief Copway made a long, windy, wordy speech, extremely ungrammatical and incoherent."[61] Another friend who dropped away, Francis Parkman, now questioned Copway's integrity. As early as November 1849 he remarked to George Squier that "Copway is endowed with a discursive imagination and facts grow under his hands into a preposterous shape and dimensions. His scheme of settling the Indians is a flash in the pan, or rather he has no settled scheme at all, and never had any." The historian also resented the Indian author's repeated requests for money. Once he appeared on Parkman's doorstep at five o'clock in the morning (Parkman 1: 66, 78).

As he fell from grace the Indian writer and lecturer edged more and more toward the crude positions of a nativist group who called themselves "native Americans." The members of this anti-immigrant, anti–Roman Catholic movement later organized the political party termed the "Know-Nothings" (see Knobel, "Know-Nothings" and *Paddy* 156–60). (Like the Masonic lodges, the party had secret grips and passwords. When asked what their purpose was, the members answered, "I know nothing.") Saluting him as a "real North American," the New York chapter of the nativist Order of United Americans elected Copway as a member early in 1852.[62]

The summer of 1851 proved a trying time for Copway. Apparently with financial support from only one individual (who donated twenty-five dollars), he struggled to bring out his weekly newspaper, *Copway's American Indian*. For three months he succeeded, but by the end of September he could not continue.[63] The final issue appeared on 4 October 1851, exactly two weeks after a New York paper destined to have a much longer life was born: the *New York Times*.

By late 1851 Copway had only two realistic options. He could return to the Rice Lake band in Canada West, or he could remain in New York. The first alternative was still open. Since his departure from Canada he had stayed in communication with his father, who once, in 1850, had visited him in Boston. He also remained on good terms with his younger brother, David.[64] But his ties with his community were not strong. He knew that many at Rice Lake recalled his casual handling of their band funds five years earlier and did not wish to see him back. Half a century later older members of the band still remembered him as the young man who "committed a forgery and fled from Justice to the United States."[65] No, he would not go home. Moreover, by this point, had he not largely adopted the viewpoints of many in the larger society? He wrote in his last book, for instance, that "man is the one for whom this world is made" (*Running Sketches* 27). He thus distanced himself from those Native American spiritual beliefs that saw human beings as part, not the center, of the universe. He had adopted the newcomers' viewpoint that the purpose of nature was to serve humans.

Anxious to succeed in New York and to duplicate his early triumphs, Copway decided to stay in the city of over half a million people and to hope for better times. Elizabeth Copway stood by her husband. She composed at least one of his letters: an appeal to James Fenimore Cooper, the author who, in eleven books, had perhaps more than anyone else impressed his romantic conception of the Indian upon America and the world at large (Keiser 101). In the note to Cooper, written in her husband's name, she requested support for *Copway's American Indian*, noting that "For of all the writers of our

43

dear native land you have done more justice to our down trodden race than any other author."[66]

Prior to their contacting Cooper tragedy had struck George and Elizabeth. Between August 1849 and January 1850 three of their four children died; the last of the three, their daughter Pocahontas, died of typhus fever in New York City.[67] There can be no question that Copway, stricken by family tragedy, forsaken by his literary friends, and bankrupt, had begun by the summer of 1851 to lose all touch with reality. The previous year in England he had become infatuated with the voice of Jenny Lind, the sensational thirty-year-old Swedish soprano. Wearing his Native costume, he had attended one of her concerts in the Liverpool Philharmonic Hall, and on the "Swedish Nightingale's" American tour he had seen her again. The Indian lecturer wrote an extraordinary letter to Abel Bingham, the Baptist minister at Sault Ste. Marie, in mid-July 1851. To the straightlaced clergyman, renowned for his "heavy, dull, traditional tirades against the evil nature of mankind," the impoverished newspaper editor announced that it was "likely" that "Miss Jenny Lind" would accompany him and "Mr. Willis The Poet" (probably Nathaniel P. Willis) on a forthcoming visit to the "west."[68]

Copway's review of Francis Parkman's *History of the Conspiracy of Pontiac*, or that which he approved for the next-to-last issue of his newspaper, provides evidence of his mental collapse. Even the most casual reader of Parkman's book would sense the author's hatred of and disgust for Indians. Rather than portraying them in positive terms as Irving and Cooper had (and as Longfellow would), Parkman conjured up the old American frontiersman's hatred of the "savage." He stressed torture, scalping, and murder and overlooked the peaceful tendencies of Indian culture. As one modern critic, Robert Shulman, has written, "his racist view of Indian culture and character did violence to the Indian's humanity, to his very status as a person" (235; Jennings). Yet *Copway's American Indian* reported on 27 September 1851, "his [Parkman's] style is lucid and interesting, devoid of flowery extravagance yet manifesting a poetic spirit. As an historian, he confines himself strictly to facts and weaves so interesting a chain about his readers that it is with regret we must lay him down until next week."

After late 1851, Copway descended further into poverty and obscurity, while apparently still living in New York, the city that he had described but two years earlier: "The walls, how high the streets, how hard. All rush by me with arrow-like speed. Silks and rags go side by side in Broadway. Here are the world's extremes. I cannot remain here long."[69] He supported his family through lectures, but it proved difficult to make a living at this.[70]

The little evidence that survives hints at his confused mental state. In Buffalo, New York, in 1852 he, together with a businessman and an undertaker, removed the bones of Red Jacket (c. 1758–1830), the famous Seneca chief, from a cemetery on a former Indian reservation to a more secure place. But Copway failed to notify the Senecas. When they learned that Copway and the two Americans had violated the grave, the Senecas, highly incensed, demanded the remains, which they gave to the favorite stepdaughter of Red Jacket.[71]

Copway's financial state appears to have been desperate. In 1852 he wrote a Mr. E. Corning, probably Erastus Corning, a prominent New York State railway developer, "Let me have $6 dollars and I go to Phil[adelphia] where I can get enough money to get home."[72] Another surviving Copway letter, dated April 1854, to a Rev. S. K. Lothrop, asks if Lothrop will donate eighty dollars to help pay for the schooling of Copway's son, George Albert. Copway briefly abandoned Elizabeth in the summer of 1856, a period in which he wrote a rather incoherent letter that appeared in the *New York Times* on 8 September 1856.[73]

Copway had long viewed his wife as an appendage to himself and constantly used her to advance his own career. Before their eventual reunion she considered leaving him forever, writing to her sister Sarah on 24 July 1856, "It is very desirable to be loved but to be a slave to an unworthy object is revolting to our pride."[74] Still, she loved him deeply. In 1858 Elizabeth asked to be reunited with him; they had another child, a daughter, born in 1860 or 1861.[75]

A number of George Copway's letters, all written in 1858, have survived, and they indicate that despite seven years of failure he remained determined to regain fame and influence among the Americans. The collection, now held in the Library of Congress, includes receipts made out to him for ads—presumably for his lectures—in an unidentified Washington paper and in the *Philadelphia Evening Bulletin*. He also sought a federal government job, for the collection of letters and receipts in the Library of Congress contains a petition, with text and signatures (all written in a suspiciously similar hand) from eighteen chiefs, warriors, and interpreters in the Kansas and Nebraska Territories. The petition requests that $2,750 be paid to Copway and $2,250 to another educated Indian, "to defray the expenses of the Agents in visiting the settlements of our various nations in order that we may avail ourselves of their advice and suggestions in repeated visits for the promotion of civilization among our Tribes."[76]

By the summer of 1858 he wanted work so badly that he, again unsuccessfully, volunteered to convince the remaining Seminole Indians in Florida to leave for the Indian Territory (present-day Oklahoma). About fifteen years earlier the U.S. government had captured and deported roughly forty-four hundred Seminoles west of the Mississippi, but several hundred escaped transport to Oklahoma by fleeing to the Everglades and the Big Cypress Swamp in southern Florida. Now Copway suggested that he assist the U.S. government to expel them from the state.[77]

The most telling reference to how far the once celebrated Indian writer and lecturer had fallen appeared in the *Boston Daily Journal* on 15 October 1858: "George Copway, the educated Indian Lecturer, who was to have delivered a lecture last evening in Mercantile Hall, but declined, owing to the small number of persons in attendance, was arrested last evening by Constable Farr, for a debt of $20, at the suit of J.A. Robie, and committed to jail for safe keeping until such time as he can give security, or be heard before a Commissioner."[78]

A reference to Copway in a letter written by Longfellow to the German poet Ferdinand Freiligrath in December 1858 provides further documentary evidence of his descent in popularity. Longfellow told Freiligrath, "Ka[h]gegahga[h]bow[h] is still extant. But I fear he is developing the Pau-Puk-Keewis element rather strongly" (H. Longfellow 4: 109). Longfellow's perceptive comparison of Copway and Pau-Puk-Keewis, the mischief-maker in his *Song of Hiawatha* (completed in 1855), betrays his loss of faith in his Indian friend. This final defection must have hurt Copway greatly. He so enjoyed Longfellow's poem that he named his last-born daughter Minnehaha, or "Laughing Water," after the wife of Hiawatha.[79]

After 1858 Copway's trail becomes ever more difficult to follow. On 24 January 1860 he announced to Erastus Corning a forthcoming lecture tour to England and a trip to the Holy Land, as he wished to become "the first Indian who will have visited that country." He asked Corning for "one hundred dollars for six weeks" and reported that since the previous November he had ceased "to take any 'firewater' in any shape."[80]

Copway's cousin, John Johnson, believed that Copway died at Pontiac, Michigan, about 1863, and many others have cited this as his death date.[81] Rev. Chauncey Hobart, a former Methodist colleague in Minnesota, understood the former temperance speaker "finally drank himself to death" (Hobart 28). In reality, however, Copway remained very much alive after 1863. In October 1863 he lived in the town of Geneva, near Rochester, New York.[82] In 1864 he worked with his brother David as a Union Army recruiter in the Civil War.[83]

George and David collected a bounty for enlisting Canadian Indians in the Civil War. According to a report of the Canadian Indian Department dated 8 October 1864, "two Indians named David and George Copway, the former belonging to the Rice Lake Band and the other from the United States have unlawfully enticed & carried away by false pretenses to the United States several young Indians and enlisted them in the American Army."[84] Apparently the Copway brothers signed up, among others, the son of one of the Rice Lake Chiefs. The young man caught a fever in Washington and died, returning home in a metal coffin.[85] Copway's only living son, George Albert, who he had once hoped would enter Dartmouth College, served in the Third Regiment of the New York Light Artillery, from 1862 to 1864, when he was discharged.[86]

The Union Army's Indian recruiter resurfaced after the war, once again living in an American community. In 1867 a "Kah-ge-ga-gah-bowh" appeared in Detroit, advertising his services as a practitioner of the "healing art." His notices in the *Detroit Free Press* invited the sick to "come and be cured."[87]

In the summer of 1868 Copway returned again to Canada, which had recently become a much larger country than in the days of the Union of the Canadas. The previous summer the Canadas, now called Ontario and Quebec, had united in a new confederation with New Brunswick and Nova Scotia.

The fifty-year-old Indian appeared alone at the Lake of Two Mountains, a large Algonquin-Iroquois mission in Quebec, about thirty miles northwest of Montreal. His wife, with their young daughter, had left him to live near her father and her relatives at Port Dover, Ontario.[88] Copway's ties with the Rice Lake band had long been cut. When he met the Abbé Jean-André Cuoq, the resident Sulpician missionary, he told the Roman Catholic priest that he was a "pagan." At the time of his arrival the Iroquois at the station, ironically, were on the point of turning Methodist to protest the Catholics' claim of ownership of the reserve. Initially, on account of his remarkable cures with herbs, leaves, flowers, bark, and roots, Copway became quite popular with both nations. But once the ex-Methodist preacher announced that he had come to study and embrace Roman Catholicism, the Iroquois avoided him.

Copway immediately became the priests' Native champion. When the Iroquois' Methodist allies brought Charles Chiniquy, the famous French-Canadian apostate, to the Lake of Two Mountains, Copway convinced most of the Algonquins to stay away from Chiniquy's services. The Sulpicians baptized "Kakikekapo" (better known, the Abbé Cuoq writes, under the title of "Doctor Copway") as "Joseph-Antoine" on 11 January 1869. Several days later their important convert, once renowned as an author, lecturer, and most recently as an herbal doctor, suddenly died, just before his first communion as a member of the Roman Catholic Church.[89]

Recently, Canada's first Indian writer has been rediscovered, brought back in part by a new interest in North American Indian culture and history and as a result of a desperate need for Native-produced source materials. Over the last twenty-five years, publishers in Canada and the United States have reissued his writings.[90] The *Saturday Evening Post* even included one of its former contributor's stories in its collection *Best of the Post 1728 to 1976*.[91] Educators in Minnesota have included him in an important school resource unit on Ojibwe history.[92] Canadian and U.S. editors have run excerpts from his writings in their anthologies of North American Indian literature.[93] Academic writers cite him.[94]

Another important reason exists for the return of Kahgegagahbow: the very readable quality of his best writing. M. T. Kelly, the respected Canadian fiction writer and poet, once described Copway's *Traditional History* as "heart-breaking, haunting, luminous" (qtd. in Colombo). His *Life*, in its numerous editions, shares the same qualities.

## NOTES

1. Copway is termed "Canada's first literary celebrity in the United States" with the knowledge that the Nova Scotian author Thomas Chandler Hal-

iburton (1796–1865) also enjoyed great popularity (with his stories about "Sam Slick" in the late 1840s and early 1850s). But Haliburton was a British North American rather than a Canadian author, as Nova Scotia was, until 1867, a separate colony from the Canadas.

2. I have used Copway's *Life* as a source throughout this essay, and particularly for information on Copway's early life.

3. Copway himself translated his name, Kahgegagahbowh, as "Firm Standing." See the inscribed copy of the engraving of Copway that appears as the frontispiece of his autobiography in the New York State Archives, Albany, New York. The handwritten inscription on the engraving reads:

Kah-ge-ga-gah-bowh
Firm Standing
George Copway
Feby 10th 1860

"Standing Firm," or "Committed," is a better arrangement of the two words (my thanks to James Clifton for this point). Jones translated the name as "he who stands forever" (113).

4. For background on the Mississauga see my articles "Who Are the Mississauga?" and "The Dispossession." Copway (*Traditional History* 53) states that he once walked seventy-five miles in a day. Peter Jones wrote of the Ojibwe on the north shore of Lake Ontario: "The Indian men are swift travelers on foot. I have known them to walk with ease fifty and sixty miles a day, and some have accomplished the journey from Niagara to Toronto, a distance of eighty miles, in one day, and that too when there was only a narrow Indian footpath. Whenever they go on a journey they carry with them their blankets, guns, pipes, tomahawks, and provisions" (*History* 75).

5. Copway mentioned that his father was a veteran of the War of 1812 in his address to the Virginia legislature in early 1849. See the clipping from the *Richmond (VA) Southerner* 15 January 1849, Henry Rowe Schoolcraft Papers, Library of Congress, reel 60. The newspaper reports Copway as stating, "my father, . . . was engaged in the Battle of Lundy's Lane and other places."

For a short review of the vision quest, see Brown 222–23. Copway mentions once fasting as a boy for four or five days (*Traditional History* 154). On the concept of "power," see Black.

6. The explanation of the conversion of the Mississauga to Christianity is very complex. For a fuller treatment of the subject, see my *Sacred Feathers* 52–97.

7. Letter from James Evans, Rice Lake, 28 December 1829, *Christian Guardian* (Toronto) 9 January 1830. Rev. Daniel McMullen reported that 130 adults and 90 children lived at the mission in February 1830 (*Christian Guardian* 13 March 1830).

8. See also Copway's reference to his father's anti-British viewpoint in his address to the Virginia legislature, reported in the *Richmond (VA) Southerner* 15 January 1849, Henry Rowe Schoolcraft Papers, Library of Congress, reel 60. In his *Life* (chap. 6), Copway stated that the sole and only payment was "the sum of £750." In actual fact, the *annual* payment was £740. See Treaty no. 20 in *Indian Treaties* (1: 48–49). Copway, in another reference to the treaty, does include the correct reference—in citing the Bagot Commission Report of 1844 he notes payment was "an annuity of £740" (chap. 17, "7. Chippewas at Rice Lake").

9. The ages of Cahbeach (sometimes written *Kahbeege*) and Taunchey are given in "Indian Missions," *Christian Guardian* 9 October 1833. John Johnson's age is estimated in Jackson 473.

10. W. Case, "Canada Missions," *Christian Advocate* 26 September 1834; Peter Jones, "George Kahbooway and the Sioux," Peter Jones anecdote book, no. 15, Victoria University Library, Toronto, Peter Jones Collection (henceforth cited as VUL, PJC). According to Copway's account, he went separately with his uncle, John Taunchey, so perhaps there were two parties to the Sault.

11. Edmund Franklin Ely, entry for 24 August 1835, La Pointe, journal nos. 6, 7, 8, Writing Book, 1 January 1835–21 September 1835. Ely Papers, Diaries, Box 1, Minnesota Historical Society, St. Paul (henceforth cited as MHS). See also Prindle 24–26. Chandler, a non-Native Methodist missionary, served at Keweenaw during the winter of 1834–35.

12. MHS, Grace Lee Nute Papers, CBX9 N976, Transcript, S. Hall to D. Greene, La Pointe, Lake Superior, 15 February 1847, American Board of Commissioners for Foreign Missions (ABCFM), MSS 245: no. 67-ALS, Northwest Mission Papers, compiled by Grace Lee Nute, CBX9 N976, MHS (hereafter cited as Nute Papers).

13. Transcript, Illinois Conference Missionary Society Minutes, Rushville, 10 October 1836, Nute Papers.

14. Johnson later commented that as missionaries' helpers they "were looked upon as holy men in keeping with the duties they performed for the clergy" ("Enmekahbowh alias John Johnson," Crow Wing, Minnesota, 24 February 1862, in *Petaubun* 2.2 (March 1862); translated into English by Aylmer Plain, Chief, Sarnia Indian Reserve; published by George L. Smith, Bright's Cove, Ontario, February 1976).

15. Boyle 20. An account of the Ebenezer manual labor school, by Charles N. Akers, appeared in the *Jacksonville Weekly Journal* in 1910. The clipping is in the Samuel Spates Papers, A-S738, MHS.

16. N. C. "Kah-ge-ga-gah-bow the Chippewa Indian," *Boston Daily Journal* 23 February 1849, transcript in Nute Papers.

17. Copway to Rev. J. F. Wright, Lebanon, Illinois, 26 May 1838, Chicago Historical Society.

18. Carroll 4: 372; obituary of Sarah Howell Wilson, *Port Hope Evening Guide* (Ontario) 3 December 1894. My thanks to Wilson Hamly, Sarah Howell Wilson's grandson, for this reference.

193. Sproat 206; Transcript, S. Hall to D. Greene, La Pointe, 15 February 1847, MSS 265: no. 67-ALS, Nute Papers.

20. Peter Jones, anecdote book, "Oojebway names given by Kahkewaquonaby, Credit Mission Decr. 20th, 1839," Wahbegoonequay ("the Female White Flower") VUL, PJC; Credit Mission Church Registry, marriage record of George Copway and Elizabeth Howell, 1 June 1840, United Church Archives, Toronto.

Dr. D. H. Hamly of Hawkesbury, Ontario, the grandson of Elizabeth Howell Copway's sister Sarah, informed me that he had been told that the Howell family had disapproved of the marriage. Hamly to Donald B. Smith, Hawkesbury, Ontario, 18 September 1984. Dr. Hamly passed away in November 1984.

21. Copway to Jones, 2 June 1840, in Peter Jones album, 1831–32, in the possession of Louise Thorp, Aldergrove, B.C.

22. Mrs. E. Copway to Eliza Jones, Credit, 2 June 1840, Eliza Jones album, in the possession of Louise Thorp, Aldergrove, B.C.

23. "Mrs. George Copway's Death," unidentified newspaper, probably from a newspaper in Port Dover, Ontario, 19 January 1904; a photostat of the clipping in the Howell family Bible was sent to me by Dr. Hamly.

24. Elizabeth Howell Copway to Sarah Howell Wilson, 24 July 1856; Dr. Hamly sent me a photostat of the letter. Elizabeth Howell Copway to Sarah Howell, Goderich, 18 June 1845, in the possession of Wilson Hamly, Elora, Ontario. A third letter, undated but presumably written in 1858, is in the Miscellaneous Manuscripts Collection, box 57, George Copway materials (twenty items received from the Chester County [PA] Historical Society in 1952), Library of Congress, Washington DC. The letter is from "E" (Elizabeth Copway) to George Copway.

25. For an example of a letter apparently written without the help of his wife, see George Copway's letter dated New York, 5 September 1856, published in the *New York Times* 8 September 1856. He had abandoned his wife early in July 1856; Elizabeth Howell mentions this in her letter to her sister, Sarah Howell Wilson, 24 July 1856, copy in author's possession. See also Copway's note to Charles Norton, 20 May 1850, for an indication of his awkward writing style. The letter to Norton, now in the Charles E. Norton Collection, Houghton Library, Harvard University, begins: "The last time we met was at that lovely place of your fathers in the famed City of Cambridge, and you were to have seen for me all the strange sights which you should meet and there I was to have eaten all the Buffalo meat which should be placed in my way."

26. Rev. S. G. Wright made the comment in reference to the Ojibwe at Red Lake, Minnesota, in 1843; see Foster, "The Oberlin Ojibway Mission" 7.

27. Transcript, Rev. W. Boutwell quoted in S. Hall to D. Greene, La Pointe, 1 April 1847, ABCFM, MSS 245: no. 68-ACS, Nute Papers. For background information on Boutwell see Hickerson.

28. Brunson, *A Western Pioneer* 2: 81. I am assuming here that the three Christian Indians indeed wore European clothes, as this would be a sign of their "civilization" and their commitment to it.

29. T. M. Higginson to S. P. Jarvis, 20 September 1844, R. G. 10, Indian Affairs Records, vol. 510, p. 76, microfilm C-13,344, National Archives of Canada (herafter cited as NAC).

30. Peter Jones to George Vardon, Edinburgh, 1 August 1845, George Vardon Papers, M. G. 19 F23, NAC.

31. T. M. Higginson to George Copway, 30 August 1845, R. G. 10, vol. 511, p. 79, microfilm C-13,344, NAC.

32. Transcript, S. Hall to D. Greene, La Pointe, Lake Superior, 15 February 1847, ABCFM, MSS 245: no. 67-ALS, Nute Papers.

33. "Address to the Governor General from the Chiefs of the Chippewa Assembled in General Council," 3 July 1845, R. G. 10, vol. 268, p. 163946, microfilm C-12,653; Jacob Mittiquab to T. G. Anderson, Owen Sound, 23 December 1845, vol. 409, pp. 732–33, microfilm C-9,615; T. G. Anderson to George Copway, Toronto, 10 February 1846, vol. 532, p. 135; T. M. Higginson to T. G. Anderson, Montreal, 4 May 1846, vol. 511, p. 344; George Paudash, John Crow, John Taunchey to T. G. Anderson, Rice Lake, 13 May 1846, vol. 409, n.p. All in NAC.

One should perhaps not be too harsh about Copway's unfamiliarity with mid-nineteenth-century accounting procedures, when one realizes that even an important civil servant such as Samuel Peters Jarvis had the same shortcoming. In the mid-1840s the former chief superintendent for Indian affairs for Upper Canada (1837–45) could not account for a sum between four thousand and nine thousand pounds. Jarvis retired in disgrace but was never forced to replace the missing funds. See Douglas Leighton and Robert J. Burns, "Samuel Peters Jarvis," *Dictionary of Canadian Biography*, 1983 ed.

34. George Copway to T. G. Anderson, Peterboro, 17 May 1846, R. G. 10, vol. 408, pp. 498–99, microfilm C-9,614, NAC. Very little evidence has survived and it is unclear how he spent the funds. The Europeans' accounting procedures would be totally new to the Indian bands, as would money itself. Copway claimed to have spent some of the money from the Saugeen band to pay for the education of Moses Alexander, a son of Chief Alexander of the Saugeen; Moses Alexander lived with the Copway family. See Copway to T. G. Anderson, Rice Lake, 22 January 1846, vol. 408, p. 486, microfilm C-9,614; and Copway to George Vardon, Toronto, 15 October 1845, vol. 410, p. 759, microfilm C-9,616, NAC.

35. T. G. Anderson to J. M. Higginson, Toronto, 9 June 1846, R. G. 10, vol. 532, p. 249; George Vardon to T. G. Anderson, 17 June 1846, vol. 511, p. 380, NAC.

36. "Expelled from the Connexion at Conference," *Christian Guardian* 12 August 1846; Peter Jones to Eliza Jones, 4 June 1846, Letterbook, VUL, PJC.

37. Transcript, D. Greene to S. Hall, Missionary House, Boston, 8 December 1846, ABCFM, Indians, vol. 10, p. 14-LBPC, Nute Papers.

38. The information about the book's registration appears on the back side of the title page.

39. The subsequent editions of Copway's *Life* are listed in the American Library Association, *The National Union Catalog Pre-1956 Imprints* (London: Mansell, 1970), 122: 349–50. For a review of one of his first lectures, see *Albany (NY) Argus*, 11 March 1847.

40. George Copway to Samuel Miller, Philadelphia, 28 September 1847, Princeton University Libraries. "As I am to be in Princeton next Sabbath I have an important matter to request of you & that is to Baptize our little girl about 7 months old to be called 'Pocahontas.'"

41. John Johnson, superintendent general of Indian affairs, identifies the "Potaganasee" as Ojibwe in his letter to Colonel Darling, Montreal, 28 October 1824, R. G. 10, vol. 494, p. 31008, NAC.

42. Alexander Winchell, diary entry for 20 September 1847, Alexander Winchell Papers, Bentley Historical Library, University of Michigan, Ann Arbor. For details on Winchell's life see *Dictionary of American Biography*, 1936 ed. My thanks to Nancy Bartlett, reference archivist at the Bentley Historical Library, for these references.

Alexander Winchell has accurately reported what George Copway said, as an earlier letter of Copway's dated 29 June 1847 also survives. On that date he wrote F. W. Porter of the Sunday School Union in Philadelphia, stating that he was "an agent" for "the Indian Manual Labor School . . . those who have sent me abroad—the Christianized Chiefs of the Chippewa nation to get funds." Copway elaborated on the plan to build the school, northeast of Toronto, at Alderville, Rice Lake. Optimistically, he added, "we hope in the first to accommodate about 500 students. . . . We will supply the Presbyterian Baptist, and Methodist Missionaries, with suitable teachers interpreters and Missionaries to further the great work of saving my poor brothers from ruin & death." Miscellaneous Manuscript Collection, American Philosophical Society, Philadelphia.

43. "The Indian Orator—Temperance Meeting Extraordinary," datelined Washington, 27 October 1847, *Baltimore Clipper* 28 October 1847: p. 4, col. 1. My thanks to Daniel F. Littlefield Jr. of the American Native Press Archives, University of Arkansas at Little Rock, for this reference.

44. Transcript, D., "Letters from Washington, Washington," 22 February

1848, *New York Observer* 26 February 1848, Box 13; transcript of address, George Copway to President Zachary Taylor, 7 March 1849, Office of Indian Affairs, Washington, 7 March 1849, Box 14, Nute Papers. The announcement of his forthcoming Philadelphia talk appears in "The North American Indians," *Philadelphia Public Ledger* 30 March 1848. My thanks to Donna Jekabson for this reference.

The word *Kahgega* is translated in Copway, *Organization* 19.

45. For information on the Methodist Ojibwes' attempts to establish an Indian territory in the fertile Saugeen district of Upper Canada in the mid-1830s to the mid-1840s, see Donald B. Smith, "The Mississauga, Peter Jones and the White Man: The Algonkians' Adjustment to the Europeans on the North Shore of Lake Ontario to 1860," Ph.D. thesis, University of Toronto, 1975, 239–41, 274. For the reference to the petition of 1836 see Joshua Wawanash, Head Chief; Edward Oojebegun, Gordon Megezeense, Peter Shuhdawgun, Chiefs; "Ahonejewuhnoong [The rapids of the St. Clair River], July 5, 1836," *Christian Guardian* 20 July 1836. For the recommendation of the Council of 1845, see Copway, *Life*, chap. 16.

46. I am grateful to James Clifton for this point. For Doty's plan see A. Smith 256–62.

47. The Algonquin (or Algonkin) nation that lived in the Ottawa Valley (in present-day Ontario and Quebec) during the seventeenth century gave its name to the Algonquian (or Algonkian) linguistic family. (Note that the name of the nation ends in *-quin* and that of the linguistic family in *-quian*.) The Algonquian linguistic family, the largest group in Canada, extends from the Atlantic coast to the Rockies.

48. Copway, *History* 260, 271, 277, 285–86. His father's statement appears in chapter 2 in this volume. Copway explains the territory should be "150 miles square" (*History* 185), but by this he means 150 miles by 150 miles, or 12,500 square miles (see also Copway, *Organization* 18). My thanks to the South Dakota State Library, Pierre, South Dakota, for their help with this point. Knobel reviewed Copway's project, see particularly 179. A short account of the "Kahgega" proposal appears in Copway, "Indian Civilization, no. III," *Saturday Evening Post* 13 April 1850 (rpt. in Copway, *History* 271–78). He advanced one of the earliest versions of his plan in an address in Columbia, South Carolina, on 15 December 1848; see the *Charleston (SC) Courier* 22 December 1848 (rpt. this volume, "Address before Both Houses of the Legislature of South Carolina").

49. See the "Letters" in Copway, *Organization* 26–32; Transcript, George Copway to President Zachary Taylor, Washington, 7 March 1849, Office of Indian Affairs, Box 14, Nute Papers.

50. From the west he wrote Francis Parkman. See his letter dated 1 October 1849, Massachusetts Historical Society, Boston.

51. Transcript, George Copway to Thomas Ewing, Washington, 12 May 1849. Office of Indian Affairs, Box 14, Nute Papers.

52. J. F. Sanford to Henry H. Sibley, New York, 28 July [1849], Henry H. Sibley Papers, Minnesota Historical Society Research Center, St. Paul. For details on Sanford see Hodder, particularly 3–7.

53. Clark, *The Ojibue Conquest* v; a copy of this volume is in the library of the Minnesota Historical Society. Copway published the poem under his own name as *The Ojibway Conquest*.

Information on Clark (1814–1908) appears in Clark's "Reminiscences of the Chippewa Chief" 378; see also the sketch by Keyes.

54. Copway to Henry W. Longfellow, New York, 29 November 1849, Henry W. Longfellow Collection, Houghton Library, Harvard University. The presentation copies to Parkman (Boston, 17 June 1850) and to Longfellow (Cambridge, 12 June 1850) are now in the Houghton Library, Harvard University.

55. Copway's presence at the signing of the treaty at Fort Snelling in 1837 is mentioned by Brunson (*A Western Pioneer* 2: 82–83). Copway discusses the treaty at La Pointe in 1842 in this volume, chapter 15.

Clifton fully examines the removal question in "Wisconsin Death March"; see also his "The Tribal History" 91–92.

56. Transcript, William Medill to Thomas Ewing, secretary of the interior, Office of Indian Affairs, 21 March 1849, Box 14, Nute Papers. Medill's own proposal of tribal reservations is outlined in Trennert 30–31.

57. Apess's *A Son of the Forest* (1829) was the first published, full-life history written by a North American Indian. See Ruoff, "Three Nineteenth-Century American Indian Autobiographers," 253. Barry O'Connell has included the revised edition (1831) of *A Son of the Forest* in *On Our Own Ground*.

58. W. Roger Buffalohead provides a short sketch of Warren's life in his introduction to the most recent edition of Warren's *History* (1984), ix–xvii. Warren completed his manuscript in 1852, but it was published in 1885.

59. Merle C. Curti, "Elihu Burritt," *Dictionary of American Biography*, 1929 ed.

60. Transcript, *New York Daily Tribune* 4 September 1851, Nute Papers.

61. Diary entry for 24 August 1850, Burritt's diaries, New Britain Public Library, Local History Room, New Britain CT. My thanks to Curator Arlene C. Palmer for forwarding the reference. Another negative assessment was made in a Newark, New Jersey, newspaper in early February 1851. The listener judged the Indian lecturer a speaker of limited ability, one who loved pleasantries and words "lugged in by the shoulders, and without much reference to the sense they may make" (cited in Dippie 280).

62. "A Real North American," *The Republic* 3 (February 1852): 105. My thanks to Dale Knobel for this reference.

63. *Copway's American Indian* 4 October 1851. Copway published the paper in New York from 10 July to 4 October 1851. To the best of my knowledge the only complete set of the newspaper is in the Newspaper collection at Colindale, British Library, London.

64. Copway to J. W. Thornton, New York, 3 July 1850, Chicago Historical Society. See also his letters to his father in *Copway's American Indian* 19 and 26 July 1851. David Copway is mentioned in the census for the Rice Lake Reserve, Canada West Census, 1851 (available on microfilm at the Archives of Ontario and the National Archives of Canada). His age is given as twenty-eight, and his occupation listed as "carpenter."

65. William McFarlane, Indian Agent, Mud and Rice Lake Reserves, to the Department of Indian Affairs, Keene, Ontario, 13 October 1902, R. G. 10, vol. 3058, file 251780, NAC.

66. Copway to James F. Cooper, New York, 12 June 1851, Beinecke Library, Yale University, New Haven, CT. The statement that Elizabeth composed this letter is based on a comparison of it and the letter Elizabeth Howell Copway sent to Sarah Howell Wilson 24 July 1856, photostat copy supplied to the author by the late Dr. Hamly. Axel Sjoberg, a handwriting analyst, examined these two letters and judges them to have been executed by the same person. "The style of writing is identical and the similarities in mid-zone strokes confirm my view" (Sjoberg to author, Saskatoon, Saskatchewan, 13 February 1987).

67. The reference to the death of the three Copway children appears in Transcript, *Boston Post* 11 January 1850, Box 15, Nute Papers. The short notice states, "The only daughter of Mr. Copway, the Indian Chief, died on Saturday, at the Western Hotel, N. York, of typhus fever; she was four years old. About a month ago, Mr. Copway lost his youngest son, and in August lost his youngest child." Actually this young girl, named Pocahontas, would have only have been three, as she was born in 1847. Copway also wrote Charles Norton on 20 May 1850 that he had "traveled through the North West Indian Territory, Michigan Wisconsin Minnesota Iowa, Missouri and Nebraska Territories last summer to see the Indians and saw over 17000 . . . and returned to NY quite late when I lost 2 of my children again besides the one I lost in Wisconsin while I was traveling" (Charles E. Norton Collection, Houghton Library, Harvard University).

68. Cumming 225. Copway mentions Jenny Lind at great length in *Running Sketches* 149–52. His presence at her concert at the Liverpool Philharmonic Hall is confirmed in the Liverpool *Standard* 20 August 1850. My thanks to Ken Thomas for this reference. Copway's letter to Abel Bingham, New York, 14 July 1851, is in the Bingham Papers, Clarke Library, Central Michigan University, Mount Pleasant. My thanks to Janet Chute for this reference.

69. This volume, Letter 1. Copway sent a letter to the editor of the *New York Times*, New York, 5 September 1856 (*New York Times* 8 September 1856). His wife also mentions that he was living in the city in the summer of 1856. Elizabeth Howell Copway to Sarah Howell Wilson, Buffalo, 24 July 1856, photostat supplied by Dr. D. H. Hamly.

70. See, for example, the references in the *Chicago Democratic Press* 1 and 2 February and 11 May 1855.

71. William C. Bryant to Gen. Ely S. Parker, Buffalo, 25 June 1884, in appendix 10 of "Obsequies of Red Jacket at Buffalo, October 9th, 1884," *Transactions of the Buffalo Historical Society*, vol. 3 (Buffalo NY: Buffalo Historical Society, 1885), 63. My thanks to Daniel F. Littlefield Jr. of the American Native Press Archives, University of Arkansas at Little Rock, for this reference. William N. Fenton informs me that reference to the incident also appears in Parker 204–5 and Armstrong 178.

72. Copway to E. Corning, 18 March 1852, Chicago Historical Society. Corning wrote a letter on Copway's behalf on 16 March 1858. See Erastus Corning to J. Thompson, secretary of the interior, Washington, 16 March 1858, in Miscellaneous Manuscripts Collection, Box 57, George Copway materials, Library of Congress, Washington DC. For a sketch of Corning's life see Frank Haigh Dixon, "Erastus Corning," *Dictionary of American Biography*, 1930 ed.

73. Transcript, George Copway to S. K. Lothrop, New Port, 10 April 1854. S.P.G.I., MSS VI-ALS, Nute Papers.

74. Elizabeth Howell Copway to Sarah Howell Wilson, Buffalo, 24 July 1856, photostat supplied by Dr. D. H. Hamly.

75. The letter from "E" (Elizabeth Copway) to George Copway, written presumably in 1858, indicates her wish for a reconciliation: "Oh George reflect for one moment for Heaven's sake have mercy upon me let your heart relent and breath the word *forgiveness*, have you never needed it." The letter is contained in Miscellaneous Manuscripts Collection, Box 57, George Copway materials, Library of Congress, Washington DC.

76. Twenty items, all apparently completed in 1858, are included in the Miscellaneous Manuscripts Collection, Box 57, George Copway materials, Library of Congress, Washington, DC. These items were received from the Chester County (PA) Historical Society in 1952.

77. Copway to J. B. Floyd, secretary of war, Washington, 23 July 1858, Lawrence Lande Collection, MG53 B55, microfilm reel H-1463, NAC. My thanks to Jim Morrison for this reference. For a short review of Seminole history see Sturtevant.

78. Transcript, *Boston Daily Journal* 15 October 1858, "*Boston Daily Journal*, Extracts of Minnesota Interest, 1842–1859," MHS.

79. P. E. Jones to L. Vankoughnet, Hagersville, 10 May 1883, R. G. 10, vol.

2221, file 43432, NAC. John Johnson, Copway's cousin, also ranked the *Song of Hiawatha* as the greatest poem of the white man. Others agreed. In 1860 the name of the Rice Lake reservation was changed to "Hiawatha" (Martin et al. 40). According to Martin et al., the Prince of Wales chose the name on the occasion of his visit to Rice Lake on his Canadian tour.

80. Copway to Erastus Corning, New York, 24 January 1860, Historical Society of Pennsylvania.

81. Pilling 93. Genzmer repeats the error, as do most of the general biographical reference works.

82. Copway to E. Corning, Rochester, 7 October 1863, New York Historical Society.

83. G. S. Walcot to Chas. Dupont, Indian Office, Manitowaning, Quebec, Indian Department, 8 October 1864, R. G. 10, vol. 615, pp. 336–38, NAC. My thanks to both Jim Morrison and Janet Chute for this reference.

84. G. S. Walcot to Chas. Dupont, Indian Office, Manitowaning, Quebec, Indian Department, 8 October 1864, R. G. 10, vol. 615, pp. 336–38, NAC.

85. G. H. Hale, "A Hiawatha Indian (dated Orillia, January 29, 1903)," *Gazette* (Montreal) 14 February 1903: 10.

86. George A. Copway, Battery E.G. 3 N.Y.L. Art'y, Bookmark 11900 D (EB) 1886, National Archives and Records Administration, General Reference Branch (NNRG-P) Washington DC. In his letter to Erastus Corning of 27 January 1860 (Historical Society of Pennsylvania), Copway wrote, "Having only one son the only child I have I have make the necessary arrangements for him to go to Dartmouth College free as you know—and he is now 18 yrs. old."

87. "Local Matters: Indian Doctor," *Detroit Free Press* 6 September 1867; "Today's Advertisements," *Detroit Free Press* 1 October 1867. Interestingly, his brother David's occupation in 1861 is also listed as "Indian root doctor" (Rice Lake Reserve, Canada West Census, 1861).

88. P. E. Jones to L. Vankoughnet, Hagersville, 10 May 1883, R. G. 10, vol. 2221, file 43432, NAC. Jones states that "Minnehaha" Copway was then "an estimable young lady 22 years of age." Hence she would have been born in 1860 or 1861. The dates on her gravestone are 27 September 1863–21 March 1921 (gravestone of Frances M. Copway Passmore, Greenwood Cemetery, Brantford, Ontario).

Elizabeth Copway and her daughter Frances (Minnehaha) Copway are listed as living in Woodhouse Township near Port Dover in the census of 1871 (see District 11, Sub-District Woodhouse). Elizabeth's father died at Port Dover in April 1869 (see the *Norfolk Reformer* [Simcoe] 15 April 1869). Her mother had died in Port Dover in 1864 (see the *Norfolk Reformer* 6 January 1865). My thanks to Nancy Kiefer for references. Henry Howell mentions "my daughter Elizabeth Copway, wife of George Copway" in his will, dated 3

April 1869, Norfolk County Surrogate Court Index 1858–1900, Eva Brook Donly Museum, Simcoe, Ontario. My thanks to Helen Coomber of Hamilton, Ontario, for this reference. Elizabeth Copway died in 1904 (gravestone located in graveyard of Woodhouse United Church near Port Dover, Ontario).

89. All the details on Copway's sojourn at the Lake of Two Mountains are from Abbé Cuoq, "Notes historiques pour servir à l'histoire de la Mission du lac des Deux Montagnes," M.G. 17, A 7-2-6, vol. 18, NAC.

90. In 1970 a Canadian reprint house (Canadiana in Toronto) reprinted the British edition of his autobiography, titled *Recollections of a Forest Life*. A major Toronto publisher (Coles) reissued his *Traditional History* (British ed., 1850) in 1972; AMS Press in New York also reprinted the book, in 1978 under the title *Indian Life and Indian History*.

91. Copway, "The End of the Trail." My thanks to Dr. Francis Paul Prucha for this reference.

92. The unit contains twenty-eight components, one of which is the attractive posters, the "Biography banners. Designed for classroom display, these eight banners present a gallery of outstanding Ojibwe men and women, each of whom contributed in some special way to the history of his people" (*The Ojibwe: A History Resource Unit*, produced by the Ojibwe Curriculum Committee in cooperation with the American Indian Studies Department, University of Minnesota, and the Educational Services Division, Minnesota Historical Society, n.d. [early 1970s]). Copway is the subject of one of the eight biographical banners.

93. Kent Gooderham, ed., *I Am an Indian* (Toronto: J. M. Dent, 1969), 133–34; Charles Hamilton, ed., *Cry of the Thunderbird: The American Indian's Own Story*, 2nd ed. (Norman: University of Oklahoma Press, 1972), 27–31, 42–43, 46–48, 52, 60–63, 66–67, 75–75; Abraham Chapman, ed., *Literature of the American Indians: Views and Interpretations. A Gathering of Indian Memories, Symbolic Contexts, and Literary Criticism* (New York: New American Library, 1975), 31–52; Bernd Peyer, ed., *The Elders Wrote: An Anthology of Early Prose by North American Indians 1768–1931* (Berlin: Reimer, 1982), 75–94; Penny Petrone, ed., *First People First Voices* (Toronto: University of Toronto Press, 1983), 106–10; Daniel David Moses and Terry Goldie, eds., *Anthology of Canadian Native Literature of English* (Toronto: Oxford University Press, 1992), 17–25; Margaret Conrad, Alvin Finkel, Cornelius Jaenen, *History of the Canadian Peoples. Beginnings to 1867* (Toronto: Copp Clark Pitmann, 1993), 27–28; Paul Lauter et al., eds., *The Heath Anthology of American Literature*, 2nd ed., vol. 1 (Lexington MA: D. C. Heath, 1994), 1484–97.

94. Several examples include: Calvin Martin, *Keepers of the Game: Indian-Animal Relationships and the Fur Trade* (Berkeley: University of California Press, 1978), 71–72, 74–75, 95, 202, 204, 208; Vecsey 31, 55–56, 168–69;

Francis Jennings, *The Ambiguous Iroquois Empire* (New York: W. W. Norton, 1984), 21–22; Bruce G. Trigger, *Natives and Newcomers: Canada's "Heroic Age" Reconsidered* (Kingston: McGill-Queen's University Press, 1985), 167; Schmalz 12, 21–22, 24, 134, 152, 156, 162–63. Grace Rajnovich, *Reading Rock Art. Interpreting the Indian Rock Paintings of the Canadian Shield* (Toronto: Natural Heritage/Natural History Inc., 1994), 20, 22, 26, 88, 131–32, 140, 162–63.

# The Life, Letters and Speeches of
# Kah-ge-ga-gah-bowh
## or, G. Copway, *Chief Ojibway Nation*.

A Missionary for many years in the North-West;
now the projector of the Concentration
of the North-Western Indian Tribes, for the
Better Promotion of their Physical
Improvement.

To the clergy and laity of
the American and British dominions,
this brief history of a child of the forest,
and of his nation, is most respectfully
and affectionately inscribed by
the author.

# Preface

In presenting my life to the public, I do so with the greatest diffidence, and at the earnest solicitation of numerous friends. I am an Indian, and am well aware of the difficulties I have to encounter to win the favorable notice of the white man. Yet one great object prompts me to persevere, and that is, that I may, in connection with my life, present the *present state* and *prospects* of my poor countrymen—feeling that the friends of humanity may still labor and direct their benevolence to those who were once the lords of the land on which the white man lives—and assist in rescuing them from an untimely and unchristian grave.

I have noticed some of our prominent chiefs now living; the missionaries laboring amongst my people; the extent of the missionary field; and an appeal to all who feel interested in the welfare of the Indian race.

If ever I see the day when my people shall become happy and prosperous, I shall then feel great and lasting pleasure, which will more than repay me for the pain, both of body and mind, which I have endured for the last twelve years. My motto is—"*My poor People.*"

In all my crooked paths, I have endeavored to mean well. I thank my friends for their kind gifts and wishes. Yet still as much, and more, remains to be accomplished.

Pray for us—that *religion* and *science* may lead us on to intelligence and virtue; that we may imitate the good white man, who, like the eagle, builds its nest on the top of some high rock—*science*; that we may educate our children, and turn their minds to God. Help us, O help us to live—and teach us to die a Christian's death, that our spirits may mingle with the blessed above.

KAH-GE-GA-GAH-BOWH.

# A Word to the Reader

It would be presumptuous in one, who has but recently been brought out of a wild and savage state; and who has since received but three years' schooling, to undertake, without any assistance, to publish to the world a work of any kind. It is but a few years since I began to speak the English language. An unexpected opportunity occurred of submitting my manuscript to a friend, who has kindly corrected all *serious* grammatical errors, leaving the unimportant ones wholly untouched, that my own style may be exhibited as truly as possible. The public and myself are indebted to him for his kind aid, and he has my most sincere thanks. The language, (except in a few short sentences,) the plan, and the arrangement are all my own; and I am wholly responsible for all the statements, and the remaining defects. My work is now accomplished; and I am too well aware of the many faults which are still to be found therein. Little could I imagine, that I should have to contend with so many obstacles. All along, have I felt my great deficiency; and my inadequacy for such an undertaking. I would fain hope, however, that the kind Reader will throw the mantle of charity over errors of every kind. I am a stranger in a strange land! And often, when the sun is sinking in the western sky, I think of my former home; my heart yearns for the loved of other days, and tears flow like the summer rain. How the heart of the wanderer and pilgrim, after long years of absence, beats, and his eyes fill, as he catches a glance at the hills of his nativity, and reflects upon the time when he pressed the lips of a mother, or sister, now cold in death. Should I live, this painful pleasure will yet be mine. *"Blessed be the Lord, who hath helped me hitherto."*

KAH-GE-GA-GAH-BOWH
alias
GEORGE COPWAY.
July 1847.

# The Life of Kah-ge-ga-gah-bowh

### CHAPTER 1

The Christian will no doubt feel for my poor people, when he hears the story of one brought from that unfortunate race called the Indians. The lover of humanity will be glad to see that that once powerful race can be made to enjoy the blessings of life.

What was once impossible—or rather thought to be—is made possible through my experience. I have made many close observations of men, and things around me; but, I regret to say, that I do not think I have made as good use of my opportunities as I might have done. It will be seen that I know but little—yet O how precious *that little!*—I would rather lose my right hand than be deprived of it.

I loved the woods, and the chase. I had the nature for it, and gloried in nothing else. The mind for letters was in me, *but was asleep,* till the dawn of Christianity arose, and awoke the slumbers of the soul into energy and action.

You will see that I served the imaginary gods of my poor blind father. I was out early and late in quest of the favors of the *Mon-e-doos* (spirits,) who, it was said, were numerous—who filled the air! At early dawn I watched the rising of the *palace* of the Great Spirit—*the sun*—who, it was said, made the world!

Early as I can recollect, I was taught that it was the gift of the many spirits to be a good hunter and warrior; and much of my time I devoted in search of their favors. On the mountain top, or along the valley, or the water brook, I searched for some kind intimation from the spirits who made their residence in the noise of the waterfalls.

I dreaded to hear the voice of the angry spirit in the gathering clouds. I looked with anxiety to catch a glimpse of the wings of the Great Spirit, who shrouded himself in rolling white and dark clouds—who, with his wings, fanned the earth, and laid low the tall pines and hemlock in his course—who rode in whirlwinds and tornadoes, and plucked the trees from their woven roots—who chased other gods from his course—who drive the Bad Spirit from the surface of the earth, down to the dark caverns of the deep. Yet he was a kind spirit. My father taught me to call that spirit Ke-sha-mon-e-doo—*Benevolent spirit*—for his ancestors taught him no other name to give to that spirit who made the earth, with all its variety and smiling beauty. His benevolence I saw in the running of the streams, for the animals to quench their thirst and the fishes to live; the fruit of the earth teemed wherever I looked. Every thing I saw smilingly said Ke-sha-mon-e-doo nin-ge-oo-she-ig—*the Benevolent spirit made me.*

Where is he? My father pointed to the sun. What is his will concerning me, and the rest of the Indian race? This was a question that I found no one could answer, until a beam from heaven shone on my pathway, which was very dark, when first I saw that there was a true heaven—not in the far-setting sun, where the Indian anticipated a rest, a home for his spirit—but in the bosom of the Highest.

I view my life like the mariner on the wide ocean, without a compass, in the dark night, as he watches the heavens for the north star, which his eye having discovered, he makes his way amidst surging seas, and tossed by angry billows into the very jaws of death, till he arrives safely anchored at port. I have been tossed with hope and fear in this life; no star-light shone on my way, until the men of God pointed me to a Star in the East, as it rose with all its splendor and glory. It was the Star of Bethlehem. I could no say in the language of the poet—

"Once on the raging seas I rode,
  The storm was loud, the night was dark;
The ocean yawned, and rudely blowed
  The wind that tossed my foundering bark."

Yes, I hope to sing some day in the realms of bliss—

"It was my guide, my light, my all!
  It bade my dark foreboding cease;
And through the storm and danger's thrall,
  It led me to the port of peace."

I have not the happiness of being able to refer to written records in narrating the history of my forefathers; but I can reveal to the world what has long been laid up in my memory; so that when "I go the way of all the earth," the crooked and singular paths which I have made in the world, may not only be a warning to others, but may inspire them with a trust in God. And not only a warning and a trust, but also that the world may learn that there once lived such a man as Kah-ge-ga-gah-bowh, when they read his griefs and his joys.

My parents were of the Ojebwa nation, who lived on the lake back of Cobourg, on the shores of Lake Ontario Canada West. The lake was called Rice Lake, where there was a quantity of wild rice, and much game of different kinds, before the whites cleared away the woods, where the deer and bear then resorted.

My father and mother were taught the religion of their nation. My father became a medicine man in the early part of his life, and always had by him the implements of war, which generally distinguish our head men. He was a good hunter as any in the tribe. Very few brought more furs than he did in the spring. Every spring they returned from their hunting grounds. The Ojebwas each claimed, and claim to this day, hunting grounds, rivers, lakes, and whole districts of country. No one hunted on each other's ground. My father had the northern fork of the river Trent, above Bellmont Lake.

My great-grandfather was the first who ventured to settle at Rice Lake, after the Ojebwa nation defeated the Hurons, who once inhabited all the lakes in Western Canada, and who had a large village just on the top of the hill of the Anderson farm, (which was afterwards occupied by the Ojebwas,) and which furnished a magnificent view of the lakes and surrounding country. He was of the *Crane tribe*, i. e. had a crane for totem—*coat of arms*—which now forms the totem of the villagers, excepting those who have since come amongst us from other villages by intermarriage, for there was a law that no one was to marry one of the same totem, for all considered each other as being related. He must have been a daring adventurer—*a warrior*— for no one would have ventured to go and settle down on the land from which they had just driven the Hurons, whom the Ojebwas conquered and reduced, unless he was a great hero. It is said that he lived about the islands of Rice Lake, secreting himself from the enemy for several years, until some others came and joined him, when they formed a settlement on one of the islands. He must have been a great hunter, for this was one of the principal inducements that made him venture there, for there must have been abundance of game of every kind. The Ojebwas are called, here and all around, Massissuagays, because they came from Me-sey Sah-gieng, at the head of Lake Huron, as you go up to Sault St. Marie falls.

Here he lived in jeopardy—with his life in his hand—enduring the unpleasant idea that he lived in the land of bones—*amidst the gloom*, which shrouded the once happy and populous village of the Hurons; here their bones lay broad-cast around his wigwam; where, among these woods once rang the war cry of the Hurons, echoing along the valley of the river Trent, but whose sinewed arms now laid low, with their badges and arms of war, in one common grave, near the residence of Peter Anderson, Esq. Their graves, forming a hillock, are now all that remain of this once powerful nation. Their bones, gun barrels, tomahawks, war spears, large scalping knives, are yet to be found there. This must have taken place soon after the formation of the settlement in Quebec.

The *Crane tribe* became the sole proprietors of this part of the Ojebwa land; the descendants of this tribe will continue to wear the dinstiguishing sign; except in a few instances, the chiefs are of this tribe.

My grandfather lived here about this time, and held some friendly intercourse with the whites. My father here learned the manners, customs, and worship of the nation. He, and others, became acquainted with the early settlers, and have ever been friendly with the whites. And I know the day when he used to shake the hand of the white man, and, *very friendly*, the white man would say, "*take some whiskey*." When he saw any hungering for venison, he gave them to eat; and some, in return for his kindness, have repaid him after they became good and great farmers.

My mother was of the *Eagle tribe*; she was a sensible woman; she was as good a hunter as any of the Indians; she could shoot the deer, and the ducks flying, as well as they. Nature had done a great deal for her, for she was active; and she was much more cleanly than the majority of our women in those days. She lived to see the day when most of her children were given up to the Lord in Christian baptism; while she experienced a change of heart, and the fulness of God in man, for she lived daily in the enjoyment of God's favors. I will speak more of her at a proper time, respecting her life and happy death.

My father still lives; he is from sixty-five to seventy years old, and is one of the chiefs of Rice Lake Indian Village. He used to live fire-water before he was converted to God, but now lives in the enjoyment of religion, and he is happy without the devil's spittal—*whiskey*. If Christianity had not come, and the grace of God had not taken possession of his heart, his head would soon have been laid low beneath the fallen leaves of the forest, and I, left, in my youthful days, an orphan. But to God be all the praise for his timely deliverance.

The reader will see that I cannot boast of an exalted parentage, nor trace the past history to some renowned warrior in days of yore; but let the above suffice. My fathers were those who endured much; who first took possession of the conquered lands of the Hurons.

I was born in *nature's wide domain!* The trees were all that sheltered my infant limbs—the blue heavens all that covered me. I am one of Nature's children; I have always admired her; she shall be my glory; her features—her robes, and the wreath about her brow—the seasons—her stately oaks, and the evergreen—her hair—ringlets over the earth, all contribute to my enduring love of her; and wherever I see her, emotions of pleasure roll in my breast, and swell and burst like waves on the shores of the ocean, in prayer and praise to Him who has placed me in her hand. It is thought great to be born in palaces, surrounded with wealth—but to be born in nature's wide domain is greater still!

I was born sometime in the fall of 1818, near the mouth of the river Trent, called in our language, Sah-ge-dah-we-ge-wah-noong, while my father and mother were attending the annual distribution of the presents from the government to the Indians. I was the third of our family; a brother and sister being older, both of whom died. My brother died without the knowledge of the Saviour, but my sister experienced the power of the loving grace of God. One brother, and two step-brothers, are still alive.

I remember the tall trees, and the dark woods—the swamp just by, where the little wren sang so melodiously after the going down of the sun in the west—the current of the broad river Trent—the skipping of the fish, and the noise of the rapids a little above. It was here I first saw the light; a little fallen down shelter, made of evergreens, and a few dead embers, the remains of the last fire that shed its genial warmth around, were all that marked the spot. When I last visited it, nothing but fur poles stuck in the ground, and they were leaning on account of decay. Is this dear spot, made green by the tears of memory, any less enticing and hallowed than the palaces where princes are born? I would much more glory in this birth-place, with the broad canopy of heaven above me, and the giant arms of the forest trees for my shelter, than to be born in palaces of marble, studded with pillars of gold! Nature will be nature still, while palaces shall decay and fall in ruins. Yes, Niagara will be Niagara a thousand years hence! the rainbow, a wreath over her brow, shall continue as long as the sun, and the flowing of the river! While the work of art, however impregnable, shall in atoms fall.

Our wigwam we always carried with us wherever we went. It was made in the following manner: Poles were cut about fifteen feet long; three with crotches at the end, which were stuck in the ground some distance apart, the upper ends meeting, and fastened with bark; and then other poles were cut in circular form and bound round the first, and then covered with plaited reeds, or sewed birch bark, leaving an opening on top for the smoke to escape. The skins of animals formed a covering for a gap, which answered for a door. The family all seated tailor-fashion on mats. In the fall and winter they were generally made more secure, for the purpose of keeping out the rain and cold. The covering of our wigwam was always carried by my mother, whenever we went through the woods. In the summer it was easier and pleasanter to move about from place to place, than in the winter. In the summer we had birch bark canoes, and with these we travelled very rapidly and easily. In the winter everything was carried upon the back. I have known some Indians to carry a whole deer—not a small one, but a buck. If an Indian could lift up his pack off the ground by means of his arms, it was a good load, not too light nor too heavy. I once carried one hundred and ninety-six weight of flour, twelve pounds of shot, five pounds of coffee, and some sugar, about a quarter of a mile, without resting—the flour was in two bags. It felt very heavy. This was since I travelled with the missionaries, in going over one of the portages in the west.

Our summer houses were made like those in gardens among the whites, except that the skeleton is covered with bark.

The hunting grounds of the Indians were secured by right, a law and custom among themselves. No one was allowed to hunt on another's land, without invitation or permission. If any person was found trespassing on the ground of another, all his things were taken from him, except a handful of shot, powder sufficient to serve him in going *straight* home, a gun, a tomahawk, and a knife; all the fur, and other things, were taken from him. If he were found a second time trespassing, all his things were taken away from him, except food sufficient to subsist on while going home. And should he still come a third time to trespass on the same, or another man's hunting grounds, his nation, or tribe, are then informed of it, who take up his case. If still he disobey, he is banished from his tribe.

My father's hunting ground was at the head of Crow River, a branch of the river Trent, north of the Prince Edward District, Canada West. There are two branches of this river—one belongs to George Poudash, one of the principal chiefs of our nation; the other to my father; and the Crow River belongs to another chief by the name of John Crow. During the last war the Indians did not hunt or fish much for nearly six years, and at the end of that time there were large quantities of beaver, otter, minks, lynx, fishes, &c.

These hunting grounds abound with rivers and lakes; the face of the country is swampy and rocky; the deer and the bear abound in these woods; part of the surrendered territory is included in it. In the year 1818, 1,800,000 acres of it were surrendered to the British government. For how much, do you ask? For $2,960 per annum! What a *great sum* for British generosity!

Much of the back country still remains unsold, and I hope the scales will be removed from the eyes of my poor countrymen, that they may see the robberies perpetrated upon them, before they surrender another foot of territory.

From these lakes and rivers come the best furs that are caught in Western Canada. Buyers of fur get large quantities from here. They are then shipped to New York city, or to England. Whenever fruit is plenty, bears are also plenty, and there is much bear hunting. Before the whites came amongst us, the skins of these animals served for clothing; they are now sold from three to eight dollars apiece.

My father generally took one or two families with him when he went to hunt; all were to hunt, and place their gains into one common stock till spring, (for they were often out all winter,) when a division took place.

### CHAPTER 2

In the fall we gathered the wild rice, and in the winter we were in the interior. Some winters we suffered most severely, on account of the depth of snow, and the cold; our wigwams were often buried in snow. We not only suffered from the snow and the cold, but from hunger. Our party would be unable to hunt, and being far from the white settlements, we were often in want of food. I will narrate a circumstance of our sufferings, when I come to speak of the actual condition of our people, before Christianity was introduced among us, which, when I think of it, I cannot but bless God for his preserving kindness to us, in sparing us to hear his blessed word.

Soon after being Christianized, my father and another Indian, by the name of Big John, and myself, went out hunting; my father left his family near the mission station, living in the wigwam. While we were out on the hunting grounds, we found out that some Indians had gone before us on the route up the river, and every day we gained upon them: their tracks were fresh. The river and the lakes were frozen, and we had to walk on the ice. For some days together we did not fire a gun, for fear they would hear it and go from us, where we could not find them. At length we found them by the banks of the river, they were Nah-doo-ways or Mohawks, from Bay Quinty; they were seven of them, tall fellows. We shook hands with them: they received us kindly. My father had determined to take all they had, if we should overtake them. After they gave us a good dinner of boiled beaver, my father stepped across the fire and ripped open two packs of beaver furs, that were just by him. He said to them "We have only one custom among us, and that is well known to all; this river, and all that is in it are mine: I have come up the river behind you, and you appear to have killed all before you. This is mine, and this is mine," he said, as he touched with the handle of his tomahawk each of the packs of beaver, otter, and muskrat skins. I expected every moment to see my father knocked down with a tomahawk, but none dared touch him; he counted the skins and then threw them across the fire-place to us. After this was done, the same thing took place with the guns; only one was left them to use on their way home. He talked to them by signs, and bade them, as the sailors say, "weigh anchor and soon be under way;" they left, and we took possession of the temporary wigwam they had built. We never saw them afterwards on our hunting grounds, though some of them have been there since.

My father was ever kind and affectionate to me, particularly after the death of my brother, which was occasioned by the going off of a gun, the load passing through the arm, and so fractured it that it soon mortified and caused his death. He believed in persuasion; I know not that he ever used harsh means, but would talk to me for hours together. As soon as it was dark he would call me to his side and begin to talk, and tell me that the Great Spirit would bless me

76

with a long life if I should love my friends, and particularly the aged. He would always take me with him when going any where near, and I learned his movements, for I watched him going through the woods. Often would he tell me that when I should be a man that I must do so, and so, and do as he did, while fording the rivers, shooting the deer, trapping the beaver, etc., etc. I always imitated him while I was a hunter.

My mother was also kind and affectionate; she seemed to be happy when she saw us enjoying ourselves by her; often she would not eat much for days together; she would leave all for us! She was an industrious woman; in the spring she made more sugar than any one else; she was never idle while the season for gathering wild rice lasted.

I was taught early to hunt the deer. It was a part of our father's duty to teach us how to handle the gun as well as the bow and arrow. I was early reminded to hunt for myself; and thirst to excel in hunting began to increase; no pains were spared, no fatigue was too great, and at all seasons I found something to stimulate me to exertion, that I might become a good hunter. For years I followed my father, observed how he approached the deer, the manner of getting it upon his shoulders to carry it home. The appearance of the sky, the sound of the distant water-falls in the morning, the appearance of the clouds and the winds, were to be noticed. The step, and the gesture, in travelling in search of the deer, were to be observed.

Many a lecture I received when the deer lay bleeding at the feet of my father; he would give me an account of the nobleness of the hunter's deeds, and said that I should never be in want whenever there was any game, and that many a poor aged man could be assisted by me. "*If you reverence the aged, many will be glad to hear of your name*," were the words of my father. "The poor man will say to his children, 'my children, let us go to him, for he is a great hunter, and is kind to the poor, he will not turn us away empty.' The Great Spirit, who has given the aged a long life, will bless you. You must never laugh at any suffering object, for you know not how soon you may be in the same condition: never kill any game needlessly." Such was his language when we were alone in the woods. Ah! they were lessons directed from heaven.

In the spring but few deer were killed, because they were not in good order, the venison being poor, and the skin so thin, that it was no object to kill them. To hunt deer in the summer was my great delight, which I did in the following manner:—During the day I looked for their tracks, as they came on the shore of the lake or river during the night; they came there to feed. If they came on the bank of the river, I lighted pitch pine, and the current of the river took the canoe along the shore. My lantern was so constructed that the light could not fall on one spot, but sweep along the shore. The deer could see the light, but were not alarmed by it, and continued feeding on the weeds. In this way, I have approached so close that I could have reached them with my paddle. In this manner our forefathers shot them, not with a gun, as I did, but with the bow and arrow. Bows were made strong enough, so that the arrows might pierce through them.

Another mode of hunting on the lakes, preferred by some, is shooting without a light. Many were so expert, and possessed such an accuracy in hearing, that they could shoot successfully in the dark, with no other guide than the noise of the deer in the water; the position of the deer being well known, in this way, the darkest night. I will here relate an occurrence which took place in 1834. My father and I were hunting on the river Trent, in the night; after we had shot two deer, and while returning homewards, we heard the noise of a deer's footsteps. The night was dark as pitch. We approached the deer. I asked my father at what part of the animal I should aim. He replied, "at the head or neck." I poised my gun and fired; hearing no noise, I concluded that my game was sure. I lighted some pitch pine and walked towards the spot from which the noise had come. The deer lay dead and bleeding. On examination I found that I had shot it just below the ear. In the fall of the year, also, I was accustomed to hunt; the meat was very fine, and the skins, (from which our moccasons were made,) were much thicker at this season. Those that could track the deer on fallen leaves and shoot one each day, were considered first rate hunters. The fall is the best time to determine the skill of the huntsman.

Of all animals the bear is the most dangerous to hunt. I had heard so many stories about its cunning that I dreaded to meet one. One day a party of us were going out to hunt the bear, just below Crooke's rapids. After we had made a temporary place to stay for several days, we marched in file; after a while we halted, each took a different direction. My father said, "my son you had better loiter behind the rest. Do not go far, for you may lose yourself." We parted—I took my course, and the rest theirs. I trembled for fear I should see what I was hunting for! I went only where I least expected to see a bear, and every noise I heard in the woods, I thought must be one. As I stood on an old mossy log, there was such a crack on the side of the hill that my heart leaped within me. As I turned and looked, there was a large bear running towards me! I hid myself behind a tree; but on he came; I watched him; he came like a hogshead rolling down hill; there were no signs of stopping; when a few feet from me, I jumped aside, and cried *Yah!* (an exclamation of fear.) I fired my gun without taking sight; in turning suddenly to avoid me, he threw up the earth and leaves; for an instant I was led to believe that the bear was upon me. I dropped my gun and fell backwards, while the bear lay sprawling just by me. Having recovered, I took up my gun and went a few feet from where I fell, and loaded my gun in a hurry. I then sought for a long pole, and with it, I poked it on its side, to see if it was really dead. It did not move, it was dead; but even then I had not courage to go and touch it with my hands. When all was over, and I had told my father I had killed a bear, I felt as though my little leggings could hardly contain me. In examining it, I found the ball had gone through its heart.

Bear meet is like pork. It can be kept a long time when cured. For some weeks together this was the only kind of food we used to eat.

The oil of the bear is used for various purposes. One use is, to prevent the falling out of the hair. The apothecaries buy it from the Indians for about five dollars a gallon.

The skins of bears are what our forefathers wore, before the white people came amongst us, as blankets; but now *land-sharks*, called traders, buy them from the Indians for a mere trifle.

I loved to hunt the bear, the beaver, and the deer but now, the occupation has no charms for me. I will now take the goose quil, for my *bow*, and its point for my *arrow*. If perchance I may yet speak; when my poor aching head lies low in the grave; when the hand that wrote these recollections shall have crumbled into dust; then these pages will not have been written in vain.

> "O! Land of rest for thee I sigh—
>   When will the season come,
> When I shall lay my armor by,
>   And dwell in peace at home."

The beaver was hunted in the spring and fall. They were either trapped or shot. Among all the animals that live in the water, the beaver is of the kindest disposition, when tamed; it is a very cleanly animal; sits on it broad tail on the ground while feeding; feeds all night, and sleeps most of the day. The beaver skin was once worth from eight to ten dollars apiece, or four dollars per pound.

The otter, too, is much valued. The whites buy the skins, and make caps of them. They are mostly caught in traps. In the fall and spring they are always on the move.

The otter is a greedy animal; it can be tamed, but when hungry becomes cross, and often bites. If it be a half mile off, it will scent any food preparing in the wigwam.

When about five years old, I commenced shooting birds, with a small bow and arrow. I have shot many a bird, but am no more a marksman. I used to feel proud when I used to carry home my own game. The first thing that any of the hunters shot, was cooked by the grand-father and grand-mother, and there was great rejoicing, to inspire the youthful hunter with fresh ardor. Day after day I searched for the grey squirrel, the woodpecker, the snipe, and the snow bird, for this was all my employment.

The gun was another instrument put into my hands, which I was taught to use both carefully and skilfully. Seldom do accidents occur from the use of fire arms among our people. I delighted in running after the deer, in order to head and shoot them. It was a well known fact that I ranked high among the hunters. I remember the first deer I ever shot, it was about one mile north of the village of Keene. The Indians, as has just been said, once had a custom, which is now done away, of making a great feast of the first deer that a younger hunter caught: the young hunter, however, was not to partake of any of it, but wait upon the others. All the satisfaction he could realize, was to thump his heels on the ground, while he and others were singing the following hunter's song:

"Ah yah ba wah, ne gah me koo nah vah!
Ah yah wa seeh, ne gah me koo nah nah."*
   The fattest of the bucks I'll take,
   The choicest of all animals I'll take

In the days of our ignorance we used to dance around the fire. I

*These lines are sung over and over again, for about half an hour.

shudder when I think of those days of our darkness. I thought the Spirit would be kind to me if I danced before the old men; and day after day, or night after night, I have been employed with others in this way. I thank God that those days will never return.

CHAPTER 3

The Ojebwas, as well as many others, acknowledged that there was but one Great Spirit, who made the world; they gave him the name of good or benevolent; *kesha* is benevolent, *monedoo* is spirit; Ke-sha-mon-e-doo. They supposed he lived in the heavens; but the most of the time he was in the *Sun*. They said it was from him they received all that was good through life, and that he seldom needs the offering of his Red children, for he was seldom angry.

They also said he could hear all his children, and see them. He was the author of all things that they saw, and made the other spirits that were acknowledged by the Ojebwas. It was said that these other spirits took special care of the various departments of nature. The god of the *hunter* was one who presided over the animals; the god of *war* was one who controlled the destinies of men; the god of *medicine* was one who presided over the herbs of the earth. The fishes had theirs, and there was another over the moon and stars!

"Millions of spiritual creatures walk the earth
Unseen, both when we sleep and when we wake."

There was one unappeasable spirit, called Bad Spirit, Mah-je-mah-ne-doo. He, it was thought, lived under the earth; and to him was attributed all that was not good, bad luck, sickness, even death. To him they offered sacrifices more than to any other spirit, things most dear to them. There were three things that were generally offered to the Bad Spirit, viz. a dog, whiskey and tobacco, a fit offering, with the exception of the poor dog. The poor dog was painted red on its paws, with a large stone and five plugs of tobacco tied about its neck; it was then sunk in the water; while the beating of the drum took place upon the shore, and words were chanted to the Bad Spirit.

The whiskey was thus offered to the Bad Spirit:—When the Indians were seated around the wigwam, or on the grass, and the person who deals out the whiskey had given all the Indians a dram, then

81

the devil was to have his share; it was poured on the ground, and if it went down quickly, it was thought he accepted the offering.

Fire water was sometimes poured out near the head of the graves of the deceased, that their spirits might drink with their former friends. I have often seen them sit around the grave, and, as they drank, make mention of the name of their dead, and pour some whiskey on the ground.

Our religion consisted in observing certain ceremonies every spring. Most of the Ojebwas around us used to come and worship the Great Spirit with us at Rice Lake. At this festival a great many of the youth were initiated into the medical mysteries of the nation. We were taught the virtues of herbs, and the various kinds of minerals used in our medicine. I will here describe the Me-tae-we-gah-mig or Grand Medicine Lodge. It was a wigwam 150 feet long and 15 feet wide. The clan of medicine men and women alone were allowed to be inside, at each sitting, with their medicine badge, on each side of the wigwam. Then there were four old men who took the lead in singing, and beating the drum, as they stood near the centre. Before them were a company who were to take degrees. There were four grades in the institution; and, as I have thought, somewhat similar to the Masonic institution.

After the singing commenced, the whole company arose and danced, as they moved from one end of the wigwam to the other. As they go round, one-half of them cast their heads down upon their bosoms, as if affected by the medicine, which was kept in small skins, and which they pretended to thrust at each other; this was done to deceive the ignorant. These forms were continued several days. The party to be made medicine men and women, looked on in the mean time, to see what they would have to do themselves. Then they are taken to another place with our medicine men, and are taught the science of medicine. After receiving instructions, another day was allotted to give them instruction on morality. They were advised on various subjects. All were to keep silence, and endeavor to retain what they were taught. I will here give some of the sayings of our medicine men:

"If you are a good hunter, warrior, and a medicine man, when you die, you will have no difficulty in getting to the far west in the spirit land."

"Listen to the words of your parents, never be impatient, then the Great Spirit will give you a long life."

"Never pass by any indigent person without giving him something to eat. Owh wah-yah-bak-mek ke-gah-shah-wa-ne-mig—the spirit that sees you will bless you."

"If you see an orphan in want, help him; for you will be rewarded by his friends here, or thanked by his parents in the land of spirits."

"If you own a good hunting dog, give it to the first poor man who really needs it."

"When you kill a deer, or bear, never appropriate it to yourself alone, if others are in want; never withhold from them what the Great Spirit has blessed you with."

"When you eat, share with the poor children who are near you, for when you are old they will administer to your wants."

"Never use improper medicine to the injury of another, lest you yourself receive the same treatment."

"When an opportunity offers, call the aged together, and provide for them venison properly cooked, and give them a hearty welcome; then the gods that have favored them will be your friends."

These are a few specimens of the advice given by our fathers, and by adhering to their counsels the lives, peace, and happiness of the Indian race were secured; for then there was no whiskey among them. O! that accursed thing. O! why did the white man give it to my poor fathers? None but fiends in human shape could have introduced it among us.

I recollect the day when my people in Canada were both numerous and happy; and since then, to my sorrow, they have faded away like frost before the heat of the sun! Where are now that once numerous and happy people? The voice of but few is heard.

When I think of them, I feel pained to know that many have fallen a prey to its soul and body-destroying influence. I could adopt the language of the poet:

"I will go to my tent and lie down in despair,
I will paint me with black, and sever my hair,
I will sit on the shore where the hurricane blows,
And relate to the God of the tempest my woes;
For my kindred are gone to the mounds of the dead,
But they died not of hunger nor wasting decay,
For the drink of the white man hath swept them away."

The Ojebwa nation, that unconquered nation, has fallen a prey to the withering influence of intemperance. Their buoyant spirits could once mount the air as on the wings of a bird. Now they have no spirits. They are hedged in, bound, and maltreated, by both the American and British governments. They have no other hope, than that at some day they will be relieved from their privations and trials by death. The fire-water has rolled towards them like the waves of the sea. Alas! alas! my poor people! The tribe became dissipated, and consequently improvident, and often suffered intensely.

It was in visiting the interior that we always suffered most. I will here narrate a single circumstance which will convey a correct idea of the sufferings to which the Indians were often exposed. To collect furs of different kinds for the traders, we had to travel far in to the woods and remain there the whole winter. Once we left Rice Lake in the fall, and ascended the river in canoes, above Bellmont Lake. There were five families about to hunt with my father, on his grounds. The winter began to set in, and the river having frozen over, we left the canoes, the dried venison, the beaver, and some flour and pork; and when we had gone farther north, say about sixty miles from the whites, for the purpose of hunting, the snow fell for five days in succession to such a depth that it was impossible to shoot or trap anything. Our provisions were exhausted, and we had no means to procure any more. Here we were. The snow about five feet deep; our wigwam buried; the branches of the trees falling around us, and cracking from the weight of the snow.

Our mother boiled birch bark for my sister and myself, that we might not starve. On the seventh day some of them were so weak that they could not raise themselves, and others could not stand alone. They could only crawl in and out of the wigwam. We parched beaver skins and old moccasons for food. On the ninth day none of the men were able to go abroad, except my father and uncle. On the tenth day, still being without food, those only who were able to walk about the wigwam were my father, my grand-mother, my sister, and my-self. O how distressing to see the starving Indians lying about the wigwam with hungry and eager looks; the children would cry for something to eat. My poor mother would heave *bitter sighs of despair*, the tears falling from her cheeks profusely as she kissed us. Wood, though plenty, could not be obtained, on account of the feebleness of our limbs.

My father, at times, would draw near the fire, and rehearse some prayer to the gods. It appeared to him that there was no way of escape; the men, women and children dying; some of them were speechless. The wigwam was cold and dark, and covered with snow. On the eleventh day, just before daylight, my father fell into a sleep; he soon awoke and said to me, "My son, the Great Spirit is about to bless us; this night in my dream I saw a person coming from the east, walking on the tops of the trees. He told me that we should obtain two beavers this morning about nine o'clock. Put on your moccasons and go along with me to the river, and we will hunt the beaver, perhaps for the last time." I saw that his countenance beamed with delight; he was full of confidence. I put on my moccasons and carried my snow shoes, staggering along behind him, about half a mile. Having made a fire near the river, where there was an air hole, through which the beaver had come up during the night, my father tied a gun to a stump, with the muzzle towards the air hole; he also tied a string to the trigger, and said "should you see the beaver rise, pull the string and you will kill it." I stood by the fire with the string in my hand. I soon heard a noise occasioned by the blow of his tomakawk; he had killed a beaver, and he brought it to me. As he laid it down, he said "then the Great Spirit will not let us die here;" adding, as before, "if you see the beaver rise, pull the string." He left me, I soon saw the nose of one; but I did not shoot. Presently another came up; I pulled the trigger, and off the gun went. I could not see for some time for the smoke. My father ran towards me, took the two beavers and laid them side by side; then pointing to the sun, said, "Do you see the sun? The Great Spirit informed me that we should kill these two about this time this morning. We will yet see our relatives at Rice Lake; now let us go home and see if they are still alive." We hastened home, and arrived just in time to save them from death. Since which, we visited the same spot, the year after the missionaries came among us. My father, with feelings of gratitude, knelt down on the spot where we had nearly perished. Glory to God! But what have I done for him since? Comparatively nothing. We were just at death's door, when Christianity rescued us. I have heard of many, who have perished in this way, far in the woods. In my travels to the west, I have met many whose families had perished, and who had themselves merely escaped starvation. May God forgive me, for my ingratitude and indolence in his blessed cause!

I will here introduce a favorite war song of the Ojebwa nation. It was accompanied by dancing, and an occasional war-whoop. At the end of each stanza, a warrior rehearsed some former victories, which inspired them with ardor for war. Unchristianized Indians are often like greedy lions after their prey; yes, at times, they are indeed cruel and blood thirsty. I have met with warriors, who, when they had killed their enemies, cut open their breasts, took out their hearts, and drank their blood; and all this was out of mere *revenge*. But to the *War Song*, which was first translated for Col. McKinney, *"the Indian's friend,"* on the shore of Lake Superior.

"On that day when our heroes lay low—lay low—
On that day when our heroes lay low,
I fought by their side, and thought ere I died,
Just vengeance to take on the foe—the foe—
Just vengeance to take on the foe.

"On that day when our chieftains lay dead—lay dead—
On that day when our chieftains lay dead,
I fought hand to hand, at the head of my band,
And *here, on my breast*, have I bled—have I bled—
And here, on my breast, have I bled.

"Our chiefs shall return no more—no more—
Our chiefs shall return no more—
And their brothers in war who can't show scar for scar,
Like women their fates shall deplore—shall deplore—
Like women, their fates shall deplore.

"Five winters in hunting we'll spend—we'll spend—
Five winters in hunting we'll spend—
Then our youths grown to men, to the war lead again,
And our days like our fathers', we'll end—we'll end—
And our days like our fathers', we'll end."

## CHAPTER 4

Our people believed much in omens. The barking of foxes and of wolves, the bleating of the deer, the screeching of owls, bad luck in hunting, the flight of uncommon kinds of birds, the moaning noise of a partridge, the noise of a *chuck chack ske sey*,* were ominous of ill;

*To this bird I have given its *Indian* name, because I have not been able to discover it among the collection of the various birds in the books and in the museums. It is about the size of the smaller kind of parrot. The color of its feathers is like those of a jay, having short wings small and broad peak, with an upper and

the two last were certain omens of death. But the sailing of an eagle to and fro, and the noise of a raven, were omens of good.

Dreams, too, were much relied on by our nation. They thought the spirits revealed to them what they were to do, and what they should be, viz. good hunters, warriors, and medicine men. I would fast sometimes two, and sometimes even four days. When fasting, we were to leave the wigwam early in the morning, and travel all day from one place to another, in search of the favor of the gods. I was taught to believe that the gods would communicate with me, in the shape of birds, animals, etc., etc. When I fell asleep in the woods, and dreamed some strange dream, I felt confident that it was from the spirits. I will now relate what I dreamed when I was but twelve years old, and also my father's interpretation of my dream.

Myself and others were sleeping far from the wigwam, near a large pine. I saw, in my dream, a person coming from the east; he approached, walking on the air: he looked down upon me, and said, "Is this where you are?" I said "yes." "Do you see this pine?" "Yes, I see it." "It is a great and high tree." I observed that the tree was lofty, reaching towards the heavens. Its branches extended overland and water, and its roots were very deep. "Look on it while I sing, yes, gaze upon the tree." He sang, and pointed to the tree; it commenced waving its top; the earth about its roots was heaved up, and the waters roared and tossed from one side of their beds to the other. As soon as he stopped singing, and let fall his hands, every thing became perfectly still and quiet. "Now," said he, "sing the words which I have sung." I commenced as follows:—

"It is I who travel in the winds,
It is I who whisper in the breeze,
  I shake the trees.
  I shake the earth,
I trouble the waters on every land."

While singing, I heard the winds whistle, saw the tree waving its top, the earth heaving, heard the waters roaring, because they were all troubled and agitated. Then said he, "I am from the rising of the

lower row of teeth, like a human being. In this last respect, it is different from any other bird. It takes its name from the sound it utters, viz. *chuck, chuck.* I hope that the celebrated ornithologist Audabon, to whom I intend to present a copy of my work, will throw some light upon this subject.

sun, I will come and see you again. You will not see me often; but you will hear me speak." Thus spoke the spirit, and then turned away towards the road from which he had come. I told my father of my dream, and after hearing all, he said, "My son, *the god of the winds* is kind to you; the aged tree, I hope, may indicate long life; the wind may indicate that you will travel much; the water which you saw, and the winds, will carry your canoe safely through the waves."

I relied much on my dream, for then I knew no better. But, however, little reliance can be placed in dreams, yet may not the Great Spirit take this method, sometimes, to bring about some good result?

There was no such thing known among our people as swearing, or profaning the name of the Great Spirit in vain. The whites first taught them to swear. I often swore, when I knew not what I said. I have seen some *white faces* with *black hearts*, who took delight in teaching them to profane the name of God. O merciless, heartless, and wicked white men, may a merciful God forgive you your enormous turpitude and recklessness!

There was a custom among us, before Christianity visited us, that when the Ojebwas intended to take a general whiskey "spree," several young men were appointed by the head chief to collect all the fire arms, knives, war-clubs and other weapons, and keep them in a secret place, till the Indians had completed their frolic. This was done to prevent them from murdering each other when intoxicated. By this means many lives have been saved; although many have been killed during their drunken fights. They would walk very far from a dram of liquor. I once heard of an individual, whom I had seen many times, who would travel all day for a single drink of fire-water. When he arrived at the trading post, he obtained and guzzled down a cup full of whiskey. When the poison had operated, he said, that he felt as if his head was going down his throat; and added, "Whah! I wish my neck was a mile long, so that I might feel and hear the whiskey running all the way down!"

A certain Indian once teased a Mrs. F. for whiskey, which he said was to cure his "*big toe*," that had been badly bruised the preceding night. Mrs. F. said, "I am afraid you will drink it." He declared he would not drink it; and after much pleading, she handed him some; he took it, and looking first at his toe, and then at the liquor, alternately, all of a sudden he slipped the whiskey down his gullet, at the same time exclaiming, as he pointed to his toe, "There, *whiskey*, go down to my poor big toe."

One of our people, who had much resolution, and was determined to seek religion, when he heard that the Methodist Indians were not to drink any more fire-water, remarked as follows:—

"*Well, if that is the case, I'll go to-night, and bid my old friend whiskey a final farewell.*" He went, and drank and caroused with his rum-companions all night. On the following day, about noon, he came staggering towards his wigwam, singing out to all whom he met, "*Me goes to Methodist; me no drink little more; me am Methodist.*" He was true to his word, for he drank no more, and the Lord blessed him in the forgiveness of all his sins. For eighteen years he was a consistent Christian, and died last June, with the brightest hopes of immortal bliss. Oh! the heights and depths of the goodness and mercy of God!

In view of these things, I have often exclaimed from the bottom of my heart, in the language of "The Indian's Regret," and which is the language of all, who have been brought from darkness, to the marvelous light of the gospel:—

"O had our Indian fathers known
   What Prophets told of Christ and heaven!
For them, we drop a tear and mourn,
   But weep for joy, our sins forgiven."


CHAPTER 5

The *traditions* handed down from father to son, were held very sacred; one half of these are not known by the white people, however far their researches may have extended. There is an unwillingness, on the part of the Indians to communicate many of their traditions. The only way to come at these is, to educate the Indians, so that they may be able to write out what they have heard, or may hear, and publish it. Should I be spared till next summer, I design to visit my people in the far west, and abide with them long enough to learn the rest of their traditions, with an account of their migration to this country. My own belief is, that they came to this country, and fought with the original inhabitants; and having overpowered them, became the owners of the soil. I will not now give my reasons for this belief, as I expect at some future day to collect all the necessary information for this purpose, from histories and discoveries, corroborated by these traditions. My readers will then be able to judge whether we are to be identified with the dispersed and "lost tribes of Israel." Can it be possible, that, had we sprung from any of the Hebrew tribes, we should be so completely ignorant of a Messiah, a Sabbath, or a single vestige of the Levitical Law? But enough of this for the present.

As far as I am able to learn, our nation has never been conquered; and have maintained their ground wherever they have conquered. The *Saxe* tribe have tried their ingenuity, power and bravery, to drive them from the south shore of Lake Superior. The *Hurons* mustered their warriors against the aggressions made by the Ojebwa nation. Their war-canoes were once directed against the Ojebwa nation, but they were obliged to turn back, and flee for protection, to the Shawnee nation. The sound of the war whoop which once rang all around the shores of Lake Huron, receded, and died away on the waters of Sandusky. The arms that once wielded the war-club, were strewed about their grounds, on account of broken treaties made in former days, and massacres at the mouth of French River. The *Iraquois*, who struck terror wherever their mere names were mentioned, also tried to check our progress, after we had conquered the Hurons. Their war whoops resounded over the dismal regions of the conquered land; but they too shared the same fate. They went as spies as far as La Pointe, on the south shore of Lake Superior; but not with their armies any farther than Ke-wa-o-non, in the copper regions. Here they were massacred by hundreds, and fell in their canoes at one of the narrow passes, on their way to the Portage, about fourteen miles from the Bay of Aunce. After these fruitless attempts to drive the Ojebwas from their land, they fought many battles with them in the regions now called Canada West; but in these they suffered much, and were defeated. It was then, probably, that the Hurons and Iraquois leagued together, hoping by their combined forces to conquer us. This accounts for the confederacy that existed when the whites came among them.

*The migration* of the Ojebwas has been traced from the upper part of Lake Superior, and even several hundred miles above its head, along the shores of Lake Superior, down to Lake Huron, St. Clair, the foot of Lake Michigan, north of Lakes Erie and Ontario, and some distance down the St. Lawrence.

They now inhabit a portion of land extending about two thousand miles east and west, and from two hundred and fifty to three hundred miles from north to south. They have in each village, a chief who governs them, besides a great number of war chiefs. Each village has a council of its own, made up of the different tribes. A tribe is a band of Indians whose sign or mark is the same; for example, such as wear the sign of the *crane*, recognize each other as relatives; and although each village may be composed of different tribes, yet they must be of the same nation.

*Councils of peace* must be held by two nations. These councils are held in high esteem. When two nations are at war, if either sues for peace, they hand to each other some token, such as a belt of wampum (or beads,) or a calumet (a long pipe.)

There was once a general council held, between the Hurons and the Ojebwas; it was conducted in the following manner:—They came together near Sault St. Marie, and agreed upon a peace for five years. After the pipe of peace was prepared, the Ojebwa and Huron warriors arranged themselves in two lines, on each side of their chiefs, and said that they must ascertain whether the Great Spirit would approve of their proceedings. Two from each nation were chosen; the Hurons held the pipe filled with tobacco, the Ojebwas, the steel, flint, and spunk. The steel was then struck against the flint, and if, on the first stroke, the spunk was ignited, so as to fire the tobacco, and thus enable the warrior to draw in, and to emit, a volume of smoke, then the evidence was complete that the Great Spirit approved of their plans and proceedings; and the whole assembly now would set up the most tremendous shout of joy. The two nations were successful in this. The shout was given, peace was secured, and these two powerful nations separated for their own homes. For three years no dark could hung over the two nations.

The Ojebwas began to trade with the whites at Quebec. It usually required all the summer to journey from the shore of Lake Superior to that place and back again. These were tedious and perilous journeys; but they were determined to obtain *"the snake which spit fire, smoke and death;"* this was their description of *a gun* to their brethren.

It was during these journeys that forty of them were massacred by the Hurons, at the mouth of French River, without the least provocation; plunder alone was their object. This, in connection with similar acts, occasioned that war which resulted in their complete extermination from Canada by our nation.

The *future state* of the Ojebwas, was in the *Far West*. They described that state or country, *as being full of game*, and with *trees loaded with fruit of every description.*

When an Indian warrior died on the field of battle, his soul, it was said, took its immediate flight to this paradise. The souls of those, however, who died in other circumstances, it was believed, departed from the grave, and journeyed in the ordinary way, although unseen by mortals, to this same land.

There was a difficult bridge near this land, over which the soul was to cross. A warrior, hunter, or medicine man, would have no difficulty in crossing this bridge. Under this bridge was a rapid stream, and he who was not a good warrior, hunter or medicine man, would either fall into the water, or lose his way, after having crossed, in some barren country, where there was no game, or fruit, although there might be, occasionally, a deer, or the like. O how barren! How dismal! A place where distress, want, and despair would continue! On the other hand, the favored warrior entered the fields of paradise, amidst the shouts and welcome of his fellow warriors, who had preceded him to this land of plenty. The deer, the moose, the elk, and all kinds of animals, fruits, flowers, and the singing of birds fill and charm the land. While the ever rolling valleys are visited with delightful and refreshing winds. To kill, eat, and shoot, are their only employments. No sickness, no fatigue, no death, will ever visit them. The valleys and the mountains are to be clothed with evergreens. No winter to chill the earth. A carnal heaven indeed! A sensual paradise! Oh! the credulous and misguided Indian.

> "Lo! the poor Indian whose untutored mind,
> Sees God in clouds, or hears him in the wind;
> Whose soul proud science never taught to stray
> Beyond the solar walk or milky way.
> Yet simple nature to his hopes has given,
> Beyond the cloud top'd hill, a humble heaven,
> Some safer world in depths of woods embrace,
> Some distant Island in the watery waste.
> Where slaves once more their native land behold,
> Nor fiends torment, no Christian thirsts for gold."
>                                              Pope.

My father often spoke of that country, while I was young. He informed me, that if I should become a great warrior, a hunter, or a medicine man, I would have no difficulty in reaching the happy spot.

Little then did he know of a *heaven revealed in the gospel*. That heaven, where angels and pure spirits dwell, and where we shall see the blessed Jesus as he is, and, what is still a greater honor, be like him.

"O for a thousand tongues to sing
  My great Redeemer's praise!
The glories of my God and King,
  The triumphs of his grace!

"Oh uh pa-gish ke che ingo' dwok,
  Neej uh ne she nah baig,
Che nuh nuh guh mo tuh wah wod
  Ning e zha Mun e-doom.

"My gracious Master, and my God,
  Assist me to proclaim,
To spread through all the earth abroad
  The honors of thy Name.

"Ning e che Noo sa weej e shin,
  Che ween duh mah ga yon,
O mah a ne gook kuh me gog
  A zhe wa be ze yun.

"Jesus! the Name that charms our fears,
  That bids our sorrows cease;
Tis music in the sinner's ears,
  'Tis life, and health, and peace."

"Jesus! kah be 'non duh we 'nung
  Kah gah see beeng wa 'nung;
Ka gait 'che me no me kah zo.
  Kah noo je mo enung."

When our warriors were dying, they told their children that they would soon reach the happy country. Their eyeballs, rolling in death, were turned towards the setting sun. O white man! why did you not tell us before, that there was a better heaven than that of the Indian's? Did not the blessed Saviour command, "Go ye into *all* the world and preach the gospel to every creature?" Reader, almost by the door of your churches, my forefathers perished for the lack of the bread of life, while you have reached out your arms, and extended your means for the relief of those *in distant lands!* O what a thought! Thousands have already perished, and thousands more will yet perish, unless converted to God. The thought of *perishing!* how *insufferable!* O how *intolerable!*

"O mercy, O mercy, look down from above;
Great Creator, on us, thy sad children, with love;
When beneath to their darkness the wicked are driven,
May our justified souls find a welcome in heaven."

### CHAPTER 6

Rice Lake, that beautiful lake, extends about twenty-five miles, and is from two to three miles in breadth, running from northeast to southwest. It contains about twenty islands. Large quantities of wild rice abound in almost every part of the lake; it resembles fields of wheat. As ducks of all kinds resort here in great abundance, to feed upon the rice, consequently, there is much good game in the fall of the year. They fly in large flocks, and often appear like clouds. Some of the islands just referred to, are beautiful; for example, *Sugar Island*, with its beautiful edge of evergreens near the water; *Spoke Island*, a place of fashionable summer resort. One of the largest of these islands, contains about three hundred acres.

In 1818, our people surrendered to the British government a large part of their territory, for the sum of £750; reserving, as they had good reason to believe, all the islands. As they could neither read nor write, they were ignorant of the fact that these islands were *included* in the sale. They were repeatedly told by those who purchased for the government, that the islands were *not* included in the articles of agreement. But since that time, some of us have learned to read, and to our utter astonishment, and to the everlasting disgrace of that *pseudo* Christian nation, we find that we have been most grossly abused, deceived, and cheated. Appeals have been frequently made, but all in vain.

Rice Lake contains quantities of the finest fish. In the summer, great numbers of boats may be seen trowling for *mascalounge*, a species of pike, some of which weigh about thirty pounds. Bass, eels, etc. are also found in this lake. Since locks have been made on the canal down to Crooke's rapids, much fur can be procured all around the lake, especially *muskrats*—Shah-won-dase O dah me koo mun.

This is the spot on which I roamed during my early days. Often have I gone with my birch bark canoe from island to island, in quest of ducks and fish. The plain on the south shore, is called Whortle-berry Plain. A steamboat runs from Gore's Landing to Peterboro once a day.

The village of the Ojebwas is on the north; the land gradually slopes towards the water. Its farms, church, school house, and council house can be seen at a considerable distance. It was here where the Rev. James Evans, whose obituary was noticed in the following manner in the "Albany Evening Journal," December 22, 1846, first taught an Indian school.

"Suddenly, on the 23d of November, at Keelby, England, Rev. James Evans, for many years a Wesleyan missionary in Canada, and the territory of the Hudson Bay Company. On Sunday, the 22d, he preached twice, and on Monday evening 23d, spoke at a missionary meeting, with great fervency. He had complained of a slight indisposition, previous to the meeting; but after he had finished his address, he said that 'his indisposition had been completely removed.' Soon after his head fell back, and life was gone."

He was a missionary in every sense of the word. From Rice Lake, he went to Lake Superior, and afterwards to the Hudson Bay Territory, where he labored with much success. His precious life was spent in rescuing the Ojebwa nation from misery and degradation. Fatigue and hunger were often his companions; but the power of living faith was that on which his soul feasted. O thou man of God, enviable are thy labors, thy rest, and thy glory! I, myself, still hold in sweet remembrance the sacred truths which thou didst teach me, even the commands of the Most High! *Memory*, like an angel, will still hover over the sacred spot, where first you taught me the letters of the alphabet.

There are numerous lakes near Rice Lake; about some of which the Ojebwas reside; particularly Mud, Schoogaug and Balsam Lakes. The country, in this vicinity, is rapidly increasing in population; the whites are continually settling among us. The deer was plenty a few years ago, but now only a few can be found. The Ojebwas are, at present, employed in farming instead of hunting; many of them have good and well cultivated farms. They not only raise grain enough for their own use, but often sell much to the whites.

The Canadian Commissioners on Indian affairs, in their report to Parliament in 1845, remarked in relation to the Rice Lake Indians, as follows: "These Indians are Methodists, and have either a resident missionary, or have been regularly visited by the missionary belonging to the Alnwick settlement. They have a school, and a school-master is supported by the Methodist Missionary Society."

CHAPTER 7

The missionaries first visited us on the island called *Be-quah-qua-yong*, in 1827, under the following circumstances. My father and I went to Port Hope, to see our principal trader, John D. Smith, in order to obtain goods and whiskey, about twelve miles from Rice Lake. After my father had obtained the goods, he asked for whiskey. Mr. Smith said, "John, do you know whiskey will yet kill you, if you do not stop drinking? Why, all the Indians at Credit River, and at Grape Island, have abandoned drinking, and are now Methodists. I cannot give you any whiskey."

"*Tah yah!* (an exclamation of surprise,) *it cannot be, I must* have whiskey to carry home; my people expect it," said my father. He wished to buy a barrel, but only obtained, after much pleading, about five gallons. My father *promised* to drink no more when the missionaries should have come to Rice Lake. We reached home the same day about one o'clock, and the Indians were awaiting our arrival, that they might have some fire-water. They assembled themselves together and began to drink and to smoke. Many of them were sitting on the grass when the whiskey began to steal away their brains. One of our number suddenly ran in the crowd, and said, "*the black coats* (missionaries) are coming, and are on the other side of the point." Each looked at the other with perfect astonishment. My father said to our informer, "invite them to come over to us;" and to the one who was dealing out whiskey, "cover the keg with your blanket, and don't let the black coats see it." The whiskey was concealed, and then came the messengers of glad tiding of great joy. They were converted Indians, saved by grace, and had been sent to preach to us, and to invite us to attend a camp meeting near Cobourg. After shaking hands all around, one of them delivered a speech to the half drunken Indians. He referred to the day when they were without the good news of *salvation*. He spoke with great earnestness, and the tears fell from his eyes. He said, "*Jesus Christ, Ke-sha-mon-e-doo O-gwe-son,* (i. e., the Benevolent Spirit's son,) came down to the world, and died to save the people; all the Indians at the Credit River, and Grape Island, are now on their road to the place where the Saviour has gone. Jesus has left a book containing his commands and sayings to all the world; your *will see it, and hear it read,* when you go to Cobourg, for the black coats have it. They wish you to come and hear it. To-morrow is the *Sabbath,* and on that day we do not hunt, or work, for it is the day which the Great Spirit made for himself." He described the way that the Son of God was crucified. I observed some of them crying; my mother heaved deep sighs; the half drunken Indians were struck dumb, and hung their heads. Not a word was uttered. The missionaries said, "We will *sing,* and then we will *kneel down* and *pray* to the Great Spirit" He gave out the following hymn:

"Jesus ish pe ming kah e zhod."
"Jesus, my all, to heaven is gone."

They stood up and sang. O what sweet melody was in their voices! The echo was so great that there appeared to be a great many more singers than we could see. After the hymn, they prayed with the same fervency as they sung.

Peter Wason prayed, and in his prayer said, "O Great Spirit! here are some of my own relatives; open their eyes and save them!" After the prayer, they said they were going to Cobourg that evening; and if any desired to go with them, they would have them do so.

My father arose and took the keg of whiskey, stepped into one of the small canoes, and paddled some thirty feet from the shore; here poured out the whiskey into the lake, and threw the keg away. He then returned and addressed us in the following manner.—"You have all heard what our brothers said to us; I am going with them this evening; if any of you will go, do so this evening; the children can attend the great meeting some other time." Every one ran at once to the paddles and canoes, and in a few minutes we were on the water. The missionaries had a skiff, in which they went from the Island to the opposite side. They sang again, and their very oars seemed to keep time on the still water. O how charming! The scenery of the water; the canoes moving in files, crossing the lake to visit their first camp meeting. When we arrived on the other side, it was about dusk, and we bought five candles for a *dollar (!)*, and obtained an old lantern. We marched on a new road the whole of Saturday night, in order to reach the camp ground. During the journey, we had to wade through deep creeks. Just before the dawn, we were about half a mile from the camp ground; here we tarried until day light, and then approached the camp.

When the Indians beheld the fence and the gate, and a great number of whites, they began to feel rather timid and suspicious, for the trader had told my father at Rice Lake, that *it was for the purpose of killing all the Indians* that the black coats had invited them to the meeting. My father told me to keep away from the ground, and hunt birds and squirrels with my bow and arrow; his object was to save my life, in the event of the Indians being killed. After remaining on the camp ground awhile, I departed; but while there, I saw a large number of converted Indians who belonged to Credit River, and Grape Island. Some of them were singing, some praying, and others lying about the ground as if dead. There were a great many preachers present.

On the third day many of our company were converted; among this number was my dear father!

As I entered the ground in the afternoon, I heard many voices, and among them my father's voice. I thought my father was dying; I ran to him, and found him lying partly on one of the seats. My father, said I, what is the matter with you? Are you sick? "Come here, my son, I am not sick, but I am happy in my heart;" he placed his hand upon his breast while he spoke. "I told you you must keep away from the ground, that your life might be spared; but I find that these are good, and not bad, people; kneel down and I will pray for you." I knelt, while he prayed. O, this was *my father's first prayer!* Methinks, that at this time the angels rejoiced in heaven. I became agitated; my bow and arrows had fallen from my hand. The Indians lay about me like dead men. All this was the effect of the power of gospel grace, that had spread amongst them. The shouts, praises, and prayers, of fathers, mothers, sons, and daughters, were heard from every quarter. Those who had just appeared as dead, arose, and shouted the praises of God! They clapped their hands, and exclaimed, "*Jesus nin ge shah wa ne mig,*" Jesus has blessed me. The feeling was so general and powerful, that the influence was felt throughout the camp, both by the Indians and the whites. This was one of the happiest seasons I ever witnessed, except the season of my own conversion. Many of my relatives were converted on this occasion. Many of them have since gone to the world of spirits, and are now singing the praises of redeeming love. This *heavenly fire* began to spread from the camp, to Mud, Schoogaug and Balsam Lakes, the homes of the Ojebwas; also to the shores of Lake Simcoe, and Lake Huron, and to the vicinity of Lake Superior.

> "Waft, waft, ye winds his story,
>     And you ye waters roll,
> Till like a sea of glory
>     It spreads from pole to pole."

On the camp ground, the Ojebwas sat in squads, giving and receiving instruction in singing, learning and teaching the Lord's prayer, and other things. Some were singing,

> "Jesus, kuh ba ke zhig
> Ning ee e nuh uh moz,
> Uh pa gish kuh ke nuh wahb' dum 'wod
> Ning ee 'nuh da moosh
> A zhe o ne zhe shing,
> O ge che o duh nuh me ah win."

> "Jesus all the day long
> Was my joy and my song;

98

O that all, his salvation might see!
   He hath lov'd me, I cried;
   He hath suffer'd and died
To redeem such a rebel as me."


## CHAPTER 8

The *conversion of my mother* took place during the summer, on Pout-ash Island, where the Indians had erected a bark chapel. For two years she lived in the enjoyment of religion. Before this chapel was ready she would call us together in the wigwam, and pray with and for us, several times a day, whether our father was at home or not. I remember well, at this moment, the language of her prayers.

She was taken sick in the winter of 1829, and was confined to her bed, most of the time, for three months; her disease was consumption. During these three months, she enjoyed much religion; there was not a day, in which she did not speak of Jesus and his promises with the greatest confidence and delight.

When she grew worse, she called for the class leaders to pray with her. She said to her mother, whom she supposed would die first, because her hair was *white*, "you will still live, but I am going to die, and will see Jesus first; soon, however, you will follow me."

The spirit of my dear mother took its flight on the 27th day of February, 1830. Just before her death, she prayed with her children; and advised us to be good Christians, to live Jesus, and meet her in heaven. She then sang her favorite hymn,

"Jesus ish pe ming kah e zhod."
"Jesus, my all, to heaven is gone."

This was the first hymn she had ever heard or learned; and it is on this account that I introduce and sing this sweet hymn whenever I lecture "On the origin, history, traditions, migration, and customs, of the Ojebwa nation." We all knelt again by her bed side, and while clapping her hands, and endeavoring to shout for joy, she swooned away in death. The last words, which she feebly uttered, were, "*Jesus, Jesus.*" Her spirit then fled, her lips were cold, and those warm hands that had so often and so faithfully administered comfort and relief, were now stiff. I looked around the wigwam; my father, sister, and brother sat near me, wringing their hands; they were filled with bitter grief, and appeared inconsolable. I then began to understand

and appreciate fully her kindness and love. Who, who can, or will, take the place of a *mother?* Who will pray for us when we are sick or in distress? Her body was consigned to the grave without any parade. No church bell was tolled; but the whistling wind sounded through the woods. I have often knelt down, at the head of her grave, and wished that the time would soon arrive when it might please God to relieve me from my troubles and cares, and conduct me to the abode of my beloved parent. My sister Sarah, too, who has since died, is doubtless with my mother. O how glorious the thought, *that both are now in heaven!* There is one spot where none will sigh for home. The flowers that blossom there, will never fade; the crystal waters that wind along those verdant vales, will never cease to send up their heavenly music; the clusters hanging from the trees overshadowing its banks, will be immortal clusters; and the friends that meet, will meet for ever.

Little then did I think that I should have to pass through so many afflictions, and so many hardships. O my mother, I am still in a *cold, uncharitable miserable world!* But the thought that thou art happy and blessed, is truly sweet and encouraging! It is this fact, and my own hopes of future bliss, that buoys me up, and sustains me in the hours of conflict and despondency. Although many years have elapsed, since her death, still, I often weep with mingled joy and grief when I think of my dear mother. "Blessed are the dead who die in the Lord." "I am not ashamed of the gospel of Christ, for it is the power of God unto salvation to every one that believeth." The gospel is the only remedy for the miseries and sins of the world.

My mother and sister's cases are not the only ones that I could related concerning the happy lives and deaths of those once degraded and benighted Indians. Many have already reached heaven; and many more are now rejoicing on the road thither. Who will now say that the poor Indians cannot be converted? The least that Christians could have done, was to send the gospel among them, after having dispossessed them of their lands; thus preparing them for usefulness here, and happiness hereafter. Let no one say that I am ungrateful in speaking thus. It was the *duty* of Christians to send us missionaries; and it is *now* their duty to send *more* of them. There are still 25,000 of my poor brethren in darkness, and without the gospel. Let the prayers of all the churches ascend to the Most High, in their behalf, that He who has power to deliver, may save the poor Indian from misery, ignorance and perdition.

## CHAPTER 9

In the summer following my mother's death (1830,) *I was converted.* The following are the circumstances connected with my conversion. My father and I attended a camp meeting near the town of Colborne. On our way from Rice Lake, to the meeting, my father held me by the hand, as I accompanied him through the woods. Several times he prayed with me, and encouraged me to seek religion at this camp meeting. We had to walk thirty miles under a hot sun, in order to reach the place of destination. Multitudes of Indians, and a large concourse of whites from various places, were on the ground when we arrived. In the evening, one of the white preachers (Wright, I believe was his name,) spoke; his text was, "For the great day of His wrath is come, and who shall be able to stand." He spoke in English, and as he closed each sentence, an Indian preacher gave its interpretation. He spoke of the plain and good road to heaven; of the characters that were walking in it; he then spoke of the bad place, the judgment, and the coming of a Saviour. I now began to feel as if I should die; *I felt very sick in my heart.* Never had I felt so before; I was deeply distressed, and knew not the cause. I resolved to go and prostrate myself at the mourner's bench, as soon as an opportunity offered. We were now invited to approach. I went to the bench and knelt down by the roots of a large tree. But how could I pray? I did not understand how to pray; and besides, I thought that the Great Spirit was *too great* to listen to the words of a poor Indian boy. What added to my misery was, that it had rained in torrents about three quarters of an hour, and I was soaking wet. The thunder was appalling, and the lightning terrific. I then tried again to pray, but I was not able. I did not know what words to use. My father then prayed with and for me. Many were praising God, all around me. The storm now ceased, and nearly all the lights had been extinguished by the rain. I still groaned and agonized over my sins. I was so agitated and alarmed that I knew not which way to turn in order to get relief. I was like a *wounded bird*, fluttering for its life. Presently and suddenly, I saw in my mind, something approaching; it was like a small but brilliant torch; it appeared to pass through the leaves of the trees. My poor body became so enfeebled that I fell; my heart trembled. The small brilliant light came near to me, and fell upon my head, and then ran all over and through me, just as if water had been copiously poured out upon me. I knew not how long I had lain after my fall; but when I recovered, my head was in a puddle of water, in a small ditch. I arose; and O! how happy I was! I felt as light as a feather. I clapped my hands, and exclaimed in English, *"Glory to Jesus."* I looked around for my father, and saw him. I told him that I had found "Jesus." He embraced me and kissed me; I threw myself into his arms. I felt as strong as a lion, yet as humble as a poor Indian boy saved by grace, by grace alone. During that night I did not sleep. The next morning, my cousin, George Shawney, and myself, went out into the woods to sing and pray. As I looked at the trees, the hills, and the vallies, O how beautiful they all appeared! I looked upon them, as it were, with new eyes and new thoughts. Amidst the smiles of creation, the birds sang sweetly, as they flew from tree to tree. We sang

"Jesus the name that charms our fears."

O how sweet the recollections of that day! "Jesus all the day long was my joy and my song." Several hundred were converted during this meeting. Many of the Indians were reluctant to leave the camp ground when the meeting was broken up. When we reached our homes at Rice Lake, every thing seemed to me as if it wore a different aspect; every thing was clothed with beauty. Before this, I had only begun to spell and read. I now resumed my studies with a new and different relish. Often, when alone, I prayed that God would help me to qualify myself to teach others how to read the word of God; this circumstance I had not told to any one. On Sabbath mornings I read a chapter in the New Testament, which had been translated for my father, before we went to meeting.

During this summer, one of our chiefs, John Sunday, with several others, departed from Rice Lake, for the west, with a design to preach to the Ojebwas. When they returned, they told us that the Indians were very eager to hear the word of God, and that many had been converted. John Sunday informed us of a certain Indian, who was so much opposed to the meetings, that he confined his wife and children to one of the islands, to prevent her attending them. But this poor woman was so anxious to obey God in attendance on worship, that she was in the habit of fording the river every night, and carrying her children on her back. Her husband was afterwards converted. He mentioned also an instance of an Indian who brought his medicine sack with him to the meeting, but on being converted, he scattered its contents to the four winds of heaven. These sacks were held very sacred among the Indians. He spoke likewise of the conversion of many chiefs, and of the flocks of children anxious to hear the word of God. He left such an impression on my mind, that often, while alone, I prayed that God might send me to instruct the children in the truths of religion.

I joined my father's class meeting; and as often as possible I attended school during the period to two years. In June, 1834, our white missionary, Daniel McMullen, received a letter from the Rev. Wm. Case, in which it was stated that a letter had been sent to him by the Rev. John Clark, who was then the Superintendent of the missions on Lake Superior. The Superintendent requested that two native preachers and two native teachers should be sent to him. John Johnson and I were told that we were to accompany Brothers John Taunchey and Caubage to Lake Superior, to aid Brother Clark.

Brother Caubage, and my cousin Johnson, took their departure. John Taunchey hesitated about going, because I was undecided, and my father felt unwilling at first to let me go.

One day I determined to leave the village so as to avoid going to Lake Superior; I hunted along the river Trent, hoping that John Taunchey would be gone before my return; I felt very unwilling to go. I was absent over two weeks; they were the longest two weeks I had ever experienced. Yet the whole time I felt dissatisfied; something seemed to whisper to me, "George, go home, and go to Lake Superior with your uncle John Taunchey." I returned to the village. The first person I saw, informed me that my uncle was waiting for me, and that my father had left it to me to decide whether to go or to stay. Here I was; the missionaries came, and said, "George, your father has left it with you to go or stay. It is your duty to go; John is waiting, and to-day you must conclude." Our school mistress, Miss Pinney, came and reasoned with me. I recollected, too, that I had prayed that God might prepare me to be useful to my brethren; and now, that I had some good reason to think that my prayers had been heard, and still to refuse to go, would perhaps be acting in opposition to the indications of God. I wept and prayed; but O! that night of struggle! I could not sleep. In the morning, I said to my father, "I have concluded to go; prepare me for my journey." That morning we were prepared; and on the 16th of July, 1834, about noon, we were on the shore. The canoe was ready; many of the Indians prayed with us on the beach. After shaking hands with my father and the rest, we bid farewell to all we loved so tenderly. We went on board the steamboat Great Britain at Cobourg, and arrived at Toronto the next day. On the 19th of July, we saw at Toronto, on the top of one of the houses, Mr. William Lyon McKenzie, who created so much trouble in Canada in the years 1837 and 1838. He was then in the height of his popularity. He was placed upon the top of a house by his friends, in company with another lawyer, with a large gold medal around his neck. There was a large concourse of his friends who had come from Hamilton for the express purpose of seeing and cheering him. On the 20th July, we left in the stage for Holland Landing; here we remained two days, for the want of a conveyance to the Snake Island Mission. At this island we tarried the whole of the Sabbath with the Indians; and had some glorious meetings. They conveyed us to the Narrows Mission. In crossing from Narrows to Cold Water Mission, we were obliged to carry our trunks on our backs. About 11 o'clock we met two runaway horses on the road to Narrows. We caught them, tied our trunks on their backs, and lead them back to Cold Water. Thus we were relieved of our heavy loads.

On Wednesday, the 26th July, we went from Cold Water Mission to Pane-ta-wa-go-shene, where we saw a great number of Ojebwas from Lake Superior, Ottowas, Menomenese, &c. Here we fell in with John Sunday, Frazer, and others, who were engaged in instructing the Indians in this vicinity.

An opportunity occurred now to go to Sault St. Marie, where the Rev. John Clark resided. We were out of provisions several times. By fishing and shooting gulls on our way, we were enabled to reach the Sault, where we met Brother Clark, John Caubage, and cousin Johnson; this took place, I believe, on the 24th of August. We stayed here about two weeks, preparing to go to the Aunce, the Ke-wa-we-non Mission. During our delay in this place, the Rev. Messrs. Chandler and Bourne (the latter a member of the Illinois Conference) arrived. Brother Chandler has since died. My cousin, H. P. Chase, was Brother Clark's interpreter. The Indians were comfortable in their new houses. We held meeting with them several nights.

Pah-we-ting with its fisheries. Thomas Shaw, a warm and open hearted half-bred Frenchman, was in the habit of scooping out of the rapids, twenty or thirty fine white fish, and boiling them for his friends.

### CHAPTER 10

I now began to feel the responsibilities resting upon me. The thought of assuming the station of a teacher of the Indians, with so few capabilities, was enough to discourage more gifted men than myself. Frequently did I enter the woods and pour out my soul to God, in agony and tears. I trembled at what was before me; and said, "who is able for these things?" But a still small voice would answer, "My grace is sufficient for you." Soothing words indeed, especially to an unlearned and feeble Red man—a mere worm of the dust.

Having provided every thing necessary for our journey, and a residence of eight months at the Ka-wa-we-non Mission, we started in company with Rev. Mr. Chandler, uncle John Taunchey, and the traders who intended to winter on the shores of Lake Superior and do business with the Ojebwas. We were more than three weeks on our journey—three hundred and fifty miles. At one place were were weather-bound for one week. Our French companions were the most wicked of men. They would gnash their teeth at each other, curse, swear, and fight among themselves. The boat, oars, the winds, water, the teachers, etc., did not escape their execrations. I thought now that I understood what *hell* was in a very clear manner. My very hairs seemed to "stand erect like quills upon a fretful porcupine," when they gave vent to their malevolence and passions. They would fight like beasts over their cooking utensils, and even while their food was in their mouths. I will just say here that I have often seen them eat boiled corn with tallow for butter.

On our road, we saw the celebrated Pictured Rocks, Sand Banks, and Grand Island. On a point of the latter place we encamped. Every Sabbath I devoted about an hour in sighing and crying after *home*. What good can I *do*, when I reach the place of labor? was a question that often occurred to my mind. Still we were going farther and farther from home. We were obliged, too, to do our own cooking, washing, and mending.

At last, in September, we arrived at the Aunce Bay. Here, our house was no better than a wigwam; and yet we had to occupy it as a dwelling, a school house, a meeting house, and a council room.

We commenced laboring among out poor people, and those that

had been christianized were exceedingly glad to see us. Brothers Sunday and Frazer had already been among them more than a year. We began to build quite late in the fall, and although we removed a house from the other side of the bay, yet we experienced much inconvenience. We visited the Indians daily, for the purpose of conversing and praying with them. There were about thirty, who had, for more than a year, professed to experience a change of heart. As my uncle was experienced in conversing with the unconverted, I endeavored to pursue his course in this respect. Each day we took a different direction in visiting the unconverted. We would sing, read the scriptures, and then pray with them. Sometimes they would be impudent, and even abusive, but this did not discourage us, or deter us from our duty. By persevering, we soon discovered that the Lord was about to bless our efforts. While my uncle was visiting some four or five wigwams, I was visiting as many others; their wigwams being near us. Our influence, with God's blessing, was now felt among them. Singing and praying were their constant employment; and some of them seemed to know nothing else but the enjoyment of the truth of the gospel, and that God can and does "forgive sin." They became the happiest of beings; their very souls were like an escaped bird, whose glad wings had saved it from danger and death. Brother Chandler preached twice every Sabbath, and taught school every other week. One Sabbath, in January, 1835, Brother Chandler preached from these words, "*And they were all filled with the Holy Ghost.*" He spoke with unusual liberty; I caught some of the *same fire* with which the sermon was delivered; and interpreted it with much ardor. O what a melting season it was! The anxious and expressive looks of the Indians; the tears streaming down their cheeks, all tended to add to the occasion. My readers, here was comfort; here was one bright spot, at least, in my checkered life, that I never can forget. My poor brethren appeared to swallow every word of the sermon as I interpreted it. One John Southwind, who had been notoriously cruel and revengeful, was among the humblest and the happiest. He had been a great *Conjurer.*

On Sabbath evenings, every converted Indian would try to induce his relatives to embrace religion, and pray in the wigwams of their unconverted relatives. These happy scenes often made me forget home.

Many of the unconverted, were very revengeful; but we let them expend their vengeance on the air. One of them, *Kah-be-wah-be-ko-*

*kay*, i. e. Spear Maker, threatened to tomahawk us, if we should come to his wigwam "with the white man's religion;" "for," said he, "already some of my family are very sick and crazy." Notwithstanding this threat, we commenced our vists, and with no other weapon than a little calico bag containing our Testament and Hymn Book. Whenever he saw us near his wigwam (we were obliged to pass near his in visiting other wigwams,) he would run out, and grumble and growl like a bear escaping from its den for life. In this way we continued our visits, and had opportunities to converse with the family, which resulted in the conversion of all his children. In the month of February, he himself came to us, and plead earnestly for our forgiveness. He had gone out to hunt the martin, with his youngest daughter, who was about ten years old. While her father was preparing a martin trap, or dead-fall, as it is sometimes called, the daughter slipped behind a tree, knelt in the snow, and prayed for her father. The Lord heard her prayer. The old man "felt sick in his heart," and every thing he looked at appeared to frown upon him, and to bid him "go to the missionaries, and they will tell you how you can be cured." He returned home three days earlier than he had intended. Just after day-dawn, we heard a number of Indians praying. John Southwind came in and said to us, "*Ke-ge-ke-wa-ye-wah, Kak-be-wah-be-koo-bay ke-che-ah-koo-sey*," i. e. your friend *Spear Maker* is very sick; he wishes you to call at his wigwam and pray with him. This was good news indeed! We went at once, and prayed with him. He could not speak; but sat sobbing and sighing over the fire. We conversed with him, and then left him; but before breakfast he entered our house with his large medicine sack containing little gods of almost every description. He stood before us, and said, "*Ah bay, ah was ah yah mook*,"—here, take this. He cast the bag, or sack, down upon the floor, and wept and sobbed bitterly, saying, "I have done all I could against you, but you have been my friends. I want you to pray for me, and to burn these gods, or throw them where I can never see them." Shortly after this interview, he obtained religion, and became truly happy in the Lord.

There were many equally interesting conversions about this time. I must here mention what was often very amusing to the missionaries, and would often create a smile, if nothing more. When some of the Indians were under *conviction*, they would take some of their own medicines (herbs) to cure their "sickness,"—for so they termed *conviction*. An old medicine man once sent a message to us, stating that his daughter was dying; and that it was caused by our singing and praying before her so much; he also added, that in the event of her death, he would have his revenge by killing us, and insisted upon it that we must come immediately, and endeavor to relieve her. We went, and after having prayed with her for some time, she revived, and expressed her confidence that the Holy Spirit had operated upon her heart. The old man soon became convinced that his daughter was not dying, except unto *sin*; he, therefore, at once, became reconciled and delighted too.

We now commenced traveling on snow shoes within fifteen or twenty miles around, where the Indians were hunting; praying, and preaching to them. The Lord owned and blessed our labors wherever we went. We held prayer meetings in the woods. All this time the *Mah-je Mon-e-doo* (Bad Spirit) was not asleep. In the spring the heathen party started in a body to visit their old friend *Spear Maker*, for the purpose of uniting with him in dancing, and in their medicine worship; but the old man had too much religion in him to gratify them. As soon as they discovered that they could not prevail upon the old man, they sent word to all, that they could excel us in worshiping the Great Spirit; and that they intended to hold their regular spring Grand Medicine Worship. Every night we held meetings. They commenced with their *paw-wahs* (singing,) and beating of the drums on the other side of the bay, and continued it for a whole week. We kept up our usual meetings; and at the end of the week, their drumming, singing, and dancing ceased. We continued our meetings for two months. The Chief of this place, was yet unconverted.

During this spring, Brother Clark, our Superintendent, arrived from Sault St. Marie, with Brother William Herkimer and family, and my cousin Johnson. These were to take our places in the mission. We had now an excellent quarterly meeting. Brother Clark preached a sensible and warm sermon; my cousin interpreted it. It was a blessed time; over twenty were baptized before the services began. There was a circumstance which rendered the occasion peculiarly interesting; an old Indian woman of about eighty years, came crawling to the meeting, for she was unable to walk; her name was Anna. The year before, she had travelled three hundred and fifty miles in a canoe, to be baptized by Brother Clark. She now lived about two miles from our mission, and on the Sabbath, was brought to meeting in a canoe. But on this Sabbath, the wind was so high that no canoe could be launched. In the morning, after the others had left, she started for meeting, and crawled over logs, through creeks and other difficult places near the edges of rocks. Old Anna made her appearance in the house, to the astonishment as well as to the delight of all. She seated herself in front of the preacher, and listened attentively to the words of eternal life. She united with others in praising God for his mercy and goodness, especially to herself. She then partook of the body and blood fo her Saviour. She spoke of the day in which she was in darkness; but now she knew, by experience, that the Lord had forgiven her sins. She cared not for the *water, mud* or *precipices*, if she could only crawl or creep to meeting, for she felt well rewarded, because the Lord blessed her. She did not, like some, fear to soil her clothes; neither was she a *fair day visitor* of meeting. Before her conversion, she was a celebrated conjurer, and a dread to the nation; every one was afraid to incur her displeasure. The last time I saw her, was in 1842, and she was still confiding in the Lord.

We were not to accompany Brother Clark to St. Marie. We started on Tuesday afternoon at about three o'clock, in our large bark canoe, which was about thirty-six feet long, five feet wide in the centre, and three feet high. We paddled about nine miles. On the next morning, we hoisted our sail before a fresh breeze and sailed at the rate of nine knots an hour. We reached the point on the Sand Banks in the evening, having previously tarried three hours with the Indians at Grand Island. The next day we sailed about six miles from the shore: it was quite boisterous; and when in the trough of the wave it was impossible for us to see the land. We now came within a few miles of White-fish Point. On the following day we hoisted our sail again, and had a favorable wind; we went down the Falls of St. Marie in handsome style, about twelve o'clock, *Waub-ke-newh** (White Eagle) walked about Sault St. Marie, attending to the interests of the missions. He was the theme of conversation in every circle, for none had ever travelled the distance in so short a time. The traders were much surprised. The Indians could hardly think it possible for any person to travel the distance in so short a time.

Note.—On our way to St. Marie, we saw that one of the Points of

*This was the name given by my poor brethren to Brother Clark, and a more appropriate one could not have been given. *The King of Birds.* They knew that he had come to be instrumental in saving their never dying souls.

Grand Island had sunk. It was formed of quicksand. It was told to the trader, Charles Holiday, by the Indians, that the Great Spirit had removed from under the point to some other point, because the Methodist missionaries had encamped there the previous fall, and had, by their *prayers*, driven the Spirit from under the point. They did not wish the missionaries to encamp any where on their Island again, fearing that the Island would sink.

### CHAPTER 11

We spent a few weeks at the Sault with the brethren, with whom we had some precious seasons. We were soon informed by our beloved Superintendent that three of us would have to go to Ottawa Lake;— Taunchey, Marksman, and myself. We had, as was supposed, provisions enough to last till we reached La Pointe, where we were to obtain a fresh supply for seven months. Brothers *Tay-yash*, and *Ma-mah-skah-wash* i. e. *Fast-sailer*, accompanied us. We had a new canoe, good oars, and a new sail. After leaving, the first place which we arrived at was about six miles above the Sault St. Marie. We here saw a porcupine on the beach; and having beat it to death, we cooked and ate it for supper. After this we were wind-bound for several days, which delayed our arrival at the Ke-wa-we-non Mission, on our way to La Pointe. On entering Aunce Bay, we were in much danger. The wind rose, with a dense fog accompanying it, and we were without a compass. We steered our course by the wind. We were very near being dashed to pieces against a large rock a few feet from us, which we espied just in time to avoid. I had been on Lake Superior, but never saw the waves run so high as on the present occasion. It was truly wonderful that our bark canoe stood the sea so well. Nor could we see any prospect of landing. Still the spray of the gigantic waves continued to roll after us in terrific fury. The canoe still struggled between the mountain waves, and then would rise on the top. The sail spread itself like a duck just ready to fly. It appeared at times that we must all perish. But God was with us. O how kind and merciful is that Being who has the winds and waves in his hands! "O Lord *I will* praise thee," etc. It is religion alone that can support in the time of danger. Faith lays hold on God. Yes, let *distress, sickness, trials, perils,* and even *death* come, yet if in thy hands, O Lord, we are secure.

Through a kind providence, we arrived at last at Brother Herkimer's, about ten o'clock, A.M. How we surprised them when they were told that we sailed all the morning through the fog. They at once saw the danger; but we could take no other course. We remained here but a few days. On Tuesday we left for La Pointe, one hundred and sixty miles. Here was another tedious journey, for we were again wind-bound for three days; in consequence of this misfortune our provisions were exhausted. We went to Ah-too-nah-kun River on Friday evening, and traveled all night to reach Porcupine Mountains, where we arrived at day-light. We stepped out of the canoe, took our blankets, wrapped them around us, and lay on the solid rocks, where we slept about an hour and a half. Saturday morning arrived, and found us with nothing but half a pound of tea; we were now eighty-eight miles from La Pointe. We rowed all the morning, when a favorable breeze sprung up, which enabled us to gain fifty miles during that day. After night-fall we toiled to reach La Pointe by twelve o'clock on Saturday night; but we were so fatigued, sleepy, and hungry, that it was impossible to continue rowing. Now and then a little land-breeze would help us along slowly, without rowing. At last we were obliged to give up rowing, as the oars were dragging in the water. I steered the boat as well as I could. We labored hard to keep awake. I thought of the tea; I chewed a mouthful of it and swallowed the juice; but in a few minutes I suffered so much from a griping pain that I was alarmed. Oh I was miserable, sick, and hungry. I could not wake any of the company; and when my pain ceased, I could scarcely keep myself awake. I now steered for the shore; it was about twelve o'clock. I threw my blanket around me, and left all hands sleeping in the boat. I threw up a little bank of sand for a pillow, and the soft wet sand was my bed. I was soon in the land of *Nod.*

Sabbath morning came. I had dreamed that we were just about sitting down to a warm breakfast, when Peter Marksman woke me, and said, "George, come, get up, *blackfast*" (breakfast, he meant, he could speak but little English) If it had not been the Sabbath, I might have been induced to retaliate. It was, indeed, a *blackfast*, dark enough; nothing to eat, and only tea to drink for breakfast, dinner and supper! and yet, only about fifteen miles from La Pointe; indeed, we could *see* the place; and had it not been that it was the Sabbath, feeble as we were, we would have proceeded. Here, then, we spent the Sabbath. I walked into the woods, and all that I could think of while reading my Bible, was *home*. I looked towards *home*, and wept at the thought of it. I said to myself, O my father, if you knew my situation to-day, you would feel for me, and fly, if possible, to assist me! I feel that your prayers ascend for me; and then descend like gentle rains, into my soul. *Home! home!* however humble, it is still *home*. This day, however, is a glorious day for my soul; but how insupportable for the body! We had a prayer meeting in the evening, which is still as fresh in my grateful memory as if it had but just taken place.

Monday morning, before the sun arose, we were on our way to La Pointe, where we arrived about ten o'clock. Mr. Warren, the trader at this place, supplied us with some necessaries. We breakfasted with him, and never did fish and potatoes taste half so sweet as now.

We called on the Rev. Mr. Hall, and others of the Presbyterian Mission. How kindly they received and entertained us; they compelled us to live in their families, while we remained in that place. We had now to prepare to depart for Ottawa Lake, where we had been appointed by Brother Clark to spend the winter, in teaching the Indians. O what a field of labor in all these regions! Indians, from every direction, congregate here every summer; those, too, who have never heard of a Saviour!

When will all my poor people "sit together in heavenly places in Christ Jesus?" When will they cease to offer up to the Bad Spirit all they possess? Shall these also perish as did the Indians on the eastern coast? The red men of the forest were then unconscious that the white man would at some future day spread his white sails on these waters, and claim their native woods; that a steamboat would make its appearance, like a monster from the deep, snorting *fire* and *smoke*, near their shores. God of mercy, save, save my poor people.

We started for the Ottawa Lake about the eighth of October, 1835. We had to carry our canoes, with the rest of our articles, over eight portages, or carrying places, one of which was nine, and another five miles long. No language can convey an idea of the hardships and toil to which we were exposed, before we reached there; for we had to carry all our things over the carrying places; and as it was too late in the fall, and on account of the disagreeableness of the weather, we were obliged to return to La Pointe. The winter set in, and we travelled one hundred and seventy miles by land. It was on one of these carrying places that I carried the heavy load mentioned on page 74.

When we arrived at Ottawa Lake, the Indians were glad to see us.

The Chief, Moose Ogeed, *Moose tail*, was particularly kind. Here we laboured with success, though at the time many of them were absent hunting. I commenced a day-school with few scholars. During the winter our provision gave out; for seven weeks we had nothing, except what we caught by spearing and shooting; but in the latter part of the winter we could neither shoot rabbits, nor spear fish. What now was to be done, except to go to La Pointe, one hundred and seventy miles, and obtain some flour. We ran nearly all day through the woods, and the next day my feet were blistered, occasioned by the strap of my snow shoes. The young man who accompanied me, suffered still more, for the blood was oozing out through his moccasons. At the expiration of two days, at about ten o'clock in the morning, we were at Rev. Mr. Hall's, at La Pointe. Brother Hall could hardly credit the fact that we had walked one hundred and seventy miles in *less* than two days.

On returning to the mission, we were one week on our journey. I had over seventy pounds of provisions to carry when I left, and my friend and companion, whom I hired, had eighty-five pounds. The Indians too were almost starving, but the spring opened just in time to save them. In their journey, down the river, we accompanied them, and had an opportunity to converse with them about religion. On our way, the Indians pointed to the battle grounds of the Ojebwas and the Sioux. How dreadful and awful was their description. The Chief, pointing to a certain spot, observed, "There I killed two Sioux, about thirteen winters ago; I cut open one of them; and when I reflected that the Sioux had cut up my own cousin, but a year before, I took out his heart, cut a piece from it, and swallowed it whole. I scooped some of his blood, while warm, with my hand, and drank as many draughts as the number of friends who had perished by their hands." As he spoke, the fierceness of the Indian gleamed from his countenance. Every half mile, trees were blazed (barked,) and notches made according to the number that had been killed.

The Sioux and the Ojebwas have been at war from time immemorial. The neutral ground of these two nations, is full of game, such as deer, bears, elks, etc. We went down to the Me-no-me-nee Mills, on the Chippewa River, where the whites were cutting down pine trees. We then returned to Ottawa Lake, and afterwards, to La Pointe.

During this winter I was with the Rev. Mr. Hall, at La Pointe, and assisted him in translating the Gospel of St. Luke, and the Acts of the Apostles, into the Ojebwa tongue. Although I have sat hour after hour in assisting him in his good work in the west, yet I can never never repay him for the kindness and affection shown to me. May God reward him for his labors of love, and for his Christian benevolence. He is like a pure and limpid stream which is ever running, and which never dries up. He is like a high rock on the sea shore, when the storms and waves have passed by, unchanging and unchanged. He is in all respects the most suitable man for this work, being devoted, humble, kind, affectionate, and benevolent, and is master of our language. I hope to see him once, if not many times more, that I may thank him again and again for his Christian goodness. May his holy and arduous life, and health, be precious in God's sight.

Here I must make a remark. In that country, we ought not to know each other as Presbyterians, Methodists, or Baptists, but only as missionaries of the cross. We should labor with and for each other; and do all the good we can. Our language should always be, "come, brethren, let us labor side by side, hold up each others hands in the work, share each others trials and privations; and spread the gospel of the blessed God." May many brother Halls be raised up for these stations; so that the poor outcast red man may soon take his station among Christians of every civilized clime. Should these observations fall under the eye of dear brother Hall, he will, I am sure, forgive me for the warm and candid confessions of a sincere heart.


## CHAPTER 12

We spent part of the summer at La Pointe, waiting for our superintendent, Rev. John Clark, who intended to go by the way of Ottawa Lake down the Mississippi. He arrived the latter part of June, with his companions. We went in two canoes up *Bad River*, and thence over the Portages, already named. We divided our provisions, bedding, etc., etc., so that each should carry an equal weight. In ascending Bad River we were nearly half of the time in the water, dragging the canoe up the stream. One day brother Clark stepped on a rock above the water, in the centre of the river, for the purpose of holding the canoe, while those that were exceedingly tired, might rest. As soon as he had put his foot on the rock, the canoe wheeled around with the current, which drew him into it, and carried him down the river. We were alarmed for some time, and it was with the greatest efforts that we could save him. At times, we could only see his white hat above the water. At first, we could not render him the least assistance. The stream conveyed him near the shore, where he seized the limb of a tree, which enabled him to reach land. We hurried to the spot where he landed, jumped out of the canoe, and ran after him, but before we could see him, we heard him cry out "*whoop*," and in a few moments saw him coming through the leaves, soaking wet. We were all thankful indeed to see him alive, and so cheerful too. On that day we would not permit him to carry but two loads or packs, the others carried three. Our wish was that he should not *at any time* carry *any thing*; but he insisted upon helping us, and to this we had to submit. This was one of those kind traits which endeared him so much to all his fellow laborers. He has also shared the last morsel of bread with us. Often has he carried the canoe on his back; and when we were discouraged and faint, he would encourage us by his cheerful countenance, and words of consolation. Our sinking hearts have often been made to beat with emotions of joy; for during these journeys we had ample reasons and time for desponding. But according to our trials, did we enjoy the smiles of heaven.

We were three days going over the Nine Mile Portage, where we spent the Sabbath. We had three loads each; and the two canoes were also to be carried, each one taking his turn every half mile. We were now completely jaded out; our bones ached. This was the hardest journey that I ever made, with the exception of the one which will hereafter be related.

After severe toil and privations, we arrived at Ottawa Lake, where Brother Clark met the chief and some of his warriors in council. He explained the object of our visit, viz. to live among them and teach them; to which the chief assented.

Brother Clark now left Johnson, Marksman, and myself here, to do all the good we could. On departing, we accompanied him down the river for two days; and on the first of August we bade each other farewell.

That day, Peter and John were inconsolable because Brother Clark and the rest had left us for a whole year. I felt so "choked up" and deserted, that I talked but little during the day. After praying, as Brother Clark was parting with us, and our heads were resting on the canoe, he said, "Brethren, take courage; do all the good you can.

Pray much; trust in God; tell the Indians how the Saviour died; we will pray for you; good bye; and may the Lord bless you and your labors."

We returned to Ottawa Lake, and built a house, where we resided during the year. Quite late in the fall, Johnson and Marksman left me, and went to La Pointe, where they remained all the winter. It is true, there were but few Indians here, but yet, too many for one teacher. They wished me to go with them, but I preferred, from a sense of duty, to spend the winter and spring in teaching, singing, and praying among the people here. In the spring an interesting conversion took place; the convert committed the fourteenth chapter of St. John before he had learned the alphabet. This young man had been remarkably kind, and humane, before his conversion; he was more like a Christain than any unconverted man I ever saw. I never heard any thing proceed from his mouth that was censurable. One Sabbath morning, while we were in the woods, I was reading to him, "God so loved the world, that he gave his only begotten Son, that whosoever believeth on him, might not perish, but have everlasting life." This was like an arrow in his heart; he prayed, and wrestled with God, until the Lord spoke peace to his soul.

In the summer, when Johnson and Marksman arrived, John and I went down to Prairie Du Chien, on the Mississippi. On our way, we had to pass through the land of the Sioux, the enemies of the Ojebwas, and we knew not what would be our fate. However, we pursued our course and ventured at their village. As soon as we approached, they raised the war-whoop and fired some guns over our heads, and the bullets either splashed in front of our canoe, or whizzed about our heads. Still, we kept on our course, and as soon as we stepped from our canoe, they seized us, and kept us prisoners for nearly three days. When we told them (through an interpreter) that we were missionaries, they released us, and treated us kindly. On the third day we were on the water again, on our way to Prairie Du Chien, which place we reached, and there saw Brother Brunson, the Superintendent for that year. We accompanied him to St. Peters, near the Falls of St. Anthony; and the same summer, through the kindness of Brother Clark, we were sent to school near Jacksonville, Illinois. To Brother Clark, under God, I owe all the education (little as it is) which I now possess. Before this, I could neither speak nor read five words correctly. Brothers Johnson, Marksman, and myself, were placed under the care of the Rev. Jno. Mitchell, now an assistant at the Book Concern, in Cincinnati. For two years we attended school at the Ebenezer Seminary, about two miles north of Jacksonville. At this institution, I passed some of the happiest seasons of my life. Many who were with me at this school, are now ministers of the Gospel, both among the whites and the Indians. The groves seemed vocal with the praises of God. The camp meeting, and the quarterly meetings, which I then attended, are still fresh in my memory. The remembrance of the many delightful acquaintances formed, the appointments filled, the interesting meetings I attended in different parts, about Jacksonville, at Lynville, Manchester, Rushville, and Versailes, will always hold a seat in my heart. It was here that I learned to read the word of God, and often, for hours together, upon my knees, in the groves, have I been thus engaged. O the sweet communion I then had with God!

Among the many letters which I have since received from my school mates, I will trouble the reader only with the following:

Mt. Sterling, *Brown Co., Ill.*
February 8th, 1845

Dear Brother Copway,

With pleasure I improve this privilege of answering your kind epistle, and taking a "paper talk" with you. By the blessings of the good Lord, we are well. But I hear you say "What does he mean by *we?*"— Only myself, my wife, and boy! Now if you will pardon me this time for marrying young, I will promise never to do so again. But I think you will not be severe in your censure, inasmuch as I have a worthy precedent in you. Brother Troy travelled three years, and married Brother Stratten's daughter, of Pike county; and I, who commenced three years after him, preached two years, and married another; so we, who had long been brothers, became brothers-in-law. Brother Wm. Piper was married since conference, to squire Baynes' daughter, near Columbus. Harden Wallace married Miss Bronson, of Athens, one year since. Brother S. Spates is on a visit to his friends, and has the ague; neither he nor Reason is married, but have "good desires." I visited Brother George, two weeks since.

We have glorious times in religion. O it would have done you good to have heard Dr. Akers tell his experience in our last quarterly meeting. In speaking of his sanctification he said, with a peculiar emphasis, while his lips trembled and tears filled his eyes. "*It was the revelation of the Son of God in me.*" But time would fail to tell of these "Ebenezer" boys, who through faith, preach "big sermons," exhort thousands, "who are valiant in fight," who slaughter many a sinner, and wear the marks of many a well fought field, although death has done his work among us! Our faithful teacher, and a beloved schoolmate, Brothers Troy and Piper, are no more; they fell victims to fever just after conference; but they fell like martyrs; they died at their post. Brother Troy and I, attended Brother Piper's funeral (the sermon was preached by Brother Berryman) at Barry. It was a solemn time. While I stood by his coffin, I thought of you all, and of Brother *Huddlestun*, who had gone before him. The day before I left, Father Stratten, Brother Troy, and I, walked out on the Mississippi bluffs, while the bright surface of the river reflected upon us the last rays of the setting sun. We talked of the happy days of other years, spent with kindred spirits now scattered over the world. His breast seemed warmed at the recollection. The flame of his zeal mounted high, and pointing to the bright waters that rolled in the distance, he said, "I feel like preaching till the last sinner on the last tributary of that stream is converted to God." Alas! he had even then preached his last sermon. Peace to their memory. "They taught us how to *live*, and, O how high the price of knowledge, taught us how to *die*." Sister Piper, and her two children, live at her own home in Barry; Sister Troy, with one child, lives with her father. You have, perhaps, read the obituaries of Brothers Benson, Otwell, Corey, Edmunson, and Hale—gone home. Brother N. W. Allen, married down south, and John Mathers to Miss Julia Tucker. Brother Heddenburg is in Springfield. I believe M. has concluded not to marry, but to keep house for her father. Moses C. lives and prospers in Petersburgh Circuit.

*March 13th.* I commence again, not having time to finish when I commenced. I record with sorrow the death of our child, aged eight months. The affliction of one short week, carried him beyond the sorrows incident to mortality, to rest with God. O it was a trial to see him sink in death, and bear him to the grave. But now, thank God,

"The storm that wrecks the winter sky,
  No more disturbs his sweet repose,
Than summer evening's latest sigh,
  That shuts the rose."

The Lord has given us some tokens for good; we have some glorious prayer and class meetings. Thirteen joined on my last round. I expect Brother Wallace with me at a protracted meeting next week: can you not come too?

Well, Brother George, how do you get along in religion? This is the subject *all important*. Time, in its rapid roll, still bears us on. The sun stood still in Gibeon, but time did not stand still. The sun went back ten degrees on the dial of Ahaz, but time rolled on with unremitting speed. *Mutation* is written all around us. The little flower, so bright, is nopped by the untimely frost of winter. The rainbow is beautiful, but it passes away with the weeping cloud. And O how soon the fleeting years of time will be lost amid the mighty cycles of eternity. And yet, my brother, we know that on this inch of time hang everlasting things. Lord, help us to stamp every moment with improvement. Now, if God has entrusted to us the care of souls immortal, how should we pray and labor, lest we should lose a prize so dear!

Brother George, I shall never forget our band society, and "young men's" prayer meeting; these were precious seasons. Though I view my brethren falling round me, the hope of immortality makes "the valley of the shadow" flame with the glory of God. Thank God for religion that can conquer death, and view the grave as but a subterranean passage to the skies Go on—I expect to hail you in a better clime. Brother, I think I have *experienced* that the *blood of Christ cleanseth from all sin*. O glorious truth! Have you not found it too? It is by simple *Faith*.

> "*Faith* has an eye no tears can dim;
> A heart no griefs can stir;
> She bears the cross, and looks to Him
> Who bore the cross for her."

Go on, brother: the land of rest lies just across the rolling tide of Jordan. Methinks I see a Troy, a Huddlestun, and Piper, put forth their hands from the banks of glory, to beckon us onward. They look out for us; O let us not disappoint them! You know the north and south talk of division; thank God they can't divide me, nor break those ties that bind me to good brethren every where, from whom "joy, nor grief, nor time, nor place, nor life, nor death, can part."

I must close my scattering letter, though not half done. Brother come down, and I'll try and tell you the rest. We can go over to Ebenezer and have a meeting. Pitner is there now. He says that the Lord has the best market in the universe; Christian duties are always good sale there, and then we are sure to get a "back load" of grace. He says, "the Lord has a great big two-story *wave-house:* the promise of the life that now is, that's the *lower* story; and of that which is to come, this is the *upper* story. There," says he, "brethren, I'll not tell you any more, you'll have to die to know the rest."

My very best respects to your lady, and the little Copways.

Yours, fraternally

William J. Rutledge.

N. B. Dr. Vandevanter, Brother Bond, and many others, still speak of your preaching at Versailes. We have some good times there now. Brothers Billy and Cabble Patterson are married; yes, and Aquilla too. He preaches, and teaches school. Brother Saxon still goes it with a rush. The "first year" class of boys in this conference, are now first rate; some of them could almost stride a mountain. O sir, it would do you good to see Brother Billy Piper throw his searing thunder bolts and rive the forest oak, or bury them in the smoking earth. See him rise in the fulness of his strength, and exclaim, "Man fell; Heaven was robed in silence, Earth in sorrow, and Hell alone was glad." Farewell.

W. J. R.

I attended several of the Conferences; the last of which was in Bloomfield, in 1839, where I parted with some of my dearest friends and companions, for nine months. Still it was pleasant to reflect that the Conference had appointed Brothers Spates, Huddleston, Johnson, and Peter Marksman, to labor at the head of the Mississippi. Brother Kavanaugh was appointed Superintendent of the Missions for that year. I was allowed to visit home in the fall, to see my friends. I travelled to Chicago free of expense: I drove a pair of fine grey horses for an individual who was on his road to that place. We slept in our wagons every night. At Chicago* I embarked in a schooner for Buffalo; but getting tired of this, left it at Detroit, and took steamboat for Buffalo, where I arrived just about day light. I had lost my cap, the wind blew it into the lake, with my pocket book, containing $27 in bills, and $2.50 in silver, with a silk handkerchief, in which my all was wrapped. Here I was, moneyless, friendless, and hatless, and in a strange land! I had, however, a little change left. I had made up my mind to visit the East before my return to Canada. But this must now be abandoned. I walked about Buffalo quite disheartened. At last I saw on a sign "Temperance Hotel." I concluded to put up at this house, and to my surprise and joy, the landlord was a warm hearted Methodist—James Madison. At night, I accompanied him to the prayer meeting, where he told a Brother Copeland my circumstances. They made up the whole amount of my loss, and gave me a dollar over. I could now visit the East as I had purposed before my loss. The next day I started for Rochester, where I spent the Sabbath. I was very anxious to see the great cities of which I had read so much at school. I resolved to go through thick and thin for the sake

*Chicago signifies *the place of skunks.*

of seeing New York. At Rochester I stopped with Brother Colby; Miss Colby perceiving that I was not warmly clad, gave me a cloak which she obtained from Brother S. Richardson. Should either, or both, of these dear friends see these remarks concerning their kindness, I hope they will excuse me for thus mentioning their names. I must thank them again for their goodness; I often remember them in my closet and by the wayside. May God reward them and all other friends.

On Monday I left for Albany. When I reached Syracuse, I took the long-looked for rail road. We were soon on our way, moving along like a streak of lightning. In the morning I arrived in Albany in time for the morning boat for New York. I walked around this Dutch city; and as every thing appeared to be somewhat new, I was interested, especially with the vessels, &c. As I wished to be economical, I left without any breakfast. I was charmed with the steamboat. We passed down the Hudson; the towns, villages, and the splendid scenery enchanted me. I had seen but very few such magnificent scenes before.

About noon, a plain looking man approached me; I discovered at once that he was of that class of men called Quakers. He spoke of what they were doing for the Indians in New York. I was very much interested with his conversation. I felt glad and proud to have the honor and pleasure of seeing and conversing with one of Penn's descendants—the friend of the poor Indians. While conversing with him, the bell was rung for dinner; he wished me to go down and eat; I told him I was obliged to be saving, as I had but little money and was not accustomed to travelling. Upon saying this, he pulled out a dinner ticket from his pocket and said, "*Friend*, thou must take this and come down to dinner." I had an exalted opinion of the Quakers before, but this kind act increased my feelings, and confirmed all that I had ever heard of their generosity to my poor people. "God bless the Quakers," said I, silently, as I descended to dinner. After dinner we finished our conversation. He said he was on his way to Philadelphia. God bless him, wherever he is. He has my kindest wishes.

In the evening I arrived at New York, and went immediately to see Brother Mason, who directed me to go to Sister Luckey's in Broome street, where I tarried during my stay.

On the 25th of October, came that great jubilee of Methodism. In the morning I went with Dr. Bangs to meeting. He preached the centenary sermon, which was afterwards printed. In the evening I attended the Allen street Station. Oh what a happy meeting this was. Here I saw some of the greatest among them weep for joy. "Amen, halleluiah, glory to God," and similar ejaculations, rang through, and filled the house. In this vast assembly was a solitary Indian—George Copway! Never can I forget that evening! Whatever may be my future lot in this life, I will always thank God for the privilege of attending these services. May the Lord pour out his Spirit on all his churches.

The next day I visited Newark, N.J., to see brother Abraham Hedenburg, with whom I had become acquainted in Illinois, at the house of his brother James. Here I met with a great deal of kindness. Brother Bartine, of the Franklin Station, requested me to preach for him in the morning; and Brother Ayers, of the Northern Station, invited me to preach for him in the evening. Brother Ayers gave me about $8.oo worth of books, which I had the pleasure of perusing during the winter. This was a favor—a distinguished favor indeed. I have seen that dear brother but once since. May the Lord be gracious to him.

My visit to Brother Hedenburg was delightful. I met many friends here, to whom I can never be thankful enough. May God visit them in great mercy. I saw them again last summer, and partook of their kind hospitalities. I feel more and more indebted to them; especially to Brother Hedenburg.

My next journey was to Boston. Dr. Bangs gave me a letter of introduction to a brother in that city. I remained about two weeks, looking at the Yankees and their city. Boston is much overrated; there are a few very few pretty spots; the rest is crooked and narrow. It is far behind New York, Philadelphia, and perhaps Baltimore, and new Orleans. I met with a few choice spirits—Brothers King, Rand, Wise, and Smith; and on the Sabbath, I addressed the Sabbath School in Russel street. In the evening we had a delightful meeting. I remained with Brother H. Merrell's family during my sojourn, and I shall always recollect them with feelings of sincere gratitude. I visited several noted places while in that vicinage,—the Monument on Bunker's (or rather Breed's) Hill, etc.; I went also on the top of the State House when the sky was clear. It was from this point that I saw the works of the white man. The steeples, vessels arriving, and others spreading their sails for distant lands. The wharves were filled with merchandise. A few steamboats were running here and there, breathing out fire and smoke. On my left, I noticed several towns. The steam cars from Worcester rolled on from the west; others were starting for Providence, and whizzed along the flats like a troop of runaway horses. Here were factories in different directions. As I saw the prosperity of the white man, I said, while tears filled my eyes, "Happy art thou, O Israel, who is like unto the, *O people saved by the Lord!*" When I thought of the noble race of red men who once lived and roamed in all the land, and upon the waters as far as my eye could reach, the following thoughts arose in my mind, which I have since penned.

> Once more I see my fathers' land
>     Upon the beach, where oceans roar;
> Where whiten'd bones bestrew the sand,
>     Of some brave warrior of yore.
> The *groves*, where once my fathers roam'd—
>     The *rivers*, where the beaver dwelt—
> The *lakes*, where angry waters foam'd—
>     Their *charms*, with my fathers, have fled.
>
> O! tell me, ye "pale faces," tell,
>     Where have my proud ancestors gone?
> Whose smoke curled up from every dale,
>     To what land have their free spirits flown?
> Whose wigwam stood where cities rise;
>     On whose war-paths the steam-horse flies;
> And ships, like mon-e-doos in disguise,
>     Approach the shore in endless files.

I now visited the Missionary Rooms of the American Board, whose invaluable labors are felt throughout the globe. I saw some articles, wrought by our people in the west, such as bead work, porcupine quills, moccasons, war clubs, etc. I thought, that if Brother Green had seen as much of war clubs as I had, (for I have seen them stained with blood and notched according to the number of individuals they had slain,) he would conceal them from every eye.

## CHAPTER 13

About the 4th of November, I took my leave of Boston, for the great commercial emporium, on my route homewards. My travelling companion was the Rev. E. Taylor, the sailor's friend. He was on his way to Philadelphia to preach. I should suppose that a better sailor's preacher cannot be found in the Union. I was much pleased with his conversation. In one of his public addresses, I was told that he said, "When I die, smother me not under the dust; but bury me in the sea, where the sea-weed will be my winding sheet, the coral my coffin, and the sea shell my tomb stone." I heard an individual say of him, "start him where you will, he will go to sea."

I was now, once more, in the magnificent city of New York. I bought a few books at the Book Rooms. After surveying the beauties and curiosities of the city, I left in the steamboat Rochester for Albany. I spent one day in Albany, and attended a Methodist prayer meeting. The Rev. Mr. Seymour, the preacher in charge at the Division street Station, introduced me to Brother Page, who had the charge of the South Ferry street Church. At the latter church I was present at a delightful and soul-stirring meeting.

The following day I took the canal for Syracuse and Oswego. On my way from Schenectady to Utica I preached twice on board the boat; and even here I found some pious souls. I observed the tears falling from several eyes. "The Lord be praised," was the language of my heart. When shall this poor heart feel full and wholly alive to the unsurpassed favors of heaven?

I took a steamboat at Oswego, and arrived at Kingston, C. W., on the evening of Nov. 11. Here I had to pay duties on the books which I had obtained in New York. The amount to be paid was $32.50, and I had but $27. I went to Charles Oliver, Deputy Collector; and as soon as I laid my circumstances before him, he said, "pay the $27, and I will advance you the balance; and as soon as you reach home, write to Mr. McCaulay, the Inspector General, who lives in Toronto, and inform him who you are; he will, doubtless, authorize me to refund you the money." I did so, and shortly afterwards received the whole amount. In this public way I would express my most hearty thanks to these gentlemen for their acts of kindness towards an Indian stranger.

I arrived at Rice Lake on the 12th day of November, 1839, having been absent from home five years and four months. Never did I feel so rejoiced as when I stood on the top of a hill, and saw my village, seven miles across the lake. I gazed upon it with pure delight; and as I took a retrospective view of all the scenes which I had passed through, I wondered at myself, and at the great goodness of God. I knelt down and "blessed and thanked Him who liveth for ever," for his unspeakable goodness to a child of sin. While crossing the lake, I was in perfect ecstacies; my heart leaped with joy; and my thoughts and emotions were at my home long before my person. O how tedious and tardy the boat seemed to be; I wished for wings several times. But at last, I planted my foot upon the spot on which I had been reared from my infancy, and where some of the sweetest and happiest recollections of my life were centered. But "every sweet has it bitter." On enquiring for some of my relatives, I was informed that they had left this, for a better life. Many of my old friends and acquaintances had gone to try the realities of another world. Numbers were bathed in tears, and the wounds of their hearts were re-opened. My own heart seemed to bleed at every pore. What a painful interview! I now requested to be shown the graves of my dear relatives and friends. I wended my way to these consecrated grounds, and sighed and wept over them. My reflections were solemn indeed! I followed many of them, in my thoughts, to heaven, whither they doubtless now are, celebrating the praises of God around the throne of the blessed Redeemer. This was great consolation amidst my griefs; and I felt now determined, with God's assistance, to follow them, so far as they followed Christ, and thus be prepared to unite with them in the songs of the upper world, whenever God shall see fit to call me hence.

Brother John Sunday, was at this time, stationed in our village. The Lord soon visited this Mission with a glorious revival; many were converted, and others reclaimed. The tracts that I had received at the Book Rooms, and the books from the American Tract Society (N.Y.,) I distributed among those that could read, and they were duly appreciated. I believe that these were the means which prepared their minds to relinquish the world, and place their hope in God.

I will now speak of Christmas and New Year. When Christmas arrived, we were invited to a centenary tea party, in company with the Rev. William Case, the well known friend of the Indians. The party met at Alderville, eight miles from the Mission. This was a season of much joy and happiness. The Chiefs referred to the time when they were without the gospel. One of them said, "Before I heard the gospel, when Christmas came, I began to thank the Great Spirit for the day on which I could get plenty of *whiskey*. Brothers, you know how often I was dragged through the snow to my wigwam, where my wife and children were cold and hungry. Now, I drink *tea* instead of *whiskey*, and have religion with it; now my house is comfortable; and my children are pious and happy. I expect to pursue a Christian course till I arrive in heaven. My fond hope is to meet these good missionaries in the land of bliss; and not only these, but also the good John Wesley, with whom I expect to shake hands there." John Sunday's brother (Big Jacob,) said, "When the Methodists were preaching to our people, I heard that the chiefs and warriors were frequently in tears. I then said, I would not shed tears were I to hear them. Still, I wished to understand for myself. I went, with a full determination not to behave myself like a *woman*, I mean by crying. I sat near the door. The preacher was speaking about the Saviour's dying on the cross, while the Indians all around were sobbing. I began to feel serious, and then the tears feel involuntarily. Frequently I wiped my eyes, but still the tears *would flow*. I asked myself, *am I crying too?* Brethren, I was ashamed to exhibit tears; but now [here he raised his hand to heaven] it is not through cowardice that I cry, for I never shed a tear on the battle field, nor even when my children or my friends lay dead before me. No! I never dropped a tear. I feel to-night very happy and thankful to know that the Great Spirit did not, while I was in darkness, say, 'I will never bless this Indian.' I feel an ardent love for you all. I love *Jesus*, who has done so much for sinful me." He then sat down; Brother John Sunday now arose, and interpreted what his brother had just said; and at the close of his remarks, he turned to the whites, who had come here from Cobourg, and several other places, and said, "Brothers, that was a *great big mercy*, for that *great big man*."

I might add other cases here, but it is scarcely necessary. Suffice it to say that we enjoyed the services throughout. As I looked around, I recognized some, whom I knew, and had often seen before the gospel reached us, and who had usually spent Christmas in the gutter,—degraded, miserable, and starving. The language of the Psalmist might well have been quoted by each of these poor brethren:—"Thou hast raised me up out of the filthiest sink (English translation, *'the miry clay,'*) and hast planted my feet firmly on a rock." Yes, the rock Christ Jesus.

New Year's day was observed in the same religious manner. And I cannot but remark here, that it is to be greatly regretted that so many

Christians in the States spend this day in gadding about from house to house, and indulging in luxuries to excess. Nay, more; I have been informed that not a few professors entertain their visitors with *fire-water* or *devil's spittle*, on that day. What a contradiction this would be in the estimation of converted Indians, were they to witness these scenes.

During the winter, the General Council of the Nation was held at the Credit River Mission. Chief Joseph Sawyer was elected President of the Council. This noble chief has filled the chair several times since, with great credit. Several petitions, and other important documents were drawn up and signed by the different chiefs, to be presented to the Government of Canada. The whole Council waited on the Governor General, Lord Sydenham, in a body; they presented their petitions (see Note A, at the end of this chapter.) In reply, we received but little satisfaction; he closed his note, by saying, "My children, for the present, I bid you all farewell." His Lordship did not even deign to affix his *name* to the note. Since then, nothing has been heard of our papers, and therefore we must conclude that they have been laid *under* the table. But what could be expected of a *"father,"* who could smile in the presence of his *"children,"* and yet stab them in the dark? See note B, at the close of the chapter, where the reader may find an extract from his letter to Lord John Russell. To rebut his false representations, I would appeal to the Report of the Commissioners on Indian Affairs in Canada; to the missionaries; and to the whole civilized and Christianized population of the Chippewa nation. I can therefore say, without the fear of respectable contradiction, that his assertions have no foundation in truth. A few drunken Indians, it is true, may be found in Canada; and these alone, would be willing to call him *Father*.

It was at this General Council that I became acquainted with Captain Howell's family, of Toronto, formerly of England, and after an intimate acquaintance of some six months, I was united in marriage to his daughter Elizabeth. My wife has been a help meet indeed; she has shared my woes, my trials, my privations; and has faithfully labored to instruct and assist the poor Indians, whenever an opportunity occurred. I often feel astonished when I reflect upon what she has endured, considering that she does not possess much physical strength. I can truly say that she has willingly partaken of the same cup that I have, although that cup has often contained *gall*. I trust, that I have not transgressed the bounds of delicacy, in speaking of one who has sacrificed so much in becomeing the partner of an Indian missionary. I will simply add, that Mr. and Mrs. Howell, and their daughters Caroline and Elizabeth, were then, and are now, members of the Methodist Church.

In the spring which preceded my marriage, I was appointed by my people at Rice Lake, to transact some business for them at Toronto. I accordingly left Rice Lake and reached Toronto in April. Just before leaving for Rice Lake, I called to see my cousin, Thomas Kezhig, who was confined to his house by consumption. While on my journey homewards, between Toronto and Port Hope, as I was sleeping on one of the sofas of the steamboat, I had the following singular dream in relation to my cousin above mentioned:—

I found myself in a path on a wide plain, which led towards the south, between two cottages. I was impressed with a belief that it was my duty to proceed to the end of the road, which, from appearances, great multitudes had walked over. On nearing the cottages, I discovered a small gate, attended by a keeper. At first, he refused me an entrance, but after much persuasion, he permitted me to pass, extorting from me a promise, to return as soon as I should reach a certain spot, from which I could see the end of the path. I passed through the gate and traveled over a beautiful rolling country, with groves, flowers, and fruits, on my right and on my left, which delighted my eyes; while the singing of birds delighted my ears. I walked through several streams which ran smoothly over beds of beautiful pebbles. From one of these streams I drank, and felt much refreshed. In some places, I saw the impress of men's feet on the pebbles, which proved that persons had gone before me. Some time after this, I heard several voices conversing about the country to which they were traveling. I ascended a hill, from which I beheld a scene which no language can describe. In front was a large granite rock, in the form of pyramid; it was exceedingly high; had seats on each side from the bottom to the top; and on these, sat a great multitude who had died in the Lord. Here and there was a vacant seat. Some, however, were standing, and all had a pair of wings. Those that were sitting, had wings, and seemed ready to fly! On the very summit, and above the rest, there was a spacious seat, or magnificent throne. One sat on this throne who shone like the sun! Over his crowned head was a circle, resembling a rainbow, on which was written, with letters of gold, "This is the King Jesus." What a splendid sight! it dazzled my eyes. Above his head were clouds of angels; these were performing beautiful gyrations. Sometimes they descended so low, that I plainly could see the upper side of their wings, which reflected a brilliant light from the throne. I did not hear them speak, but there was a noise like a mighty rushing wind, occasioned by their wings, which were constantly in motion. There were myriads upon myriads of these winged angels; the very heavens were covered with them. I observed between me and this great rock, a river, part of which was as black as jet, and the rest as yellow as gold. It flowed gracefully along the edge of the beautiful green, near the rock. I saw two men plunge into its bosom, and swim. As soon as they reached the spot where the water was black, their clothes fell off of them, and were carried away by the current; while they themselves reached the shore on the opposite side. They now assumed forms too glorious for tongue or pen to describe; even imagination must fail here. They now seemed to rise up out of the river; and as they stood up its bed, with their long white wings majestically expanded and dripping, they clapped their hands and exclaimed, "Glory to God in the highest; glory and honor to Jesus." They now stepped out of the stream, walked side by side, and ascended to their seats midway up the rock! While they were ascending, the entire multitude cheered and welcomed them. "Glory to God," "Hallelulah," with many other exclamations, were echoed in loud peals throughout the whole region. My eyes wept big burning tears, which overflowed my face. I tried to join the happy throng in ejaculating *halleluiah*; and made several fruitless attempts to cross the river. I felt as if I were fettered, and fastened to a stake. Presently, I heard the sound of footsteps behind me; I turned around suddenly, and beheld my cousin Thomas Kezhig, passing along. I addressed him, and said, "Where are you going, cousin?" He replied, "I am going where my *mother* and *sister* have gone; but *you* must return home soon, for you are needed there; you will one day follow us to the skies." I exerted myself to approach him, but in vain. He turned about, ran down the hill to the water, plunged in, and swam like a duck. His clothes now fell off of him, as did those of the two individuals referred to above. I saw him rise; he exclaimed, "*Glory to Jesus!*" Some one exclaimed from the rock, "Thomas Kezhig is come, Thomas Kezhig is come." Immediately, two flew from their seats, and presented themselves before him, near the edge of the water.

They embraced each other, and clapped their wings, as if filled with joy. O what a happy, happy scene! The immense throng of angelic beings witnessed this sight, and lowered their flight. Those on the rock, now stood up at his approach, and flapped their wings. The two who had flown to him, led him by the hand to a seat. Every eye was now upon him; and the whole heavens seemed to echo, *"Welcome to thy rest, thou child of affliction."* I recognized in these two, his mother and sister, who had died a few years before, with a hope full of glory. I could have given worlds for permission to cross the river. I wept sorely, and felt it incumbent to return, according to my promise, to the keeper of the gate. The keeper inquired, "well did you see them?" But my heart was too full to give utterance to my thoughts. I now awoke, much agitated, and still weeping. I looked at my watch, and discovered that it was a quarter past one o'clock, P. M.

In the evening I met one of my step-brothers at Port Hope; he had just arrived. The first words that he uttered, were, "Our cousin is no more." I inquired, "When did he die?" He replied, "To-day, about one o'clock." "Then," said I, "he is happy in the realms of bliss." The next day, as I stooped over his cold remains, I could still see his glorified spirit as in my dream, welcomed to the land of angels. O! "Let me die the death of the righteous, and let my last end be like his." I loved him tenderly, and had good reason to believe that he also loved me. My readers will, I trust, excuse me for having inflicted upon them this dream. It is even now so vivid in my recollection, and being somewhat curious and peculiar, that I have ventured to give it. It is but a dream, and I wish it to go for what it is worth, and no more.

I left Toronto for the west, on the third of June, and arrived at Buffalo the same evening, just in time to fulfil an engagement. I was to address the Sunday School Missionary Society at the Methodist Episcopal Church. I was obliged to leave Mrs. Copway at Toronto, as she was not quite prepared to depart; but the following day she met me in Buffalo. Here the brethren prevailed on us to stay over the Sabbath. Sabbath morning I preached at Black Rock, and in Buffalo in the evening. What a curious, inquisitive, and teasing people, some of the Yankees are! Yet, they are very friendly withal, for every one seemed to be striving to induce us to go to their homes to take tea and to pass the night. I had been married but a few days, and the following were some of the questions put to me:—"How did you obtain your wife?" "Where were you married?" "Did her father consent?"

"How many of your people have married our white women?" These and similar inquiries were constantly made, and were exceedingly annoying. But notwithstanding all this, I could say "farewell *dear friends* of Buffalo; thank you for your kindness, your good wishes, and your prayers. Farewell Sister Dobson, Brother M., and Brother Vanderpool"—a *noble* hearted and whole-souled man.

On the 7th of June, we parted with my wife's sister, Caroline, who had come with my wife from Toronto as far as Buffalo. We were soon sailing on Lake Erie. On the 8th we were in Cleveland. Here we were obliged to stop, as the regular boat was engaged to convey persons to the great Whig Convention at Fort Meigs. But we passed a very agreeable time, however, especially with Mr. and Mrs. Peet. On the 12th, an opportunity offered by which we could go as far as Amherstburg, on our way to Detroit. The steamboat Milwaukie stopped at Cleveland on her route upwards and on board of her we went. Soon we fell in with Rev. John Clark, who was on his way from the General Conference to Chicago, in company with Rev. Mr. Colclazier, of Detroit. It was my design to preach on board, but was prevented on account of the rolling of the boat, which caused much seasickness, and our early arrival at Amherstburg. Here we staid one week, and passed many happy hours, especially with Sister Scott. From Amherstburg we went to Detroit. On the 18th we started from Detroit for Mackinaw, on board the steamboat Robert Fulton, which place we reached on the 20th; here we remained a few days with B. Chapman, Esq. Here I heard of the death of one of our traders, Lavaque, a pious man and a particular friend. I preached his funeral sermon, and then his remains were consigned to the grave. Many wept on this occasion, for he was much beloved. Mrs. Copway was now suffering from chills and fever, which she first contracted at Toronto. On the 23rd, we took passage on board the steamboat Fairport, and arrived at Green Bay early the next morning. Mrs. Copway's indisposition induced me to remain here until she should feel better. Brother Chenoworth, the stationed preacher, was absent, and it devolved on me to fill his pulpit on the Sabbath. We had a most interesting season in waiting on the Lord. Mrs. Copway's fevers continued three weeks, and when it was thought that she had recovered, we took land carriage to Prairie Du Chien. But before we had gone many miles, she was again seized with chills and fever, and we were obliged to tarry at the house of a Mr. McCarty. His family were kind, and would not receive any compensation for their trouble. I now proposed to Mrs. C. to return to Green Bay, but she would not consent, saying, that as we had started, it were better to keep on. Every other day she had the fever. O how it distressed me to witness her affliction. We passed through the villages of the Stockbrige and Brother Town Indians. Their lands are good, and it is to be hoped that they will continue to conduct themselves well.

On the 17th July, we arrived at Winnebago Lake, where we took dinner with Brother White. After leaving this place, we had to kindle up a fire in the groves several times, in order to cook something for breakfast, and for the rest of the day; there being no settlers within twenty miles. Some men seem to have come to these "diggings" only for the purpose of defrauding travellers out of their goods and money. For every slim and dirty meal, we had to pay fifty cents. There is a house between Fort Winnebago and Prairie Du Chien which I can never forget. We had to pay fifty cents for each meal (?); twenty-five cents for lodging in beds swarming with fleas and bugs. Sleep was out of the question; so I spent the hours of the night on the seat of what was called a chair. August 23d, we arrived at Prairie Du Chien, after much fatigue, having traveled ten days. Brother Kavanaugh had just arrived from St. Peters, and had us conveyed to Dubuque, in a canoe. Here Mrs. Copway remained, till I returned from the Conference, which was held at Mount Morris. From Dubuque we went to Prairie Du Chien, in a steamboat; on the 26th we were compelled to go in our canoe to St. Peters, on account of the shallowness of the river. Our company consisted of Brothers Spates, Huddleston, Brown, Jones, Mrs. Copway, her sister, and myself. We encamped, occasionally, on the banks of the Mississippi. We were more than two weeks traveling three hundred miles, to St. Peters. We had a tent which we pitched every night. On the 26th September, we had to mount the bluffs of the Mississippi river; here we found a number of Indian deities, made of stone. Mrs. Copway and her sister tumbled them all down into the river. Their worshippers must have been astounded and mortified when they returned, and discovered that their gods had vanished. On several occasions we were dripping wet. On the 9th of October we arrived at St. Peters; we here had the happiness and privilege of associating with the Presbyterian missionaries three weeks; they were affectionate and truly kind to us. These were Brothers Garvin, Pond, Denton, and their wives. We had yet to journey nearly three hundred miles. After some delay in getting ready, we started in our canoe. On the 27th of October we went about fifteen miles up the river; on the 28th we could proceed no farther on account of the ice. Now what was to be done? If the winter sets in, while we are on our journey, we shall have to suffer much. We therefore concluded to go by land to Elk River mission. On the 19th we hired a Frenchman to convey our things in his cart. It being late when we started, we walked but five miles the first day; we really dreaded the journey. On the thirtieth, while we were crossing the Rice River, the cart was upset; our provisions and clothes were filled with water; and many of our things were floating down the river. I made a fire, and we passed the rest of the day in drying our articles; fortunately, not one of us was in the cart. Mrs. Copway exhibited much patience and fortitude; she reproved us for murmuring, on account of this and other mishaps; and laughed, while our pies and cakes were sailing down the river. On the 31st we walked the whole day, and reached Rum River,—called so, because a barrel of rum had been concealed there. It would be too tedious to narrate *all* the circumstances connected with the rest of our journey.

On the 6th of November we arrived at the mission, having traveled, in all, about two thousand and eighty miles. The Indians had fled from this mission, on account of their enemies, the Sioux, whom they dreaded. Here, then, we had no employment; no one to instruct! We now endured much suffering. I was taken sick with the dysentery, and remained so four months, although, occasionally, I could move about. Brother Huddleston, also, became sick; he was taken on the 25th of December, and died on the 30th, of dysentery. This was truly a time of trial. We buried him near the banks of the Mississippi, on New Year's day. He had come here to do good; but O how inscrutable are the ways of God! The chief of the Ojebwas had now arrived; and addressed us in the following language:—

"Brothers, I am sorry to see you all in such afflicting circumstances. I see that you loved him; and from what little I saw and knew of him, I believe he was a good man. He came here to do us good—to teach our children. You ask me where you shall bury your Brother. I will tell you. Bury him on that little hill [pointing to it,] so that we may see his grave as we pass up and down the river. I will tell my people to keep the grave in good order, and to respect it. No grass shall be allowed to grow too near it; we will see that it is weeded. Next summer,

*I* will build a heap of stones about it; that all may see and know where the good man lies—he, who came to bless us. Tell his father that the Sioux, our enemies, will not molest his remains."

This chief was not a pious man. Three of his warriors, now went to the hill, cleared away the snow, and dug the grave according to our directions. We committed his lifeless body to the cold grave in a strange land! I never knew how much I loved him, until he was gone. Filled with tears, sobs, and sighs, Brother Spates performed the last sad office, over the remains of our dearly beloved brother, while the rude blast was blowing the snow in every direction. Just before he died, he admonished and entreated us to meet him in heaven, where he assured us he was going. "Blessed are the dead, that die in the Lord."

The chief now invited us to go and reside with him at Rabbit River; and, in February, we did so, after having traveled three days. During these three days, however, we had often to shovel away the snow, build a fire, and spread the bedding without any tent over it. We awoke one morning, and found the snow two inches deep on the bed clothes. We built a large fire, by which we warmed ourselves and boiled some coffee. Our bread was frozen; but we thawed it, and made a meal. When this was over, off we started. By the way, I ought to have mentioned that I had a pony for Mrs. Copway and her sister, on which they could ride. Through the winter he lived on rushes, and browsed like a deer. The poor fellow had to give out, about two miles before we reached Rabbit River; Mrs. Copway, therefore, had to walk this distance on the ice, which greatly fatigued her. On Saturday night quite late, we arrived at the shanty of Chief Hole-in-the-sky. In all our journeyings Mrs. C. was always ready and willing to endure every hardship. She never murmured nor appeared discontented. This often encouraged me, and afforded us much relief. I record with gratitude, that God enabled her and her sister to bear up under the severest trials and hardships. We could have no earthly gain in view; the grace of God alone, therefore, supported us by day and by night, in sickness, in perils, in storms, in fatigues, in despondency, and in solitary places. At Rabbit River we labored with considerable success; but on account of the war raging between the Sioux and the Ojebwas, these two missions, with that at Ottawa Lake, had to be abandoned.

### NOTE A.

"1st. The soil at the Credit is generally very poor, and, consequently, the crops are light, and this, in a great measure, discourages our people from becoming good farmers. The situation of the Credit Reserve is better calculated for commercial than agricultural purposes.

"2nd. We have learned, by experience, that living together in a village, whilst endeavoring to follow farming, is attended with many disadvantages, and loss of time; it is therefore desirable, that all the Indians who wish to become planters should be settled on their own lots.

"3rd. The evil example of many of the white people around our village, exposes our people to the temptation of drinking fire-water, and of committing other vices.

"4th. We are of opinion, that, if we go and settle on a good tract of land, many of our young men, who are now spending their time in idleness, would be induced to become industrious, and attend to their farming."

### NOTE B.

"Government House,
*"Kingston, 22nd July,* 1841.

"My Lord,—I have the honor to acknowledge the receipt of your despatch of the 1st instant, No. 393, on the subject of the Indian Department in Canada. I beg to assure your Lordship that I have given the subject my attentive consideration, and I hope to be able to submit for your approval a scheme for the consolidation of the Department. At the same time the matter is attended with great difficulty, arising from the peculiarity of the duties which the officers of the Department have to perform, the extent of country comprised within their jurisdiction, and, above all, from the system pursued with regard to the Indians, which, in my opinion, is of the most mistaken character. All my observation has completely satisfied me, that the direct interference of the Government is only advantageous to the Indians who can still follow their accustomed pursuits, and that if they became settlers, they should be compelled to fall into the ranks of the rest of Her Majesty's subjects, exercising the same independent control over their own property and their own actions, and subject to the same general laws as other citizens.

"The attempt to combine a system of pupilage with the settlement of these people in civilized parts of the country, leads only to embarrassment to the Government, expense to the Crown, a waste of the resources of the Province, and an injury to the Indians themselves. Thus circumstanced, the Indian loses all the good qualities of his wild state, and acquires nothing but the vices of civilization. He does not become a good settler, he does not become an agriculturist or a mechanic. He does become a drunkard and a debauchee, and his females and family follow the same course. He occupies valuable land, unprofitably to himself and injuriously to the country. He gives infinite trouble to the Government, and adds nothing either to the wealth, the industry, or the defence of the Province.

"I have, &c.

(*Signed*,) "SYDENHAM."

"The Right Honorable

"Lord J. Russell."

## CHAPTER 14

In the spring we were out of provisions, and had to fish for a living for about three weeks. Brother Spates taught school, and cousin Johnson and myself visited the wigwams daily, for the purpose of singing and praying, and reading the word of God. They always received us kindly; and soon their minds and hearts began to feel serious, and they inclined strongly towards Christianity. It was not long after that many of them professed to have made their peace with God, and expressed their determination to obey the precepts of Jesus. Here we must acknowledge that God "made us glad according to the days wherein he has afflicted us." We had "not labored in vain, nor spent our strength for nought," although we had to confess that we were unprofitable servants. While conversing with a chief upon the importance of true religion, he became much troubled, and admitted that his own religion was not as good as the religion of the Bible; but, said he, "I will embrace your religion when I shall have returned from one more battle with the Sioux; and I will then advise my people to embrace it too." What a struggle this poor fellow had within! His name was *Bah-goo-na-ge-shig* (Hole-in-the-sky.) He had always been kind to me and mine: in the spring he presented me about eighty pounds of sugar; observing at the same time, "I have brought this from the Sugar Bush to-day; you will require some for your family; and I cheerfully give it."

Brother Brace and his family now arrived from Prairie Du Chien. What tales of sufferings did they communicate! They had traveled six hundred miles in the midst of winter; and were exposed to all winds and weathers! But, thank God, now they were with us. Their clothes were almost in strings, and their children were in rags! Expecting to find enough to live on as soon as they arrived, they brought nothing with them. Thank heaven, we were just enabled to keep them and ourselves from starving.

The Indians desired us to visit several other places, and establish ourselves there. The whole country seemed ripe for the Gospel. It was thought best that Brother Spates and myself should go down to St. Peters, by water, and obtain provision. We were four days going, and, on our arrival, a war party was just on the eve of departing for our mission, where they intended to murder all the Ojebwas they could find. I requested Brother Spates to accompany me back by land, to inform the Indians of the intention of the Sioux. He said, "there would be too much risk in going before the War Party." But my wife and sister were there; they, as well as my poor people, might be barbarously murdered. After repeated efforts to get some one to accompany me, but without success, I was determined to go alone. I trusted in the God of battles, and with his aid I was confident that I could prevent these merciless and blood-thirsty warriors from imbruing their hands in the blood of my nation. I was ready for a start; and went to chief Little Crow's village, to tell him that I was going to the Rabbit River Mission. Not thinking, that I was in earnest, or had courage enough, he said "Tell Hole-in-the-sky, I am coming to get his scalp." This took place three hours before they were ready to march. In the midst of *jeers* and *war-whoops*, I left their mission house. They did not believe that I intended to go farther than Fort Snelling. As soon as I was out of sight, I began to run as fast as I was able. I called at the Post Office, which was nine miles from the Crow Mission, got my papers and letters, and ran about seven miles over the prairie, without stopping. I bought a pony on the road, of a Frenchman, and having no saddle, I rode but three miles of the whole distance. I tied my pack on his back, and made him run all the afternoon. In the night I slept without a fire. I was so anxious to get home, that I had no appetite for eating, the first two days. I went at the rate of about seventy-five miles per day, and arrived home at noon, on the fourth day; having walked two hundred and forty miles, forded eight large streams, and crossed the broad Mississippi twice. My coat and pantaloons were in strips. I crossed the Mississippi just in front of our mission house, and, as soon as possible, I told the chief that the war party were now on their way to our mission, to kill them. I advised him to lead away the women and children, which they did, and the next day they *all* left us. We, that is, my family, myself, and the other missionaries, were now left to the mercy of the Sioux. But they did not come, although they sent spies. Brother Brace, Cousin Johnson, and I, now ventured to take our families down to St. Peters. We left in a large bark canoe, and had only *one loaf* of bread, *two quarts* of beans, and *two quarts* of molasses.

Brother Brace was so sick, that we had to lift him in and out of the canoe.

We saw tracts of the war party, on our way to St. Peters. They watched us on the river, as we heard afterwards. We encamped about one mile and a half this side of their watering place, during the night, and did not know that they knew this fact, as will be seen in the sequel. They came and held a council just across the river from our encampment; they could see the light of our fire. The war chiefs agreed that four of the warriors should swim over to us and take us all prisoners. One was to take the canoe to the other side of the river, to bring over the rest of the party. They were to kill me and my Cousin Johnson. But the chief said to them, "If you kill these men, the Great Spirit will be angry, and he will send his white children to kill us, and our children."

One of the warriors told the chief that he was a coward, and that he ought to have remained at home. To this the chief replied, "I am no coward; and we will see who are cowards when we come in front of our enemies." Thus they disputed, and even quarelled, among themselves, till day-light. The same morning, we left without breakfast, and on the morning following, we were beyond their reach.

We saw where they had raised a number of logs, so that they might lie in ambush. I ought to mention, that we were perfectly ignorant of all their plans and actions, until we arrived at St. Peters. The chief, himself, communicated to us what has been stated above, in the presence of his warriors.

This country, is, indeed, a dangerous place for the Ojebwa Missionaries; but not so for the whites, for they never pretend to interfere with them, in any way.

Before Conference, and while I was obliged to be at their mission, for there was no other road for us to go, the Sioux tried to intimidate me by pointing their guns to my breast, and by flourishing their war clubs about my head; they would say, "I wish you had *longer hair*, so that I could take a good hold of it and scalp you." I cannot describe my *feelings*, on this occasion, better, than by quoting, with a little alteration, from the immortal bard of Avon:—"They were so terrible, that they shook my soul, and made my seated heart knock at my ribs against the use of nature; cold drops of sweat hung on my trembling flesh, my blood grew chilly, and I seemed to freeze with horror." I would often go and see them in their Tepees (wigwams;) this was good policy. They frequently showed me some of the scalps of the Ojebwas, and danced the scalping dance. What awful noises they made, as they danced in their fantastic dresses, with their faces painted black. They reminded me much of his Satanic and fiendish majesty, rejoicing over a damned spirit entering hell.

During this summer, I accompanied Brother Kavanaugh to Sandy Lake Mission, at the head of the Mississippi. I returned by the Falls of St. Anthony, while Brother Kavanaugh went by the way of Lake Superior, he having business with the American Fur Company. When I arrived, I learned that the elder son of Brother Kavanaugh had been drowned; he fell from a ledge of rocks. Sister Kavanaugh felt deeply, this mercifully severe dispensation. Brother Kavanaugh now arrived; poor man! he could not speak to me for some time. I met him some distance from his house; he had heard of the circumstance, but had not, as yet, been home. "How unsearchable are God's judgments; and his ways past finding out." Yet, withal, in such dark hours, many a Christian sees parental Love. Ah! we may often exclaim, in the language of good old Jacob, "All these things are against me," but we may also say, God orders every thing for the good of his own.

That summer we went to Conference, which was held in Platteville. I was then appointed to establish a Mission at Fon du Lac, at the head of Lake Superior. Brother James Simpson was appointed school teacher.

We traveled from the Sioux Mission up the St. Croix River, crossed over to Burnt-wood River, and thence to Lake Superior. Having provided food, I departed with Mrs. Copway and her sister, John Jacob, Massey, and Brother Simpson, about the fifteenth of September. We were two weeks on the St. Croix River; and part of this time I was so sick as to become delirious. I was just able to walk over the two mile portage to Burnt-wood River. The other men, therefore, had to carry the large canoe two miles; this was hard, but it was impossible for me to help them. We were now out of provisions. I have been told, by good authority, the following singular fact. There is but one spring which forms the two rivers;—the St. Croix which runs down to the Mississippi, and the Burnt-wood River which runs down to Lake Superior.

In going down the Burnt-wood River, our progress was slow. We were out of provisions from Thursday, till Sabbath morning, when we arrived at Fon du Lac. On Saturday, Mrs. Copway and her sister had a small piece of bread between them; the rest lived upon *hope*. In the afternoon, we rowed about twenty-eight miles, and on Sabbath morning just at day-break we had to start for our station, Fon du Lac; about twelve o'clock we arrived there, and saw John Laundree, the trader, who was celebrated for his hospitality. I shook hands with him; he asked me if I was sick; and said, "You look pale." I told him, we were all hungry, and had had nothing to eat but a small piece of bread since Friday evening. "Ah, indeed!" said he, "I will soon have breakfast for you." Mrs. Laundree, after a few minutes, had every thing necessary for our cheer and comfort. While eating, I thought, that whatever might be said of Catholics, this was a truly Christian act; and heaven will not let it pass unnoticed.

In the evening I addressed a company of traders and Indians. I found the Indians in a miserable state; the cause of which I attribute wholly to their intercourse with the traders, the principal part of whom are notoriously wicked and profane. I felt very thankful, however, that we were here; yet I was filled with anxieties; for how should I begin my labors? Brother Simpson and I commenced by fitting up the old mission house, formerly occupied by the Rev. Mr. Ely, who had taught many to read and write. The school house, also, was fitted up, and in it Brother Simpson taught, till the spring. Our prospects seemed to brighten up, and we had good reason to think that the Indians were glad to have us with them; for they sent their children regularly to school, and our religious meetings were well attended. During the winter several became seriously and religiously affected; and in the spring, a few believed that they had experienced a change of heart. This encouraged us much. I can never forget the happy seasons I enjoyed, in my visits from house to house, and in the woods. I endeavored to seek out all; and the good Master was gracious to me. I have often traveled about among them on snow shoes, weeping for joy. Often, too, did I sleep alone in the woods, having had to dig away the snow to prepare a place to lie on. Though frequently hungry, faint, and lonely, I enjoyed the presence of the Lord. On one occasion I was sorely tried; I accompanied one of the traders about one hundred and eighty miles, to purchase cattle for our place. I bought a cow for my own immediate family; and in the spring it was killed and eaten by the Indians. Had they been in want, there might have been some excuse for such an act. We expected her to "come in" in about three weeks, and her milk was to be our chief dependence. It was a cruel piece of work. After having traveled, too, three hundred and sixty miles for the purpose of obtaining her, and then to be thus deprived, was a hard case truly. Had she lived, many of the children of the Indians would have shared in the milk. When will the poor Indians be instructed in right principles?

From a long experience and close observations among the Sioux and the Ojebwas, in regard to the hostile feelings existing between them, I have been brought to the following conclusions:

1. That Christianity and education alone, will check their malevolent and hostile feelings, and thus put an end to their bloody wars. For this end missionaries must be sent to both nations.

2. That it is useless to send missionaries without suitable interpreters to assist them.

3. That missions should be established in the vicinities of the borders or the neutral grounds of these two powerful and savage nations; because in these places there is but little, if anything, to excite them to revenge.

4. That wherever a mission is once established, it must never be abandoned.

5. That where any Protestant mission is established in any village, no other denomination should establish another in the same place, or interfere in any other way.

6. That missionaries ought to assist each other whenever they happen to fall in each other's way, or are requested to do so.

7. That missionaries ought not to preach their own peculiar doctrines, to the disadvantage of other denominations; for this not only lessens their own influence, but likewise that of others.

The scenery near the head of Lake Superior, is almost as splendid as that of the beautiful Hudson. There is a magnificent fall about eight miles above the mission. The Indians often kill moose, bears, and deer, in this region. In the spring, summer, and fall, they live on fish. As we had no salt, we were obliged to preserve our fish by hanging them on poles, with their heads downwards, and in this manner they would freeze. When the spring arrived, they began to thaw, and becoming soft, would fall from the poles. Late in the fall, white fish ascend the rapids, and can be scooped up with nets. In the spring, fish of every kind, and in great abundance, ascend these rapids.

On the 9th of April, 1842, it pleased the Lord to bless us with a son. This was our first child—a fine healthy boy. We thanked God for his goodness and mercy in preserving all our lives in the desert, and while surrounded by savages. I committed and commended him to God. May he live to take his station in the missionary field.

Brother Kavanaugh was kind enough to visit us; he returned by the way of Sandy Lake Mission. I accompanied him over the first Portage; here we knelt down on the green, and worshipped the God of Missions. We now parted; but I still hope to see this affectionate brother again, even in this world. But if we shall never meet on earth, I trust we shall in heaven, "where the wicked cease from troubling, and the weary are at rest."

"Where we shall forget our sorrows and pain,
And with our Redeemer in glory shall reign,
Shall sing the anthems resounding on high,
And bathe in the ocean that never shall dry."

## CHAPTER 15

We were often delightfully associated with the Presbyterian Missionaries at La Pointe, the Rev. Messrs. Hall and Wheeler, and their ami-
able families. Their benevolence and Christian courtesy are above
any praise that we can render; but we would acknowledge that our
hearts overflow with great gratitude whenever we recall them to
mind. It was here that I became acquainted with the Rev. Mr. Boutwell. I preached for these beloved brethren several times, and enjoyed sweet communion, and some thrilling seasons together.

The Council of the Ojebwa nation assembled in this place about
the first of October. The government agent, R. Stewart, of Detroit,
treated with them for their mineral regions, for which the government gave them a large amount in money. From this time, I shall
date the dissipation, misery, and ruin, of this part of our nation.

1. Because it induced speculators to visit them yearly to sell their
goods at enormous prices; and their whiskey, which inevitably ruins
both body and soul.

2. Because it opens the door for all sorts of unprincipled men and
vagabonds. The miners, too, many of whom are no better than pick-
pockets.

3. Because, in possessing so much money, without any correct
views of economy, utility, or prudence, it becomes to them "the root
of all evil"—a curse instead of a blessing.

In these appropriations, the American Government have grossly
erred. What benefit can the many thousands of dollars, which are
paid annually, be to the Indians, if they are not capable of exercising
any judgment in relation to a proper use of money? The fact is, that,
at the end of every year, they are sunk into deeper degradation. I
would now ask, what are millions of money without education? I do
not mean that an *equivalent* should not be given for lands ceded to
the government. No; but I do mean that this equivalent should be
appropriated in such a way as to produce the greatest benefits and
the happiest results. If a certain amount had been given in cash, another amount in cattle and farmer's utensils, another in clothing, another in houses and school houses, and the like; and with these, if a
few mechanics, farmers and teachers, had been sent among them,

the Indians might have become industrious, intelligent, and useful citizens. One-third of each annual payment would be sufficient to educate, and to supply all the wants of their children. It may be supposed by some, that the white people settled near them give them good advice, and urge upon them the propriety and necessity of appropriating their monies in the manner just suggested. Yet this is not only *not the case*, but these very whites, at least a large majority of them, are continually laying plans by which they can extort from these unlettered and ignorant Indians, whatever they possess. I write not at random, on these matters. I am too well acquainted with them from painful observation and bitter experience. I have been present at *ten* payments; viz. at Sault St. Marie, Mackinaw, Green Bay, Prairie Du Chien, and St. Peters. During these payments, quantities of whiskey were brought to the Indians, or else they were seduced to go elsewhere to purchase it. Poor untutored red men! you were deluded, and made drunk by white men, and then in your hellish and drunken passions, you turned around and imbrued your hands in the blood of your own relatives and brethren. And were I to narrate some of the scenes which occurred among the white faces (with black hearts) on these occasions, it would sicken the heart; nay, it would make mad the guilty, and appal the innocent. The very devil himself might shudder.

It was now two years since I left Canada; I received letters from there, from the Rev. Messrs. Stinson, Green, and Jones, requesting me to return home and labor with them. At first, I did not deem it advisable to go, because I felt under many obligations to those who had sent me to school for two years; and had rendered me other kind services. But it was not until after repeated solicitations had been made, and money to defray my traveling expenses had been remitted, that I consented. I obtained permission from my Superintendent, Rev. J. R. Goodrich, to depart. I left La Pointe, Oct. 10th, in the schooner Algonquin for Sault St. Marie. From there we took a row boat for Mackinaw, and at M. took a steamboat for Buffalo; we now proceeded onwards and arrived at Toronto on the 28th of October. My wife's parents and relatives, and very many dear friends were delighted to see us again, after an absence of two years. We found them all well, and felt grateful to God for another expression of his abundant goodness and mercy. I spent much of my time in narrating the scenes we had witnessed, and a full account of my mission.

In about a month, I was sent to Credit River, (Mrs. C. remained behind in her father's family.) Here I taught school till Christmas, when I began traveling with Rev. Wm. Ryerson, on a missionary tour towards Montreal. We were absent about three months, and preached or spoke every day. We collected about a thousand dollars per month. The eloquence and piety of Brother R. seemed to be duly appreciated wherever we went. He is the best platform speaker, that I ever heard in the Methodist connexion. I had supposed, however, that he would be dull and monotonous; but this was far, very far from the fact.

Having returned from this tour, to Toronto, I was next appointed by the Missionary Society to labor at the Saugeeng Mission, in the place of the Rev. Thomas Williams. On this journey my wife accompanied me. The distance was one hundred and sixty miles; and we reached there on the 12th of April, '43. On our way, we stopped at Goderich; and from thence we took a canoe about sixty-five miles.

I entered upon my duties as a missionary among the Christian Indians. I met with difficulties, for I could obtain nothing without money; and even when a request was made, it was not met by the Society. I could not be convinced that it was my duty to starve, and therefore concluded I must leave. My Indian brethren stepped forward at this time, and petitioned Governor Metcalf, to afford me a living from the Government. Their request was granted, and I was paid by Government $400 per year, for three years. I should have continued here, but the next year my services were demanded among my relatives at Rice Lake.

In the summer, I took Mrs. Copway to Toronto, and left her at her father's, while I was absent at Montreal with the Rev. Mr. Jones. Here we waited on the Governor General, and presented our views, and those of our people, respecting the formation of a Manual Labor School for the benefit of the Indians. The Governor expressed himself as favorably disposed, but was too sick to take an active part in it. But before this, the Canada Conference had appointed Rev. P. Jones and myself, to visit the Missions, and ascertain how much each Mission was willing to contribute for this object.* During this fall, Mr. Jones and family left for England.

I returned to Toronto and took my family back to Saugeeng Mission. While on our passage, in a schooner, our little son, who was about three years old, fell overboard; we heard him fall into the water. I ran immediately to the side of the vessel and jumped into the lake. The schooner was sailing quite rapidly, and had passed him about twenty yards. I swam as fast as possible, and saw him sink. When I reached the spot where he sank, I dove down about seven

*The amount reported from the Indians alone, was $2,800.

feet, seized hold of him, and brought him to the surface. As the waves were running high, it was with the greatest difficulty that I could keep him above the water so that he could breathe; and I was compelled at times to let him sink an instant, that I might breathe myself. I heard him cry, which was encouraging, for I was fearful that he was dying. At one time I almost despaired of saving either of our lives. I was about giving up all hope, when I saw the yawl boat near me, and I was told that I was just about sinking, when the captain rescued us from a watery grave. The captain, and all on board, were so frightened, that they lost some time in concluding what to do. Had they luffed at once, and despatched the yawl, two or three minutes might have been saved. But, I ought not to complain; our lives were spared, and thanks be to a kind Providence for his timely deliverance. I then gave him up to God, and prayed that he might be preserved, and be devoted to the cause of Christ.

We now resumed our labors at the Mission. While at this station there where many hopeful conversions. A remarkable circumstance is, that during the whole three years of my sojourn in this field of labor, I never knew but *one single case* in which fire-water was used. I must not omit noticing here, a very faithful teacher in my charge, Jacob Jackson; his influence was of the best kind; he was also a very pleasant and interesting singer. It has been but a few years since these Indians were converted. They now have good farms, dwellings, school houses, meeting houses, and a saw mill. How wonderful are the effects of the gospel! They also take delight in praying, and in singing the praises of God. Had the American Government adopted the same course towards the La Pointe Indians, that the British Government adopted toward these, the same lasting blessings would have ensued.

## CHAPTER 16

Of late, the General Councils of the Christianized Ojebwas have been convened, and conducted, in the same manner as public and other business meetings are conducted among the whites. The last General Council, which consisted of Ojebwas and Ottawas, was held at Saugeeng. The chiefs came from Lakes St. Clair, Huron, Ontario, and Simcoe, and from Rice and Mud Lakes. The object of this convention was to devise plans by which the tract of land now owned by the Saugeeng Indians, could be held for the sole benefit of the

Ojebwa Nation; to petition the Government for aid in establishing a Manual Labor School; to ascertain the views and feelings of the chiefs in relation to forming one large settlement among themselves at Owen's Sound, there to live in future; and to attend to other things of minor importance. There were forty-eight chiefs present, from Canada West alone. Chief Sawyer took the chair, and the writer had the honor of being Vice President. Chief John Jones, of Owen Sound, was selected to deliver the opening address, in which he was to give an outline of the subjects to be discussed. The meeting was now called to order; and after singing, and an appropriate prayer by Chief John Sunday, Chief Jones arose; all was silent, and every eye was turned towards him. After rolling his small but piercing black eye over the vast assembly, he spoke as follows:

"Brothers! You have been called from all parts of Canada, and even from the north of Georgian Bay. You are from your homes, your wives, and your children. We might regret this, were it not for the circumstances that require you here.

"Fellow Chiefs and Brothers, I have pondered with deep solicitude, our present condition; and the future welfare of our children, as well as of ourselves. I have studied deeply and anxiously, in order to arrive at a true knowledge of the proper course to be pursued to secure to us and to our descendants, and even to others around us, the greatest amount of peace, health, happiness, and usefulness. The interests of the Ojebwas and the Ottawas are near and dear to my heart; for them, I have passed many sleepless nights, and have often suffered from an agitated mind. These nations, I am proud to say, are my brothers; many of them, are bone of my bone, and for them, if needs be, I could willingly, nay, cheerfully, sacrifice any thing. Brothers, you see my heart. [Here the speaker held out a piece of *white paper*, emblematical of a *pure* heart.]

"Fellow Chiefs and Warriors! I have looked over your wigwams throughout Canada, and have arrived at the conclusion, that you are in a warm place; your neighbors, the whites, are kindling fires all around you [that is, clearing the lands.] One purpose for which you have been called together, is to devise some plan by which we can live together, and become a happy people, so that our dying fires may not go out [our nation may not become extinct,] but may be kindled in one place, which will prove a blessing to our children.

"Brothers! Some of you are living on small parcels of land, and others on Islands. We now offer you any portion of the land which we own in this region; that we may, the rest of our days, smoke the pipe of friendship; live and die together; and see our children play, and be reared on one spot. We ask no money of you. We love you; and because we love you, and feel for your children, we propose this.

"Brothers! There are many other subjects which we think ought to come under your consideration besides those already stated. But the most important are:

"1. Whether it would not be better for the whole Ojebwa Nation to reside on this, our territory.

"2. Would it not be well to devise ways and means to establish Manual Labor Schools for the benefit of the nation.

"3. Ought not a petition to be drawn up and presented to our Great Father [the Governor General,] for the purpose of fixing upon a definite time for the distribution of the annual "presents," and the small annuities of each tribe.

"4. Is it not desirable to petition the Governor General, to appoint a resident Indian interpreter, to assist the agent in Toronto.

"5. As we [the Christian part of our nation] have abandoned our former customs and ceremonies, ought we not to make our own laws, in order to give character and stability to our chiefs, as well as to empower them to treat with the Government under which we live, that they may, from time to time, present all our grievances and other matters to the General Government.

"My Chiefs, Brothers, Warriors! This morning, [the speaker now pointed his finger towards heaven] look up, and see the blue sky; there are no clouds; the sun is bright and clear. Our fathers taught us, that at such assemblies when the sky was without clouds, the Great Spirit was smiling upon them. May he now preside over us, that we may make a long, smooth, and straight path for our children. It is true, I seldom see you all; but this morning, I shake hands with you all in my heart.

"Brothers! This is all I have to say."

On taking his seat eighty-four chiefs responded "*Hah!*" an exclamation of great applause.

Several chiefs spoke, and highly approved of what had been proposed; and expressed their gratitude for the kind offer of the lands. It was proposed to petition his Excellency the Governor, to grant and secure to the Indians, the whole of this territory.

147

The following was drawn up by John Jones, Jacob Jackson, and David Wa-wa-nosh.

*The Petition of the Ojebwa Chiefs, in General Council, respecting the unceded lands north of Saugeeng and Owen's Sound, June 5th, 1845.*

To our Great Father Lord Metcalf, Governor General of British North America, and Captain General of the same, &c., &c.
The Ojebwa Chiefs in General Council assembled, HUMBLY SHEWETH:

Father—Your Petitioners having ceded a great portion of their once extensive territory about Saugeeng and Owen's Sound, and a portion of it having been restored to them since the treaty of 1836, by your Excellency's gracious commands;

Father—Your Petitioners are very anxious that the reserve (now still known as the Indian Territory) be a perpetual reserve; as a future refuge for a general colonization of the Ojebwa Nation, comprising the scattered Tribes in Canada West;

Father—And that these lands may now and for ever be opened to all the Tribes; that whenever any tribe is disposed to move, that they may have nothing to fear, but have access to any of the good lands to settle upon;

Father—You have settled your white children on those lands that once were our fathers; we ask now to let us have the only remaining land we have, to ourselves, unmolested;

Father—This is the prayer of your red children; and feeling confident that you will give it every important consideration which it requires, your red children will listen to hear the answer of their Great Father. And they, as in duty bound, will ever pray.

Forty-seven names, besides that of the President, were attached to this petition.

Never was I more delighted than with the appearance of this body. As I sat and looked at them, I contrasted their former (degraded) with their present (elevated) condition. The Gospel, I thought, had done all this. If any one had told me twenty years ago, that such would be their condition, I should have ridiculed the idea, and set the narrator down for a fool or a maniac. This assembly was not convened for the purpose of devising schemes of murder; plans by which they could kill their enemies; but to adopt measures by which peace, harmony, and love, might be secured, and a "smooth and straight path" made for their children. I see nothing at present, to hinder them from increasing in knowledge, happiness, and usefulness, except the conduct of the Government Agents, many of whom are inimical to our nation, and often prove a curse to her.

Several other papers were drawn up, and signed by the President, by order of the General Council. One of these I must be allowed to give, although it concerns myself:

> To all to whom it may concern. In the General Council of the Ojebwa nation of Indians. We, the Chiefs, of the various Tribes of the Ojebwa Indians, do hereby appoint and authorize our beloved brother, the Rev. George Copway, as our agent for the Manual Labor School, to procure subscriptions for the same, believing that this will be one of the greatest means, if established, of raising our young men, to become like our white brothers; to learn industry, economy, and to gain knowledge, that we may become a happy and a prosperous people.
>
> Signed by order of the General Council.
>
> JOSEPH SAWYER, [L. S.]
>
> President of the General Council of the Ojebwa Nation.
>
> *Saugeeng*, July 4, 1845.

> I will also give an extract of my letter to the Rev. Mr. Wilkinson, who was then President of the Canada Conference, immediately after the close of the General Council.
>
> [*Extract from Letter Book, Page* 151.]
>
> Saugeeng Mission,
>
> July 14, 1845.
>
> To the President of the Conference Rev. Mr. Wilkinson.
>
> \* \* \*
>
> The late General Council, have appointed me their agent for the Manual Labor School. I shall be happy to receive any instructions you may think proper to give, on my way down [to Montreal] for I am anxious to see this going on.
>
> \* \* \*
>
> I remain yours, &c.,
>
> GEORGE COPWAY.
>
> Missionary at Saugeeng.

I give these, for the benefit and instruction of those, who have been so kind as to insinuate, or assert, that I was not an *authorized agent* to forward the interests of my poor people. Those who have been the loudest and most active in this slander, have done the least, in rendering the Indians any essential service. Let them go on, with their gossippings, while I go on my way rejoicing in doing all I can for my poor people, independently of the Canada Conference. Neither have I any disposition to court the favor of this Conference. Indeed, my heart has often sickened at the divisions and subdivisions of the Canada Methodists.

The speeches of Jones, Sunday, Taunchey, McCue, D. Sawyer, J. Youngs, W. Herkermer, were excellent. That of John Sunday, particularly, was uncommonly eloquent. His keen black eyes, flashing fire; and his large brawny arms extended, gave great effect to his speech. As a matter of course, there were often differences of opinion, as well as warm discussions, upon various subjects; some would even feel that their views were not fairly treated; still, there were no unkind remarks, no calling of hard names, no abuse, no ridicule, no insults, no threats, no intrigues, no blows, and *no challenges to me on the field of* HONOR (?). The individual who had the floor, was never interrupted; profound attention was given, and a death-like silence was observed. Occasionally, it is true, there was perpetrated a pleasant, and innocent *jeu d' esprit*; an example of which, I will give.

During a protracted debate, in which Chief John Jones took a very active part, some facts were elicited, and some views were presented, which induced him to change some of his former opinions, and vote on the other side. One of the speakers at the close of his remarks, referred to this fact, and observed, very good humoredly "If he wishes to be like a *fish worm without a head*—capable of moving forwards or backwards, let him alone."

I have often been asked the question, "What is the reason that the Indians are diminishing in numbers in the midst of their white neighbors?" To state all that might be said in replying to this question, would require almost a separate volume. But the following are a few of the principal reasons:

1. The introduction of King Alcohol among them.

2. The introduction of new diseases, produced by their intercourse with the whites; and by adopting their intemperate habits.

3. Their inability to pursue that course of living, after abandoning their wigwams, which tends to health and old age.

4. Their spirits are broken down in consequence of seeing that their *race* are becoming homeless, friendless, moneyless, and trodden down by the whites.

5. Their future prospects are gloomy and cheerless—enough to break down the noblest spirits.

There are many other reasons which could be assigned for their diminution. But are not these sufficient of themselves to crush and exterminate even any *white* race, if not protected and defended by friends and wholesome laws? Our people have been driven from their homes, and have been cajoled out of the few sacred spots where the bones of their ancestors and children lie; and where they themselves expected to lie, when released from the trials and troubles of life. Were it possible to reverse the order of things, by placing the whites in the same condition, how long would it be endured? There is not a white man, who deserves the name of *man*, that would not rather die than be deprived of his home, and driven from the graves of his relatives. "Oh shame, where is thy blush!"

With all the wholesome and enlightened laws; with all the advantages and privileges of the glorious Gospel, that shines so richly and brightly all around the white man; the poor ignorant Indians are compelled, at the point of the bayonet, to forsake the sepulchres of those most dear to them, and to retire to a strange land, where there is no inhabitant to welcome them!!! May the day soon dawn, when Justice will take her seat upon the throne.

If I did not think that there were some who are alive to the interests of my people, and often shed a tear for them; if I did not think that I could discover a gleam of light and hope in the future, "I should of all men be most miserable." "Surely the bitterness of death" would be "past." I look then to the Gospel and to education as my only hope.

I will now state, in a very brief manner, what I think ought to be done, by those whose benevolent feelings lead them to commiserate the condition of the Aborigines of America.

1. They should establish missions and high schools wherever the whites have frequent intercourse with them.

2. They should use their influence, as soon as the Indians are well educated, and understand the laws of the land, to have them placed on the same footing as the whites.

3. They should try to procure for them a territorial or district government, so that they may represent their own nation.

4. They should obtain for them, deeds of their own lands; and, if qualified, according to law, urge their right to vote.

The Indians will be sure to waste and squander whatever they may receive from the American or British Government, unless *some*, at least, of the above suggestions, shall have been put into practice.

The Council was not dissolved. The President, Chief Sawyer, proceeded to His Excellency, the Governor General, and presented the petitions, in the name of the General Council. These petitions, as we learned afterwards, were received with a simple *nod!* of the head. O mercy! is this for ever to be our destiny? Common humanity, at least, might have induced his Lordship to speak a few consolatory words, if nothing else. Our reception was both discouraging and chilling. When we have a press of our own, we shall, perhaps, be able to plead our own cause. Give us but the *Bible*, and the influence of a *Press*, and we ask no more.

The General Council appointed me to go to Walpole, to present their address to the Walpole Island Indians, entreating them to embrace Christianity. I visited them in July.

## CHAPTER 17

*A Geographical Sketch of the Ojebwa, or Chippeway, Nation.*

As the Ojebwa Nation are within the bounds of the two Governments—the American and the British—I will give a separate account of each. The number of our nation, according to Drake, in 1842, was thirty thousand; and this is not far from the truth. The best work upon the Indians, however, is that deservedly popular book, by Col. McKinney, of New York; the *undoubted* friend of the red man.

I will not speak of that part of the nation who occupy places within the bounds of the United States. They inhabit all the northern part of Michigan, or the south shore of Lake Huron; the whole northern part of Wisconsin Territory; all the south shore of Lake Superior, for eight hundred miles; the upper part of the Mississippi, and Sandy, Leach, and Red Lakes.

That part of our nation who live in the British possessions, occupy from Gononaque, below Kingston, throughout all western Canada; the north of Lake Huron; the north of lake Superior; the north of Lake Winepig; the north of Red River Lake, about one hundred miles. The whole extent, therefore, occupied is over one thousand nine hundred miles east and west, and from two to three hundred miles north and south.

There are over five thousand living under the British Government, and less than twenty-five thousand under the American Government. There are about five thousand of these who receive religious instructions; missionaries of different denominations being sent from Canada and the United States. The Methodists were the first who preached to the Ojebwas, or Massisaugas (as they are frequently called.) They commenced at Credit River, in Canada West, in 1824, and at Grape Island, in 1827. The conversion of some of the Ojebwas commenced during those years. Native teachers were then sent to their brethren in the West, where the influence of Christianity is still felt. There are twenty-three Methodist Missionary Stations: six of which are in the States, and the remainder in Canada. There are four Presbyterian Missions, all of which are in the States; viz. La Pointe, Bad River, Leach Lake, and Red Lake. There are seven Episcopalian Mission Stations; all of which are in Canada, except one, which is at Green Bay. There are two Baptist Mission Stations, one at Sault St. Marie, and the other at Green Bay. The Roman Catholics have their missionaries in nearly all the principal places in the west.

Those who are not under religious instruction, although accessible, are wandering without the gospel. There is a field in the Territory of Wisconsin where missionaries should be sent. There are Indians all around the shores of Lake Superior who have, from time to time, called for missionaries, and have not yet been supplied. The Hudson's Bay Company have, of late, adopted a plan which in my opinion does them much credit; they employ Missionaries to give instruction to the Indians and their children in the principles of Christianity. There are persons who once belonged to other nations, who now live in the territory of the Ojebwas.

The present state of the christianized Ojebwas is such, that they are fully ripe for greater advancement in religion, literature, and the arts and sciences. Multitudes have left their wigwams, their woods, and the chase, and are now endeavoring to tread in the footsteps of worthy white men. The reasons for all this, are the following:

1. Their chiefs have seen the necessity of making a "smooth, strait path for their children," by appropriating as much of their means as they could spare.

2. The rising generation are beginning to thirst for learning, and are cultivating a taste for improvement more than ever.

3. Native teachers are now being trained to go to their brethren, and preach to them in their own language, Christ, and him crucified. By this means the nation must be elevated.

Our prospects as a nation, are becoming brighter through missionary efforts. There are many in Wisconsin, and at Lake du Flambeau, who have requested that missionaries be sent along the south shore of Lake Superior. The same may be said of those residing about Winepeg and Red Lakes. Much of the western part of Red Lake, is full of "the habitations of cruelty;" for the Chippewas and Sioux are habitually destroying each other.

I will here give extracts from the Report of the Commissioners, in 1842, to the Provincial Parliament, relative to the Mission Stations; also subjoin the names of the villages with their condition, and the chiefs of each village, as far as I could ascertain them, which will show their progress, and their present state; and also those who have abandoned the wigwam and the chase, and resort to farming for a living.

### 1. CHIPPEWAS ON THE RIVER THAMES.

The Chippewas and Munsees occupy a tract of land containing about 9000 acres, in the Township of Caradoc, within the London District, a distance of about twenty-five miles from the Moravian village. It is only within ten years that the Chippewas have been reclaimed from a wandering life, and settled in their present location. The Munsees have been settled since the year 1800, on land belonging to the Chippewas, with the consent of that tribe. The present number of Chippewas is 378, and of Munsees 242.

The Chippewas and Munsees are not collected in a village, but live on small farms scattered over their tract. Some of the Chippewas are settled on surveyed lots of twenty acres each. This tribe occupies 76 log houses, and six wigwams; they possess 25 barns. They have 450 acres under cultivation. Their stock consists of 30 oxen, 27 cows, 44 heifers, 82 horses and colts, and 400 swine. Their agricultural implements include 9 ploughs, 9 harrows, 23 scythes and sickles, 19 ox chains, a fanning mill, 4 wagons and carts, 7 spades, &c.; they have a blacksmith's forge, and two and a half setts of carpenter's tools

John Riley, *Chief.*

### 2. THE CHIPPEWAS AT AMHERSTBURG.

They all profess Christianity, and several of them are examples of true piety. The majority are Wesleyan Methodists, and the others Roman Catholics. They have no place of worship of their own. They can command the means. The Methodist minister, however, who is stationed in the town of Amherstburg, visits those of his persuasion every Sunday, and with the aid of an Interpreter, preaches, reads, and expounds the Scriptures to them. They also have a general Prayer Meeting among themselves, once a fortnight, and they meet occasionally more privately for social prayer; some of them maintain family worship. The Roman Catholics attend chapel at Amherstburg, which is about three miles from their settlement.

There is at present no school among them, but they have expressed their desire to establish one, and would gladly avail themselves of instruction for their children. When there was one, the attendance of the scholars was very irregular, but their ability in acquiring knowledge was in no way inferior to that of the white children.

### 3. CHIPPEWAS OF THE ST. CLAIR.

These Indians are among the first whom Sir John Colborne endeavored to settle and civilize. Previously to 1830, they were wandering heathen like their brethren elsewhere, scattered over the western part of the Upper Province; they were drunken and dissipated in their habits, and without either religious or moral restraint. In 1830 and 31, a number of them were collected on a reserve in the Township of Sarnia, near the head of the River St. Clair, and containing 10,280 acres. A number of houses were built for them, and an officer was appointed for their superintendence. Their conversion to Christianity and their progress in religious knowledge, and in the acquisition of sober, orderly, and industrious habits, have been, under the care of missionaries of the Wesleyan Methodist Society, both rapid and uniform. From the formation of the mission 221 adults and 239 children have been baptized and admitted into the Methodist community. The total number up to the year 1839–40 does not appear to have exceeded 350. Since then their number has increased greatly by immigration, chiefly from the Saginaw Bay, in the State of Michigan, and by the settlement of wandering Indians; and in 1842, as many as 741 received presents.

The Indians of the River aux Sables have about sixty acres under improvement, and one log house. Those at Kettle Point have twenty acres of improved land and two log houses. The land on the Upper Reserve was regularly surveyed and laid out into farms. The chief, with the approval of the Superintendent, placed most of the present occupants on these lands, but it is not indispensable that he should be consulted, as the members of the tribe may choose any unoccupied spot; when once in possession they are secure from intrusion, but repeated ill conduct or drunkenness would subject them to be expelled from the reserve of the chief.

Wa-wa-nosh, &#125; *Chiefs.*
Salt,

### 4. CHIPPEWAS AT WALPOLE ISLAND.

These Indians are also known under the name of Chippewas of Chenaille Ecarte. The Chippewas who have long hunted over the waste lands about the Chenaille Ecarte and Bear Creek, are a branch of the same nation which is settled in Sarnia, and share in the same annuity.

The Pottawatamies are recent immigrants from the United States.

The settlement at Walpole Island was commenced at the close of the American war, when Col. M'Kie, called by the Indians "White Elk," collected and placed upon the island which lies at the junction of the River and Lake St. Clair, the scattered remains of some tribes of Chippewas who had been engaged on the British side. Being left for many years without any interference or assistance on the part of the Government, they became a prey to the profligate whites settled on the frontier, who, by various frauds and in moments of intoxication, obtained leases and took possession of the most fertile and valuable part of the island.

### 5. CHIPPEWAS OF THE RIVER CREDIT.

These Indians are the remnant of a tribe which formerly possessed a considerable portion of the Home and Gore Districts, of which in 1818, they surrendered the greater part, for an annuity of £532.10, reserving only certain small tracts at the River Credit, and at Sixteen and Twelve Mile Creeks. They were the first tribe converted to Christianity in Upper Canada.

Previous to the year 1823, they were wandering pagans. In that year, Messrs. Peter and John Jones, the sons of a white surveyor and a Mississaga woman, having been converted to Christianity, and admitted members of the Wesleyan Methodist Church, became anxious to redeem their countrymen from their degraded state of heathenism and destitution. They, accordingly, collected a considerable number together, and by rote and frequent repetitions, taught the first principles of Christianity to the adults, who were too far advanced in years to learn to read and write. In this manner the Lord's Prayer, the Creed, and the Commandments, were committed to memory. As soon as the tribes were converted, they perceived the evils attendant on their former state of ignorance and vagrancy. They began to work, which they never had done before; they recognized the advantage of cultivating the soil; they totally gave up drinking, to which they had been greatly addicted, and became sober, industrious, and consistent Christians.

J. Sawyer, }
P. Jones, } *Chiefs.*
J. Jones, *War Chief*

### 6. THE CHIPPEWAS OF ALNWICK.

These Indians were converted to Christianity in the years 1826–7. They were then pagans, wandering in the neighborhood of Bellville, Kingston, and Gananoque, and were known under the name of the

Mississagas of the Bay of Quinte; in those years, between 200 and 300 were received into the Wesleyan Methodist Church, and settled on Grape Island, in the Bay of Quinte, six miles from Bellville, where they commenced planting, and where schools were established by the missionary for their instruction. On this island they resided eleven years, subsisting by agriculture and hunting. Their houses were erected partly by their own labor, and partly at the expense of the Methodist Missionary Society. The number, at length, amounted to twenty-three; besides which, they had a commodious building for religious service and school, another room for an infant school, a hospital, smithery, a shoemaker's shop, and a building for joiners' and cabinet work.

Sunday,  
Simpson, } *Chiefs.*  
G. Comego, *Ch. & M. Inter.*

### 7. CHIPPEWAS AT RICE LAKE.

These Indians belong to the same tribe, the Mississagas, or Chippewas of Rice Lake, who, in 1818, surrendered the greater part of the tract now forming the New Castle District, for an annuity of £740. They have all been reclaimed from their primitive wandering life, and settled in their present locations within the last ten or twelve years.

The Rice Lake settlement is on the northern side of the lake, and at about twelve miles from Peterborough. The number of Indians is 114. They possess about 1550 acres of land, which are subdivided into 50 acre lots; of this, 1120 acres were granted in April, 1834, to trustees, "in trust, to hold the same for the benefit of the Indian tribes in the Province, and with a view to their conversion and civilization;" and the remaining 430 have been since purchased with their own funds. They have rather more land cleared than the Indians of Alnwick, about 400 acres; but the cultivation is not so good. The village contains thirty houses, three barns, a schoolhouse, and a chapel with a bell. The head chief of the tribe resides here. For some time these Indians were under the charge of an officer appointed by the Indian Department, who assisted in their settlement; but at present they have no special Superintendent.

Poudash,  
Copway, } *Chiefs.*  
Crow,

### 8. CHIPPEWAS AT MUD LAKE.

The Mud Lake Indians are settled on a point of land on the Mud or Chemong Lake, sixteen miles north-west of Peterborough. They are ninety-four in number, and possess twenty dwelling houses, with three stables. They occupy a grant of 1600 acres in the township of Smith, made to the New England Company for their benefit, in April, 1837, of which about 200 acres are in cultivation. These Indians were for some time under the management of the late Mr. Scott, agent for the the New England Company, and belong to the Wesleyan Methodist Church. A chapel is in the course of erection at the village, where there is already a mission house and a school.

Nogee,
Iron,     } *Chiefs.*
McKue,

### 9. CHIPPEWAS AT BALSAM LAKE.

The Balsam Lake Indians, ninety in number, are at present settled within the Township of Bexley, on a point of land jutting out into Lake Balsam, which is the most northerly of the chain of lakes, running northwest across the back Townships of the district of New Castle. The reserve which was granted to them by the Crown, is 1206 acres in extent. Of this they have about 200 acres in cultivation. Their village contains twelve houses, a barn, and a commodious school-house, in which divine service is performed by a resident Methodist missionary. But within the present year, (1843,) these Indians having become dissatisfied with the climate and the quality of the land at the Balsam Lake, have purchased six hundred acres on the banks of Lake Scugog, to be paid out of their share of their annuity, and are making preparations for removing from their former settlement. Their improvements will be sold for their benefit. Their reason for removing evinces their desire to advance in the pursuit of agriculture.

Crane, *Chief.*

### 10. CHIPPEWAS OF RAMA.

These Indians formerly occupied the lands about Lake Simcoe, Holland River, and the unsettled country in the rear of the Home District. General Darling reported of them in 1828, that they had expressed a strong desire to be admitted to Christianity, and to adopt the habits of civilized life; and that in these respects they might be classed with the Mississagas of the Bay of Quinte and Rice Lake, but were then in a more savage state. In 1830, Lieutenant-Governor Sir J. Colborne, collected them on a tract of land on the northwest shore of Lake Simcoe, of 9800 acres in extent, where they cleared a road between that lake and Lake Huron. They consisted of three tribes of Chippewas, under chiefs Yellowhead, Aisance, and Snake, and a band of Pottawatamies from Drummond Island; their number was about 500, under the care of Mr. Anderson, now the Superintendent at Manitoulin, who was appointed to take charge of their settlement and civilization; they made a rapid progress. The tribe under the chief Yellowhead, now settled at Rama, were located at the Narrows on Lake Simcoe; Aisance's tribe, at present residing at Beausoleil, Matchadash Bay, was settled at Coldwater at the other extremity of the reserve, the distance between them being fourteen miles.

Yellowhead,
Na-nah-ge-skung, } *Chiefs.*
Big Shillinge,

### 11. CHIPPEWAS OF BEAUSOLIEL ISLAND, MATCHADASH BAY, LAKE HURON.

This band, under the chief "Aisance," is the same which was settled by Sir John Colborne, at Coldwater. Their present village, which is not very distant from the former settlement, was only commenced last year. It contains fourteen houses, and a barn; the number of the band is 232. They have about 100 acres under cultivation.

The majority of these Indians are Roman Catholics. They have not as yet any place of worship, or school. In the former settlement they were occasionally visited by the Roman Catholic priest, resident at Penetanguishene.

Aisance,
James Ka-dah-ge-quon, } *Chiefs.*

### 12. CHIPPEWAS OF SNAKE ISLAND, LAKE SIMCOE.

This body of Indians was one of the three bands established at Cold water and the Narrows, and separated from them on the abandonment of those settlements. They now occupy one of the three Islands on Lake Simcoe, which was set apart for this tribe many years ago. They are 109 in number, and occupy twelve dwelling houses. They have also two barns and a school-house, in which their children are instructed by a respectable teacher, and Divine Service is performed by a resident Missionary of the Methodist persuasion, to which these Indians belong. They have about 150 acres in cultivation, and are improving in habits of industry and agricultural skill. Their missionary, who has been acquainted with them since July, 1839, states that the majority of them are strictly moral in their character, that most of the adults are decidedly pious, and that many of them for consistency of character, would not suffer by a comparison with white Christians of any denomination.

J. Snake, *Chief.*

### 13. CHIPPEWAS OF SAUGEEN, (LAKE HURON.)

It was from these Indians, and their brethren, since settled at Owen's Sound, that Sir Francis Head, in 1836, obtained a surrender of the vast tract of land lying north of the London and Gore Districts, and between the Home District and Lake Huron, containing 1,600,000 acres. He reserved, at the same time, for the Indians, the extensive peninsula, lying between Lake Huron and Georgian Bay, north of Owen's Sound, and supposed to contain about 450,000 acres.

J. Metegoub,
Alexander, } *Chiefs.*
Ah-yah-bance,

### 14. CHIPPEWAS OF BIG BAY, IN OWEN'S SOUND, LAKE HURON.

These Indians were formerly either wanderers in the Saugeen tract, surrendered to Sir F. Head, or lived in scattered wigwams, on the shores of Big Bay. According to the agreement then made with them, it was proposed that they should either repair to Manitoulin or to that part of their former territory which lies north of Owen's Sound; upon which it was promised "that houses should be built for them, and proper assistance given, to enable them to become civilized, and to cultivate land."

John Jones, } *Chiefs.*
Peter,

### 15. CHIPPEWAS AND OTHERS, IN THE TOWNSHIP OF BEDFORD.

Within a few years past, some stragglers from the Rice Lake tribe have settled in the township of Bedford, about twenty-five miles north of the town of Kingston; and recently, they have been joined by a band of eighty-one Indians from Lower Canada; belonging to the post of the Lake of Two Mountains. As the settlement is of recent formation, and the claim of these Indians upon the attention of the Department of Upper Canada has only been brought forward last year, they have not yet been visited by any officer of the Department, and no account can be given of the settlement. By Instructions issued in 1843, they were transferred from the Roll of Lower Canada to that of the Upper Province, and, accordingly, received their presents for the first time in that Province.

My beloved Reader—I am now about closing my narrative, and in doing this there are but a few things to say. Throughout the work, I have confined my remarks chiefly to my own nation. But it must not be supposed, on this account, that I am forgetful of my brethren of the other Indian nations. The prayers and benevolent efforts of all Christendom should be directed towards all men every where. The gospel should be preached to every creature; and the field is the *wide* WORLD.

The Menomenees in Wisconsin, the Winebagoes and Potawatamies in Iowa, the warlike nations of the Sacs and Foxes, the Osages, Pawnees, Mandans, Kansas, Creeks, Omahas, Otoes, Delawares, Iowas, and a number of others elsewhere, must perish as did their brethren in the Eastern States, unless the white man send them the Gospel, and the blessings of education. There is field enough for all denominations to labor in, without interfering with each other. It is too late in the day to assert that the Indians cannot be raised up out of their degraded state, and educated for God and heaven. None need be discouraged since the Ojebwas in Western Canada have been converted. No language is adequate to portray the misery, wretchedness, and degradation in which we were, when the word of God was first brought and preached to us.

It is not necessary to detail each and every wrong, that my poor people have suffered at the hands of the white man. Enough has already been said in various parts of the work, to prove that they have been most grossly abused, peeled, and wronged. Nor shall I notice the *personal wrongs* that I myself have received; and from those, too, of whom I had good reason to hope better things. I once thought, that there were some things that I could never forgive; but the religion of Jesus, and the law of love, have taught me differently. I *do* forgive them; and may God forgive them and me too.

I have sometimes heard it said, that our forefathers were cruel to the forefathers of the whites. But was not this done through ignorance, or in self defense? Had your fathers adopted the plan of the great philanthropist, William Penn, neither fields, nor clubs, nor waters, would have been crimsoned with each other's blood. The white men have been like the greedy lion, pouncing upon and devouring its prey. They have driven us from our nation, our homes, and possessions; compelled us to seek a refuge in Missouri, among strangers, and wild beasts; and will, perhaps, soon compel us to scale the Rocky Mountains; and, for aught I can tell, we may yet be driven to the Pacific ocean, there to find our graves. My only trust is, that there is a just God. Was it to perpetrate such acts that you have been exalted above all other nations? Providence intended you for a *blessing* and not a *curse* to us. You have sent your missionaries to Burmah, China, the Sandwich Islands, and to almost every part of the world; and shall the Indians *perish at your own door?*

Is it not well known that the Indians have a generous and magnanimous heart? I feel proud to mention in this connection, the names of a Pocahontas, Massasoit, Skenandoah, Logan, Kusic, Pushmataha, Philip, Tecumseh, Osceola, Petalesharro, and thousands of others. Such names are an honor to the world! Let a late Governor of

Massachusetts* speak for our fathers, when they first beheld the trembling white man:—

"Brothers! when our fathers came over the great waters, they were a small band. The red man stood upon the rock by the seaside, and saw our fathers. He might have pushed them into the water and drowned them. But he stretched out his arms to our fathers and said, 'Welcome, white men!' Our fathers were hungry, and the red man gave them corn and venison. Our fathers were cold, and the red man wrapped them up in his blanket. We are now numerous and powerful, but we remember the kindness of the red man to our fathers."

And what have we received since, in return? Is it for the deeds of a Pocahontas, a Massasoit, and a host of others, that we have been plundered and oppressed, and expelled from the hallowed graves of our ancestors? If help cannot be obtained from England and America, where else can we look? Will you then, lend us a helping hand; and make some amends for past injuries?

It is often said, that the Indians are *revengeful, cruel* and *ungovernable*. But go to them with nothing but *the* BIBLE *in your hands*, and LOVE *in your hearts*, and you may live with them in perfect safety, share their morsel with them, and, like the celebrated Bartram, return to your homes UNHARMED. They very soon learn to venerate the Bible; as a proof of this, I will give an instance, that came under my own eye:—While at the Rabbit River Mission, a chief from the west, visited me. After reading to him several chapters form the Bible, he said, with much surprise, "Is *this* the book, that I hear so much about in *my* country?" I replied, yes; and these are the word of *Ke-sha-mon-e-doo* (the Great Spirit.) "Will you not," said he, "give me one? I wish to show it to my people." I told him, not without you first promise that you will take care of it. He promised me that he would. I handed it to him; he took it, and turned it over and over, and then exclaimed, "*Wonderful, wonderful! this is the book of the Great Spirit!*" He then wrapped it up in a silk handkerchief, and the handkerchief in three or four folds of cloth. I heard, afterwards, from the trader, that the book was still kept sacred. O, if my poor brother could but *read* and *understand* that blessed volume, how soon would his dumb idols be "cast down to the moles and to the bats!" Will no one go and tell him and his nation, of the boundless, beseeching, bleeding, dying love of

*Edward Everett, Esq.

a Saviour; and urge upon them the importance of such a preparation of heart, as will enable them "to give up their account with joy?" The Great Spirit is no respecter of persons; He has made of one blood all the nations of the earth; He loves all his children alike; and his highest attributes are *love, mercy,* and *justice.* If this be so,—and who dare doubt it?—will He not stretch out his hand and help them, and avenge their wrongs? "If offences *must* come," let it be recollected, that *woe* is denounced against them "from *whom* they come."

I again propose that the territories of the Indians, in the British dominions, be annexed to that Government, and those in the American dominions to the Federal Union. And, finally, in the language of that excellent, magnanimous, and benevolent friend of the poor children of the forest, Col. Thomas McKenney, I would say,

"I have already referred, in the commencement of this proposal to annex the Indian territory to our Union, to those good men, who, in the character of missionaries, have kept side by side with the Indians in so many of their afflictions and migrations. I will again refer to them, and implore them by all the lost labor of the past, and by the hopes of the future; by the critical condition of the pacific relations that exist between the Indians and us; and by the sacredness of the cause in which they are engaged, to look well and earnestly into this subject, and learn from the past what *must* attend upon their labors in the future, if the change I propose, or some other change equivalent to it, be not brought about. And, seeing, as they must see, that the plan I propose, or some other, is indispensable to the success they seek to command, I implore them to take up the subject in all its bearings, and by the instrumentalities which they have at command, manufacture, collect, and embody public opinion, in regard to what may be determined to be done; and by memorial, and personal agencies, bring this opinion to bear upon Congress, with whom alone the power is vested, to redeem, disenthrall, and save, and bless, the remnants of this aboriginal race. And I make the same appeal to all the good, of all religious persuasions, both in the Church and out of it, and politicians of all parties, to second this attempt, feeble as I know it to be, to save the Indians, and consolidate, and perpetuate peace between them and us, and, by so doing, ward off the terrible retribution which must sooner or later, unless it be averted, fall upon this nation."

# To the Reader.

I have given two of the speeches which were delivered in the Legislature of South Carolina, Dec. 1848, and the other in Harrisburgh, Penn. Legislature, on a subject which has occupied my whole attention in behalf of my brethren, the North-West Indian Tribes.

Besides the Speeches, the Letters which have appeared in the "Flag of Our Union," a widely circulated paper in Boston. By the request of my friends, they are given, with a few Notices of the Press, (as my time has been so occupied with other matters,) as a continuation of my crooked Travels.

Kah-ge-ga-gah-bowh.

*New York, Feb. 5th,* 1850.

# Address before Both Houses of the Legislature of South Carolina.

A correspondent of the Charleston Courier, writing from Columbia, gives the following address delivered by the Rev. Geo. Copway, (or Ka-ge-ga-gah-bowh,) well and favorably known in this community, before both Houses of Legislature of South Carolina, on the subject of Indian Civilization, and the best means of promoting it:

*Gentlemen of the Legislature of South Carolina:*

My limited knowledge of your language renders it somewhat difficult for me to make myself distinctly understood. I speak with some embarrassment a language which is not my native tongue. I must beg you, therefore, to pardon any errors of diction I may commit when advocating the claims of the Indian. Extend to me personally your charity, and, at the same time, allow me to ask your sympathy for the cause in which I am engaged.

In presenting my claims before your august body, I cannot but recur to an early period in the intercourse of my forefathers with yours, 356 years ago. The Indian, then, roamed over the country unmolested. It was a vast world of grandeur. The Indian was as free as the air he breathed. He then knew no bounderies. No could appeared which foreboded dangers. The mountains were covered with the game he lived on. The vales swarmed with the natural productions of the land. The whole was his dominion. The shout of his children answered shout from peak to peak of his mountains across the vales. He was then happy.

The Paleface was then a small nation, and while he trembled with cold on Plymouth Rock, the Indian took him, and placed his billow-tossed limbs by his warm fires and nerved him to walk! We reared your forefathers; until now the country, which was then our sires', belongs to you. Here are now your plantations. The changes with my nation have been great.

In return, we now look to you as our guardians. To-day I come to lay before your body a plan, which if followed out, will ensure the salvation of the Indian; when you have listened to my remarks, you cannot, I am sure, reasonably charge me with selfishness, for I have studied the interests of your Government, as well as the wants of my nation.

My plan is this—to collect the Indians in bodies in the West, in some portion of the country, where enjoying a permanent home, they may improve in science, in agriculture, in morality, and the arts of civilized life.

Before we can do the Indians much good, we must collect them together, for thus only they will be likely to improve. The first means to be employed in accomplishing this object is, to move Congress to approtion them a tract of country, say near the bank of the upper waters of the Missouri River, about sixty miles square, more or less, as they might need for agricultural purposes. Thus, the whole of the Northern scattered tribes, the Indians north of the southern boundary of the State of Missouri, all the tribes of the Lakes, Upper Mississippi and Iowa, the Shawnees, Soukees, Foxes, Chippeways, Ottowas, Delawares, Minominees, Winebagoes, and Sioux, might be gathered together in one general settlement. This country would become the great nucleus of the Indian nations.

In advocating this plan in this country, I have been asked, "Have not the Indians homes now which the Government has asigned to them?" The answer is, Yes! they have the same kind of homes which they had East of the Mississippi, before they left their country. There have been 96,000 removals since the policy of removing the Indians commenced, and there are 24,000 more still waiting their removal Westward, according to their agreement with the Government. I am not opposed to their being removed by Government, provided they are placed in such a position in the Western country that future migration may not bring trouble upon them. What is the nature of the country they now hold as their present home? It extends, in detached portions, from Texas to the head waters of the great Mississippi. Unfortunately, the Commissioners appointed some years ago, selected a country which the Indians cannot hold, for several reasons; among others, I would notice, in the first place, that the position of the country is like a great barrier, through which emigration must necessarily pass, and the majority of it must obtain vent through their country, and this will again disturb the minds of the Indians, and prevent them from improving. They will begin to suspect that the Government are anxious, as heretofore, to get the whole of their lands. Who, in such case, will guarantee to them the undisturbed possession of their homes, when various influences, which will always continue to operate, are at work to disturb their tranquility? Rail roads must pass through their country, canals and military roads be opened, and it will be impossible to carry out these internal improvements without disturbing the Indians and preventing their peaceable enjoyment of their lands. This will be constant and fruitful cause of discontent and dissatisfaction. In the second place, I would remark that the vast quantity of land assigned to them by the Government, amounting in all to 15,000,000 acres, is decidedly injurious to my countrymen. It encourages roving habits among themselves, and holds out a perpetual temptation to the emigrant. The lands are fertile, and the Indians easily duped by artful speculators into selling them at a price vastly under their value. Thirdly, in their present situation, they have not the means of educating their children and of advancing in intelligence. They live only from day to day, and provide very little for the future. When they see the wicked white man standing by his barrel of cider, they long to partake of the intoxicating draught. They engage in drunken revels during the night, and the missionaries, consequently, however desirous to promote their temporal and spiritual welfare, do them little or no good. If you can place them in some situation where they would have opportunities for moral, intellectual and religious instruction, beyond the sphere of the temptations and mischievous influences by which they are now surrounded, you might then hope for their permanent improvement and progressive elevation in the scale of nations.

Fourthly. The Indian, as he is now situated, can live and live comfortable on the proceeds arising from *the sale of his lands*. It is very obvious, so long as this state of things continues, that he will have little or no inducement to turn his attention to agriculture. the disposition to rove, which is natural to the Indian, will still continue to form one of his marked characteristics. The children will retain all the predilections of their fathers for a roving life, hoping and expecting to fare no worse than their fathers have done. As his means of living become less and less, he will at last be compelled to sell all, and will be left without any resource.

Fifthly. *In their present situation they do not see the necessity of turning their attention to agriculture*. By circumscribing their domain, they

169

would soon learn that they had no other means of living than what was furnished by the culture and production of the soil, and they would be compelled from the force of circumstances, to adopt industrious habits. But until they see the absolute necessity of industry, they will never become industrious—never become an agricultural people, but will continue to rove through the forests in pursuit of deer and will live by hunting; and when their lands are all gone and the last deer is killed what then? They will retire to the frontier, and issuing from their fastnesses in the Rocky Mountains, they will prosecute an exterminating war against whites.

Sixthly. If the Indians remain as they now are, their peculiarities and natural traits will be perpetual. You will have to send your agents to each tribe, and the labor of civilising them, in detached portions, will be greatly increased. But bring them all together in some central spot, and you will have a better chance to break down and merge in the higher forms of civilization the distinctive peculiarities which now separate the different tribes from each other, and which prevent their acting together for their common good. Give them, as I before suggested, some sixty miles square on the banks of the Missouri, where they shall remain unobstructed by the land-speculator and the trafficker in *firewater*—that curse of the poor Indian—and you may then look for some radical changes in their condition and character for the better. Until this is done, I despair of their making much progress under their present circumstances. As to the quantity of land, sixty square miles is enough, I would not recommend a larger quantity. Let this land be properly distributed, each Indian receiving a certain number of acres to till. In this way he would become attached to the soil, and would feel a pride in cultivating it.

The results of such an arrangement would be:

1. *That the North Western Indians would remove there and have permanent homes.* Hitherto they have had to move from place to place.

2. *Seminaries of learning would not be rooted up.* They would become permanent establishments, and their effects be felt to future generations.

3. Necessity will compel them to become agriculturists. My nation has become agriculturists. This has resulted in part from their becoming Christians, for some twenty years ago my nation embraced Christianity. Ten years ago many of them were hunters. They had to go twelve or fifteen miles for deer. But they now have their little

farms, and they find it much better to stay at home and cultivate the land, than to wander abroad for an uncertain subsistance. For example, my uncle, last year, raised on his farm 978 bushels of wheat. He employed two horses to carry it to market, and got his money for it. In all ages men try to get a living in some way; and the Indian, while he holds a gun in one hand, now holds a hoe in the other. He has made this approach to civilization, and only requires encouragement and opportunity to become still more civilized and more Christianized.

4. The Indians are a remarkably social race. If they had some central interest, such as I propose to give them, their individualities would be lost as they become better acquainted with each other, and they would become one people, all having common objects and interests to promote and pursueing them with energy. I can scarcely unfold to you all the benefits which would result from the establishment of Schools among them, but I would mention one of the most important and obvious of those benefits. When the children of various nations go to a common school, their parents, however hostile they may have been heretofore, will, in the common advantages which they see their children enjoy, find new bonds of union to connect them with each other.

5. Nothing will contribute more to tranquility of mind than the assurance that they are no more to be removed from the home they occupy. This is what the Indian has always wanted. Give them settled and permanent homes and you will make them contented.

6. When that are once convinced that they derive great advantages from a common intercourse in some central position, their objections will give way to the force of argument. The Indian is not obstinate when his reason is convinced.

7. The improvements of which I speak in the condition of the Indian, though certain, will be gradual. You cannot accomplish them at once. When you give them a government, the laws should not only prohibit and punish drunkenness, but prohibit the sale of liquor to the Indians by those who now traffic in the article. The government of the United States would thus hold a hammer over those bad men, one good consequence of which would be, that quarrels and wars which now result from the intemperate use of ardent spirits, would cease.

8. A spirit of emulation would spring up among the Indians which would be attended with the happiest results. In 15 or 20 years the country would be settled, provided, in the mean time, they are not

disturbed in the occupation of their lands; but, begin to construct Rail Roads through their territory, and they will burn them as fast as you build them.

9. The present government fund for the education of the Indians amounts to $10,000; but under the present distribution of it among the scattered tribes, it does little or no good. Let seminaries of education be established; let a college be founded with the proceeds of the sale of their lands; give the Indians a single fort in this central position for their defence; give them Courts of Justice in which they should adjust their quarrels according to the laws of Indians, in connection with the Courts of the United States, and a better understanding would spring up between them and the Government of the United States, and there would no longer be any reason to apprehend hostility and war on their part.

10. Your Government expenses would be less. You now have to guard the whole of your frontier, from Texas along the whole of your Southern border. But concentrate the Indians, and give them for their defence a single fort, and you will have nothing more to fear from the incursion of the border tribes. Not one grain of powder, not a single ball will be necessary.

11. You will have to give only one price for their lands, instead of two or three prices, which you now give when you wish to remove them.

12. The expense of sending out agents will be less. You now employ many agents. You are obliged to do it: but, if my plan is adopted, only two or three agents will be necessary.

13. There need be no expense for transporting them. Give the first settlers a premium and they will go there fast enough at their own charges.

14. The Missionaries would then become permanent among them. The agents are now in the habit of slandering the Missionaries, representing them as being unfavorable to the Government.

In conclusion, in asking this favor of the American people, I have not consulted my own feelings. I ask them only to give the Indian education and literature. He loves to live by his own stream, as the bee loves to gather sweets as he flies from flower to flower. When we come among you, we like to reciprocate the friendly feelings you entertain towards us. If you are prosperous, and, sitting in halls like this, our children come to you and ask you for bread, will you give it to them? Will you put plough in their hands and teach them how to use it? Then will our children be merry around our fireside, with a Bible in their hands, and a touch of God's fire in their hearts. Then will our people participate in the blessings of religion and civilization. Then will peace, love and unity prevail; and our poor neglected race will occupy a high place in the scale of nations.

*Fanatics* have talked of extending universal suffrage, even to the colored man, but their being *silent* in reference to that which would elevate the North American Indian, proves that they assent to his downfall. He must receive something in return for giving up his whole country. In return give him but institutions of learning, and he will give you noble examples, perhaps a Patrick Henry, or a Randolph, who shall do honor to his race, and who shall handle the lightning, as a mere plaything, with a Franklin or travel with a Newton from star to star. The wide world looks with wild intensity to our shores for a model—a noble example it finds in him who loved liberty, the father of liberty, George Washington. I ask you to give the Indian that liberty, and then he will, like the eagle (the emblem of liberty) stretch his wings abroad and soar aloft.

It is my purpose to collect all the expressions of sympathy from the people and from the different Legislatures, until next March, and in this way move Congress to adopt some plan for the permanent good of the Indians in the West. I ask your favorable consideration of this plan. It is true, you have but few Indians in this State—a miserable remnant of the Catawbas. But ever remember after this, that, on the 15th day of December, an Indian dropped his tears in this Hall, when he, in a reasonable manner, presented the claims of the Indian *for your cooperation.*

Finally, for success, I depend not on these arms—nor on any natural endowments I may have been blessed with; but for success, *in the God of the Universe will I trust.*

In all my journeys on the shores of Lake Superior, while I endeavered to hold up the Cross before my brethren, I have watched the movements of Providence, step by step, and if I can but be a connecting link between the United States and my race, I shall then be happy. Those of you who pray to the Great Spirit, ask his blessing on me, that the same angel who has watched over me in the woods, may guide and shield me and them; and if, when dying, I shall be so happy as to see my children and yours enjoying prosperity and happiness, I shall die in peace.

# Address before the Legislature
# of Pennsylvania.

The following is an address delivered before the Legislature of Pennsylvania, on the 25th of January last, by Mr. George Copway, (or Kahge-ga-gah-bowh,) a chief of the Chippewa tribe. Mr. Copway has recently been in this City and lectured before respectable and interested audiences. We presume all feel an interest in the welfare of the Indians—and we place this address before our readers, feeling that they will be instructed in its reading.

*Gentlemen of the Legislature of Pennsylvania:*
My limited knowledge of your language will render it somewhat difficult for me to be understood this evening, as I speak a tongue which is not my own—which is not my native language. Permit me, however, to ask your indulgence while I endeavor to present to you the claims of the Indian, and at the same time, I solicit you to extend to me, personally, your sympathy, as well as to the cause in which I am engaged. Besides the embarrassments under which I labor at the present moment, I have had for several days past a severe cold, which, in a great degree, incapaciates me from speaking with that ease and freedom that I could wish, in order to lay my heart open to you.

In presenting the claims of my unfortunate race, I cannot resist recurring to the period when the Indian and the white man first commenced their intercourse, three hundred and fifty-six years ago. The Indian was then an inhabitant of all the Eastern Countries on which rests the different cities of the Atlantic States. The Indian was the sovereign of the whole country; the mountain echoed with his voice, and all he saw was his. The game of the forest he claimed as his own, the fish of the waters and the course of the rivers were also his. Proudly he then roamed through the country where now stand your farms and your mighty cities. There was then no cloud that the heathen saw portending his danger. The heavens were clear before his eye. He knew no bounderies; he knew no limits to his desire. And when he was found in this country, he had no extent of society, he had no extensive institutions, which have since been established where he then lived. There were no palaces, with their gaudy attendants; but, wherever you now see the mountains of your State, whether in the north, the south, or the west, you may picture to your mind's eye the noble form of the Indian standing on one of their lofty peaks. He made his native mountains his throne, and it was from thence he could see, to a limited extent, his boundless empire.

While the paleface trembled on Plymouth Rock, shivering there with cold, his billow-tossed limbs were gathered by our fathers, who brought him to their firesides, and introduced him to their people. The palefaces were then a small nation, but they have since become a great one, and the proud sons of the forest have, one by one, fallen away, like the stars that die at a distance in the skies. In return for our kindness and friendly feeling towards you, we look to you for protection, for guardianship, for instruction, as we protected and taught your fathers in the early history of this country. Several years back, with much solicitude, I endeavored to study the peculiar wants of my poor people, as well as the condition of the emigrants westward; and in order to promote the welfare and interests of both, I attempted, to the best of my ability, to mature a plan which, I think, if carried into effect, will prove highly beneficial and advantageous to both people, the whites as well as the Indians. gentlemen, I feel assured that when you shall have heard all my remarks on this important and interesting subject, you will not accuse me of selfishness on this occasion, as I have not overlooked your nation in advocating the claims of my own.

In presenting my plan before you this evening, gentlemen, permit me to state, in as few words as possible, what I have to say, as I wish to accomplish my visits to the different State Legislatures now in session, on this errend, with as little delay as possible. On the 31st of March last, you may remember that a meeting was held in the city of Philadelphia, where I attended for the first time, and broached the subject of civilization among the Indians in a more extensive and elaborate manner than on the present occasion. I found however, that it was done at a consumption of a great deal more time and an expenditure of money than I could conveniently afford. I found that the getting up of meetings in cities was a more tardy and inefficient method of obtaining the action of Congress in the matter than in personally soliciting and enlisting the aid, influence and action of the Legislatures of the several States. I have visited the different States of the Union, presented to them my views in relation to saving the Indians, and, if possible, to get their expressions of approbation of my plan, in order that their resolutions might be addressed to Congress, in the hope that they may set apart a territory in the West, in which all the Indian tribes shall be collected, and there remain unmolested for ever. Gentlemen, I have found this project, as far as I have gone, meet the views of those who have counselled me in the matter.

The object I have in view, is to call upon the General Government to grant to the Indians a part of the north western territory, west of the Iowa territory, and between the Nebraska and Minesotta territories, for the use and occupancy of all those Indians who are living there in a scattered condition, where they can enjoy permanent homes, the advantages of education and agricultural instruction, so that, after a time, when they shall have become Christianized and enlightened, they may be incorporated into the Federal Union as a State. Before we can do much good for the Indians, we must, as I have already said, provide them *permanent* homes, and by that means, secure to them peace of mind, which is absolutely necessary to ensure their improvement and progress in the arts of civilization. Much good can be effected in this way; and all the Indian tribes will assemble together, and go to their new and permanent homes, there to live in peace and harmony.

But the Indians, in their present isolated condition, are eternally at war with each other, and every influence is now brought to bear upon them, that is calculated to increase their revengeful feelings towards one another. I do not refer to the civilized, educated and enlightened portion of the Indians that are now living in different parts of the United States, as, for instance, the Indians of the State of New York, and those in Michigan, and the States of North and South Carolina, as well as Georgia. All these Indians, however, will go to the far West, and there join their brethren and form one family. I repeat, that I do not mean that the more improved and educated portion of them, will remove from their present homes but only those who are not so advanced in civilization. Let them remain where they are, and go on improving and enjoying all the blessings of civilization. I mean that those Indians that are scattered in Michigan, the territory of

Iowa, and on the banks of the Mississippi, shall go to one place, and form a great settlement among themselves.

Gentlemen, in advocating this plan in the different States of the Union, I have been asked the question—'Have not the Indians now homes in the West, which the United States have granted them, on the other side of the Mississippi?' Those Indians in Arkansas—the Chickasaws and Creeks, and several other nations have homes there, and the same kind that they had when they were east of the Mississippi river. It is said that their homes have been so secured to them that no one can buy their homes from them. That, gentlemen, is our present version of the acts of the general government with the Indians; but have they not been violated in bygone ages? Have not the laws which have been secured to this people, been violated by those who succeeded to the law-making power. Most assuredly they have. Unfortunately for the government of the United States, the commissioners appointed by it to select a territory for the Indians, selected the best portions of the west, and the consequence has been that circumstances have rendered it impossible—and unfortunately—for them to hold their lands.

In the first place, their position is such that their land extends all the way from Texas to the North, like a barrier through which emigration must press. There, roads are to be constructed and canals opened through their country. Military roads, too, will be opened for emigrants; and, no sooner do you propose to go and buy one acre of land to open those highways, than the eye of the Indian will be directed with suspicion to their Great Father, and the Indians will be removed from the last acre of land that they hold.

2. The quality of their land is another great inducement to deprive them of it, and they never can hold it. Several months ago, I was conversing on the subject with Mr. Albert Gallatin, of New York, when he remarked 'that is one of the greatest reasons why the Indians can never hold the lands which the United States has ceded to them. The quality is such, that the people living out West will tease the Indian, and also the government of the United States, that in the end the land will be bought again from the Indians by the government. Then, again, the day will come when we will see trouble, as in the State of Georgia.

3. The quantity of the land is so great that they cannot hold it. And what do the Indians want with so much land when we are attempting

to teach them the science of agriculture? for, the having so much land begets a feverish anxiety on their part for deer hunting; and, as long as there is a deer on their territory, so long will they let fall every agricultural implement from their hand and take their guns in order to maintain themselves by hunting.

4. They have no means of educating their children, because they are inhabiting so broad an extent of country, that it is impossible for the people of the United States to supply them with schools, and teachers of morality, and the arts and sciences, which are necessary to elevate their condition.

5. They depend upon the proceeds of the sales of their lands, and having a great quantity for sale, they dispose of it and will reason thus: 'my children will fare no worse than I have fared. I was living yonder; my father sold a portion of the territory, which we occupy, to the United States, upon the proceeds of which I and my children have lived, and now the United States will buy this land from us. My children will fare the same as I fared ever since I sold it to the United States. Therefore, it will not be worth while to have plantations, because they will only be a loss to us; for, no sooner have we our plantations and our farms, than we must be compelled to sell them through necessity. This moving, then, must still go on westwardly, till the last Indian shall stand on the barren peaks of the Rocky Mountains, and gaze on the land which has been taken from him. The kind-hearted, then, will drop a tear for the fate of that race which was once noble and free as the eagle that soars in the skies.

6. The scarcity of food which must follow, will produce trouble between the Indians and the government of the United States; for, as long as there is a deer or a buffalo on this side of the Rocky Mountains, no cloud of discord will be over the head of the Indian and the white man. But, no sooner will the last resource of the Indian be gone, than he will nerve himself for the worst, and take up his weapons of warfare. He will feed for a time upon the cattle on the frontier, and no sooner has he killed a bullock or a steer for his subsistence, than the newspapers abroad will proclaim that 'the Indians are coming against us, that they are killing our cattle by hundreds;' and the whole country is in danger, and soon the soldiers will be on the spot, and the rattling of their firearms be heard, giving proof of the destruction of a race that once lived in this country. And when, gentlemen, that day comes, the Indian will die with his weapons of

war—for he will not die but at the mouth of the cannon, when des-
peration has driven him to it. In order to avert this state of things, I
have addressed the Legislatures of the several States. I love peace—I
am for peace.

7. The Indians in their present distinctive position—in the isolated condition in which they are found—will perpetuate the peculiarities which characterize them as a nation apart from others. The
Sioux, the Winnebagoes, the Pottawatamies, the Osages, and the rest
of the Indians have their several peculiarities, but when you come to
throw their interest in the centre, the effect will be to unite the one
tribe to the other—an interest which the United States alone is capable of giving and controlling. What, I ask, would be the natural results of such an arrangement, if carried into operation? In the first
place, there would be a perceptible improvement in the physical, intellectual and moral condition of the Indians. Their seminaries of
learning would be permanent. There is now annually appropriated
by the generosity of the people of the United States, for the purpose
of educating the Indians, the sum of $10,000 and that is so divided in
the West, that some times two or three dollars of it come to us at the
head waters of the Mississippi and the Lake Superior. The money, in
short, is so scattered along the banks of the Mississippi river, and the
banks of the great Northern Lakes, as not to be of any perceptible
advantage to those for whom it is intended. The small sum of
$10,000 circulated over so extensive a country, and intended to be
used in paying teachers to educate the Indians, does little or no
good.

Suppose you were to go and sow seed on the ground, putting two
grains there, and one here, and another yonder, when the ground
was rich to produce fruit; and, in the spring of the year, on going to
it, you would find but a very sparse crop—a little stick here and another there only—the little birds having had access to the seed at all
times, and much of which would be destroyed by disease. This by
way of illustration. But, gentlemen, put the Indians on one territory,
in a central position, and use the fund now set apart for school purposes and you will have schools and seminiaries of learning that shall
reflect credit alike upon the Indians as the government of the
United States, the benefits and good effects of which will be felt for
ages to come. Wherever the government and the missionaries have
succeeded in educating the Indians, they have become an indus-

trious, moral, and well-behaved people. We have learned to read and write. We have tried to become like the white people, but when the Indian sees the deer bounding before him, he will let drop all his implements of husbandry, and follow the chase.

But no sooner have the Indians gone on and made improvements, and our children began to like to go to the school houses which have been erected, than we hear the cry of the United States government, 'We want your lands;' and, in going from one place to another, the Indian looses all that he had previously learned. But were they to be placed in a position, where they would forever be free from molestation, then they would profit by the establishment of schools among them, and religion and piety would increase and flourish among that people. The disastrous effects of removing the Indians has been shown on the banks of the Ohio and the Sandusky, and in Georgia and New York, where the Presbyterians, labored hard to make the Indians what they were twenty-five or thirty years ago. And no sooner did the tree of piety begin to expand its limbs, than comes the request, 'We want you to go Westward. We want your lands.' The Indian reluctantly gives up his land to the American government, not believing, at first, that they were in earnest; but, when he was convinced of the fact, and his soul being almost teased out of him, and the soldiers having dug up the trees, and taking it to the woods of Arkansas, there to plant it, he surrendered.

We have ever been told that while the eye of philosophy has ever looked on, that under all favorable circumstances, the Indian would be Indian still. And, I would ask, who, under such circumstances, would improve? We cannot find institutions of learning, even among the whites, cherished though they may be to a greater extent, always patronized according to their worth.

2. When the Indians have a permanent home given, then what they did on their plantations would of course be permanent. When you give them a home, you will find contentment around their firesides; but, if they see a probability of their being removed still further westward, the Indians will act as they have always done, showing that they have no faith in the government of the United States.

Yes! when I went to Washington last April, I saw there a Chief from Green Bay, whose name was John Quincy, to whom I opened my heart as to what I intended, if possible to accomplish. No sooner did he learn what my object was, than he rose from his seat, and stretching forth his hands—the tears running from his eyes—he said, 'I hope the Great Spirit will preserve your life till you accomplish this object, for if the day shall come when the United States shall grant to the Indians a country to the West, I will be the first one to move there, for I am tired of moving about from place to place; for, when we came from the State of New York to Green Bay, we were told that we should not have to remove again; and now, again, Col. Medilly will not settle with us for $7,000, in order that we might sell our lands again, as we did several years ago.' The poor man then sat down.

Ah, my dear friends, if there be any one here who calls himself a man, I would ask him if he would not feel for any one placed in such circumstances as these.

3. By circumscribing the domains of the Indians, you will make agriculturists of them. Twenty-five years ago, in Canada, we were all hunters and it is now 17 or 18 years since we become agriculturists. So long, as there was a deer to hunt, within a range of 18 or 20 miles, we did not regard agricultural pursuits; but no sooner was the country cleared and settled, than we became agriculturists. No sooner did they find that they could raise grain in the quantity of 1,000 bushels a year, than they were encouraged to labor.

4. The Indians are a social race. They are social among themselves, and were they to be placed in a central position, the intimacy between the several nations would soon become strong, and they would be on the most friendly terms. Their respective nationalities would, before the lapse of many years, be lost, and they would become social and kind towards each other, and thus would be brought about a peaceful state of society which is necessary in order to their improvement.

5. Contentment would be followed by all its attendant blessings. The missionary societies would have great influence, and one school teacher can be employed in educating hundreds; but, while the Indians are in a separate and isolated condition, they cannot avail themselves of these advantages. So that in forty or fifty years hence, the condition of the Indians will be greatly ameliorated and improved. I say it is impossible for you, according to your present system, to succeed in converting the whole of the North American Indians.

6. You must convince the Indians that it is for their good and their

salvation—that it will be just and right. The Indian is not a stupid being. When he is to be convinced by the advice and arguments of some kind-hearted man, that his home is never to be touched again—that his children are never to be removed, and that the fruit of his labor is never to be blasted as heretofore,—then will he accept it and act upon it.

7. The improvement of which I speak cannot be accomplished in one day, or in one year, or five years. The elements are now ripening in the far West. If the government of the United States would look to the example of Wm. Penn, and assure the Indians that their new home should be permanent, then they need never fear that one arrow is ever to be directed against it, or the people of the United States. So long as the people follow the example of that kind and good-hearted man, William Penn, towards the Indians of Delaware, when he first came to this country, they need never be at war with the Indian tribes.

8. Emulation would spring up all around them. Some may do well, and thus set an example to those who are not doing well. We do not expect much from the old men, but after they shall have passed away—have ceased to exist—their children will imbibe a different spirit from them. They will be guided and governed by Christianity on the one hand, and education on the other.

9. Your government expenses would become less. Now you are trying to fortify the whole of the West by means of barracks and garrisons. You have spent thousands upon thousands and millions upon millions of dollars, for the last 40 or 50 years, and what has it been for? Because, it is said, it is necessary to defend the frontier settlements from the encroachments of the Indians. Therefore it is, that you have sent your soldiers to your garsons from Arkansas away down to the North. Now all that we have to ask is to have but one garrison in the central part of the territory. If there is any bad feeling among the Indians, that will be a check upon them, instead of incurring so much expense and trouble in undertaking to fortify the entire far West with barracks and garrisons. I would ask the government to give us four or five hundred soldiers, to go (not as a great many have done to break down and overawe the Indian spirit, under pretext that they are encroaching upon the white people) to ward off the hard-hearted white men, who disturb the peace of the Indians by

selling them liquors—for many of them are worse than the worst kind of Indians I ever did see. (*Applause and Laughter.*)

10. In buying up the country which lies on this side of the Rocky Mountains, I would have given but one price for it—for, according to Col. McKenney's statement, you have given a quarter of a center per acre for the land to the Indians, who have afterwards sold it to the government for half a cent, by having to purchase it so often.

11. The expense of sending agents to reside among the Indians, has become a loss on the part of the government, for we would ask but one or two. You have got ten or fifteen among the Chippewas, and ten or fifteen among other nations, and consequently you have expended thousands of dollars needlessly. And some of these agents do not know the Indian character, and are, therefore, unfit to be agents. We want agents who would keep the door, and all the whites that should come among us, would have to come through them. By this means we would ward off a great many wicked men; and when there are any offenders against the laws of the United States, we will hand them over for punishment, and when also, there should happen to be any offenders against our own laws we will punish them. If there is any misunderstanding between the Indians and the agents, then the difficulty can be adjusted between the parties.

12. The expense of transporting the Indians has been great to the government, but as soon as you give a country to the Indians, you will be relieved from the trouble of removing them, for they will go there of themselves.

13. The missionary labors there would become permanent, which has not been the case since their labors have been broken up. And the Indian has always been the sufferer.

14. Gentlemen, in conclusion, I deem it necessary to give the reasons why the Indians have decreased and not improved—why they decreased in a vastly greater proportion since the introduction of the white race on this continent, than before. Prior to their landing on these shores, the small pox and many other virulent and noxious diseases, were unknown among the Indians.

The wars that have raged among themselves. Before the discovery of America, and before the introduction of fire-arms from Europe, the wars among the Indians were not so fatal and destructive as they are now. They have been taught to handle fire-arms with a great deal of skill. The history of Pennsylvania—the history of the New England States, and the history of the South, all tells in what manner those wars were conducted. Champlain, in 1612, supplied the the Indians in the North with fire arms, to oppose the Six Nations in that part of Canada, now composing a portion of the State of New York, who at length became so reduced in numbers, that they were compelled to give up the contest. And so it was with the Spaniards in the South, who, as well as the French and English, also furnished arms to the Indians. In all the wars that have been waged in this country among the European powers, the Indian was always asked to show his fearless nature on the battle field, in behalf of the English, French, Spaniards and Americans. And when the Indian has received these weapons of war from them, his heart has bled, and he has suffered. Yes! look towards the South. In 1763, the Spaniards were waging war against the French. Look in the state of New York, among that class of people, who were of German descent, who encouraged the Indian to war against each other. Look, too, among the people of the North, in Canada, where the British government furnished the Indians with munitions of war, and encouraged them to fight against the North Americans. Sometimes the Indian has been called a savage, because he has been called upon to go and show his bravery in the field.

I ask you, gentlemen, as intelligent men—men who live in an enlightened age, which was the most savage, the ones who knew not the origin of these wars, or those who did? Spirituous liquor has been the great cause of the decrease of the Indians of this country. Disease, war, and famine, have alike preyed upon the life of the Indian. But, ah, alcoholic spirits have cut off the existance of those nations who have left the records of their existance upon their rivers and their mountains. I remember well when I was but a child, that my mother related to me the introduction of liquor on the shores of Lake Superior. Some young men (said she,) were urged to go down to Montreal. They went, and returned late in the year; a council of the nation was called, and one of the men seized a war club and knocked down another. He then fled into the woods, and his brother took the place of the murderer, ordered the men to make two fires, and place a post behind him; then to paint his bare breast black, and put a white spot near the place where he felt his heart beating. And when all these things had been done, twelve warriors came forth with their bows and arrows to shoot him in the breast as soon as he

was ready. 'Don't shoot me,' he said, 'till I have sung the death song.'
When he was ready, he called out to his brother, 'I am now ready to
die in your stead, and if you can live to endure the idea, that the
world shall look upon you as a coward, you will not disgrace the clan
to which you belong, but shrinking from that which you merit; and
then he began to sing. The murderer now ran to him and pushing
him aside, pointed to his breast, and made a white spot where he felt
his heart beating. He then exclaimed, 'I am not a coward—I am not
afraid to die—I went to the woods to get sober for I would not die
drunk.' After saying this, he commenced singing the death song,
and when he gave the signal that he was ready to die, twelve arrows
pierced his heart, and he fell, one of the first victims to alcohol.

'Ah! brandy, brandy, bane of life,
Spring of tumult, source of strife;
Could I but half thy curses tell,
The wise would wish the safe in hell.'

[Here Mr. Copway read the series of resolutions which had been
passed, by the Legislatures of North Carolina and South Carolina,
respectively.]

Mr. C. resumed, saying—In conclusion, gentlemen, I will say that
I have detained you too long. I ask nothing more than what is reasonable, and in asking this of the people of the United States, I feel
more confident that my humble petition will be granted by this Legislature, at least, on account of Pennsylvania's early history, in connection with the Indians, I am convinced that there has been
friendly relations existing between the Indians and the people of the
Pennsylvania particularly. Oh, when I think of that day when peace
reigned between the Indians and William Penn. That was a glorious
period, and he was a kind-hearted and humane man.

I have ever venerated the name of William Penn, and whenever I
thought of the tree under which he made his treaty, which never has
been broken, I have often thought if I had only been under the
boughs of that old elm tree, I should have been satisfied. I sent to
Philadelphia three or four years ago, the endeavor to procure a little
piece of that tree, but I failed to obtain it. And I never succeeded in
getting hold of any of it until yesterday. Yesterday I received a card
from a lady in Philadelphia, requesting me to call at her house. I did
so, and, on entering one of the rooms, I saw a picture of the old tree.
After salutation, she said, 'there is the tree under which William

Penn made his treaty with the Indians. I have understood that you were inquiring for a piece of it, and many have tried to get it from me; and I do not know why I have not parted with it before; and now, it seems to me is the proper time to part with it. I will give it to you.'

And, I took it in my hand and pressed it to my bosom. There it is, and I hope as long as I live, and venerate the name of William Penn, that I shall keep it close to where my heart beats, for I revere the memory of that old man. I venerate the very day when he first came to negotiate with the Indians of this country. For seventy years not a cloud in the Heavens portended danger and discord. The Great Spirit even smiles upon the wild Indian and the white man, as they smoked the pipe of peace. Oh, last summer, when I was in the city of Washington, on the 4th of July, I thought to myself, when I saw the people enjoying themselves, and flocking around at the laying of the corner-stone of the monument to the memory of Washington, that if the day came when the Indians shall have peaceable possession of their homes in the West, I would get my people to raise another monument to the memory of George Washington. We will point our children to his noble form, and speak of his exalted character, and love of country, in the hope that they may emulate his spirit, and follow his glorious examples in all that was great and good.

We trust that the time may come when the Indians of the far West will have it in their power as it is their inclination, to erect a monument as well to the memory of Gen. Washington as to that of William Penn. The eagle of liberty is stretching forth his wings all over the earth, and the mountains of France and Germany have received him. The isles of the sea are celebrating their songs of liberty; and will not, I ask, the Indian participate in the glorious jubilee? You, gentlemen, have too much patriotism in your hearts,—you have too much love in your hearts, to let the Indian die without being lamented.

Many have asked—'Who is that Indian? Where has he come from, and where was he born? And what is he about?' They have asked one another these questions when I have been endeavoring to explain my views in relation to the salvation of my poor countrymen. Thank Heaven, I am an Indian. Yes; were I to be the last to stand on the peaks of the Rocky Mountains, I would still raise my hand to the world as a part of a noble speciment of humanity, the representative of the Indians who once lived in this country. I heard one gentleman say to another—'Who is that?' [Alluding to myself] 'Who is he?' Now if he is in this Hall at the present time, tell him 'I am a native American.' [Applause and laughter.]

Mr. C. in conclusion, said—'I beg this audience—highly inteligent and respectable as it is—to receive my warm acknowledgments for your kind attention this evening; and I pray the Great Spirit that you and I may, while we live, do something for the benefit of the world— that, when we are about to visit the world to come, and the Angel of Death appears to sever our bodies from our souls, that the latter may fly, like an eagle, to mansions in the skies. I trust that the white man and the Indian may meet where they shall swear eternal friendship before their God.

# Correspondence of the Flag,
## *by the Indian Chief, Ka-ge-ga-gah-bowh.*

*New York.*

Sir:

Before leaving these Atlantic Cities for the woods in the far distant west, permit me to converse with your readers, some of whom may have seen notices of the addresses and lectures of an Indian chief, in the halls of different legislatures from South to North.

The great object of my efforts has been to awaken an interest in the minds of the people of these Atlantic States, in behalf of that long neglected race, the Aborigines of America. That government might collect the Indians in one body in the west, for the purpose of forming them in one state, thus preparing the way for their improvement.

The deep interest I have seen manifested in behalf of the Indians, by the American people of the States through which I have travelled, leads me to believe that the majority of the pale-faces wish the red men well.

The North Carolina Legislature passed a joint resolution after I had addressed them, strongly recommending my plan to the consideration of the American government; and the resolution was transmitted to Congress.

My next visit was to the Legislature of South Carolina, where I was received in the kindest manner, and had the honor of addressing the members on the 15th of last December. At the expiration of a few days a resolution was passed by the House, in my favor, and concurred in by the Senate.

I then started for the north, remaining for a short time in Charleston, where the crowds who attended my lectures denoted the feeling of the people of that city, to whom I am indebted for numerous favors.

I stopped in Wilmington, N. C., addressed the Virginia Legislature, but that body was so pressed with business that no resolution was passed, but I was informed that one will be at its next session.

My address before the Pennsylvania Legislature was published in full. I greatly esteem the people of that State, for their deep regard for my efforts to educate and elevate the Indian. They are worthily the desendants of William Penn. They have always been *friends* of the Indians, and have stood at their side when all others forsook them and fled. They have taught them to handle the hoe, and taught them to love the Maker of all.

After delivering a course of lectures, by request of the mayor, and other eminent citizens in Philadelphia, I left for New York. This is the Rome of the New World. It takes full one year of close effort to interest the people, and there is but one way in which this can be done—to let the shadow of a mighty dollar, appear on the walls of their public halls.

By the advice of friends I visited your city, in which I found many warm-hearted friends. The kindness bestowed upon an Indian stranger by your worthy governor, by Amos A. Lawrence, Esq., and other influential citizens, can never be forgotten. As my friend, H. W. Longfellow, has beautifully said—

> "Friends, my soul with joy remembers!
>   How like quivering flames they start,
> When I fan the living embers,
>   On the hearth-stone of my heart."

What else could I do but love and esteem the American people? I love their Bible and their institutions. I admire their magnanimity and their perseverance. Industry, being guided by their intelligence, causes the sea to do their will, and has opened channels, through which commerce pours its treasures at their feet. The roar of the cannon speaks for its defence, and the flag that waves over it, is the charter of its rights.

While revolution after revolution follows in the Old World, and thrones crumble beneath the giant tread of freedom, our own nation stands firm in the right, and instead of blood and carnage, diffuses among its inhabitants the principles of education. The struggle in the Old World has but commenced. The fearful struggle betwen the powers of darkness and the powers of light, betwen the *lion* of despotism and the *eagle* of freedom.

America! America! I adore thee! Land of intelligence, of industry, and the fruits thereof. I have drank from thy mountain streams. I have gazed at thy lofty mountains, and floated in my birchen canoe over the calm surface of thy glassy lakes.

'America, America, heaven's blessings attend thee,
While we live we shall cherish and love and defend thee!
Tho' the scorner may sneer, and the witless defame thee,
Our hearts swells with gladness whenever we name thee.'

My letter is dated in New York. As an Indian, I walk these streets amid the palaces of the white man. The walls, how high, the streets how hard. All rush by me with arrow-like speed. Silks and rags go side by side in Broadway. Here are the world's extremes. I cannot remain here long. I must away to the western woods and lakes, to the Falls of St. Anthony, across the Prairies to the base of the Rocky Mountains. I shall take the fish-hook and pole. When I have been lucky you shall hear from me, and I will send you an invitation to partake of a feast at the foot of the Rocky Mountains.

You will hear from me at Washington, before I leave for the West.
Yours, &c.
Kah-ge-ga-gah-bowh.

### LETTER 2

*Washington, May,* 1849.

Sir:

In my last I told you that I would write from Washington, and now, not knowing how soon I may be off from here, I sit down to talk once again with your numerous readers.

Washington! What a name. The nation's pride, the centre of patriots and the model of men for centuries to come. The wide world's languages with their dialects have learned to pronounce it. The fame of the man, though silent, will speak to new-born millions. Mothers whisper this name in the ears of inocency. How appropriate for a new-born republic. Those massive pillars of the Capitol and the White House, and that shaft which is about to be reared to the skies, must wear away before the name will cease to be a motto for nations abroad, and for the two hundred States which must exist when all this American land is subdued by commerce and art.

Washington is comparatively still to what it generally is. But the same dust that rose in white columns when I first saw the city three years ago, is still here rising from the avenue. To-day the north-west winds have been rather uncourteous to aged heads, and garments play rather curious tricks.

The trees on the avenue look quite green. The song of birds among them is heard, and the tiny homes for a tiny race are being built. The flowers sweeten the air, and children sportfully play with the gold fish in the reservoir, in front of the Capitol. To-day, tired of looking at mud walls, just before sunset I went to Georgetown heights. I passed by people who had the same disagreeable disease with which Yankeedom is afflicted, namely, 'curiosity,'—white men and women, a glorious mixture—you know what I mean. Mouths were opened, 'there is that Indian chief,' said an urchin, advancing before me. I made at him as though I would *cane* him, and I have not since seen him; for, as he started he made an effort to squeal, and whirled around a corner as though he would run to the end of the world and neither stop nor look back. Scare that boy again in like manner, and he would be as white as his neighbors. Poor child, I would not harm a straight hair of your head.

After reaching the top, nearly out of breath, I glanced my eyes over the panoramic view about me. The wind, how bracing, the gentle rustling of the leaves of the trees, how musically delightful. Before me lay the waters of the Potomac clothed with white sails.

'What is yon dark streak?' inquires my friend. It is the bridge, a mile and a quarter long.

The sun began to sink. With what a gorgeous fold it enwraps itself, as the music of creation lulls it to rest. The clouds around it, attending ministers on its departure, on one side appeared as a full blaze, on the other like giant waves foaming and careering onward. It has sank behind the trees and their foliage is in a crimson hue. O, could I have a bower there. Methinks that when I slept I should dream of Eden's pleasant groves.

What a beautiful sight! A Boston poet stood before me like a statue, gazed, wondered, admired! He said nothing, but his eyes flashed with the fire of his soul. In his silence there was language! Far off on yonder branch sings the mocking bird of the south, and nearer was a robin, both chanting the praise of their Creator. Other birds flew by to their nest. Night creeping over the vale below, I turned away reluctantly from the glorious scene.

Just now I have passed the large building, the Treasury—Uncle Samuel's pocket—in which is held the common cents of the nation.

Good night! My friend has gone ahead of me, and is waiting my arrival in the land of nod.

*May* 15.—I have just learned a Washington secret, viz, that my friend ——— is to dine with the Cabinet to-day, or rather that the Cabinet is to dine with him. Mention it to no one. You can whisper it to the ladies, however—they can keep a secret.

The dust! I wish to leave it and away to the green fields of the west. I am to know to day whether I am to receive the aid of government in the prosecution of my plan to concentrate and civilize the Indians of the west. God knows that the Indians deserve aid and instruction from the American people, and they seem desirous to grant it. What the people wish to do, the government will not hinder them from doing, and, to the credit of the men at the head of national affairs be it said, they seem anxious to recompense the red men for the wrongs of the past.

I must close. The clouds are at this moment gathering in their might, and threaten to flood us with cold water.

I am yours,

Kah-ge-ga-gah-bowh

## LETTER 3

*Mount Vernon, May,* 1849.

Sir:

To-day for the first time I had the good fortune to find time to visit this place; the final resting spot of the greatest of modern men.

Mayor Seaton, of Washington, gave us a note to the present occupant, Mr. Washington—and after a ride of sixteen miles by land, in company with my friend Mr. John S. Adams, of Boston, we came in view of the spot. On our way to the tomb we were obliged to travel a most disagreeable road, ditches, rivulets, narrow passes, tangled woods, and other evils obstructed our way. We drove up to the gate and 'uncle' somebody came hobbling along to open it. In these diggins, habituate yourself in calling every negro you meet who is half a minute older than youself, 'uncle,' and you will pass anywhere.

He opened the gate and we entered, looking upon the old dilapidated brick walls on our right hand, and going up to the door, delivered my note, and was soon requested to walk in the passage.

'Dah,' said a curly-headed urchin, 'walk round and and see what you can see.'

'But where is Mr. Washington?' I inquired.

'He is in dat room dah, sir.'

'What, is he sick?'

'No sair—but you will look round de room and see what you can see.'

We strolled about the parlor, sitting-room, and passage, and used all the exertion we could to 'see what we could see.' We looked about us in vain for some person to conduct us to the tomb. When I asked the colored boy the location of it, he stuck out his long arm in a horizontal position, and pointing to a long brick wall, said, 'Dah!'

I went to the front of the once elegant mansion, and stood on the brow of a hill under the branches of a tall tree. The Potomac lay below and not a ripple was to be seen. The air was sultry and still. O, how still. Two magnolia trees in front of the house were seemingly drooping into decay, but the cool air of the evening was only needed to revive them.

The house was in a very neglected, timeworn condition; the oak trees seemed to flourish better than anything else, and the windows corresponded with other parts of the house, except two of them, which seemed to have more attention bestowed on them than did the others, being adorned with superb curtain hangings.

Seeing no white man, we availed ourselves of the guidance of an old negro. He began to speak of the greatness of George Washington, and between each word would escape a sigh.

'There,' said he, 'is the place where massa Washington sleeps.'

Here at the gate, I stood, and when I gazed on the marble coffin which contained his body, an indescribable feeling filled my soul—of pleasure and regret. Here rests the remains of a man whose fame is as boundless as the ocean—whose honor towers above the skies—whose virtues are sung in other lands, and will be a lesson to the children of generations yet to come—a model for heroes, a model for Christians. Here rests the man in whose breast burned the true flame of patriotism; the man whose voice was heard above the din of battle—whose counsels piloted the ship of freedom through tempestuous seas, and who hoisted the stars and stripes, beneath which American commerce now floats in security. It was he who fed the young eagles in their defenceless homes, in their hour of peril, till they became strong, till the hour of peril was past, and they were let loose to bear over the world the charter of freedom which Washington marked out for it. They go from east to west, and soon all shall be free, this earth a paradise, and men and angels one.

Who of all the ambitious Cæsars of the Old World could be compared with George Washington? When we speak of Napoleon, the heart is sickened with the thought of blood. But around the memory of Washington, the light of an unclouded sun is seen. The one led on his warriors with an iron sceptre—the other governed them with a smile. Both died. One soothed by the hands of an angel, the other pressed down by the thoughts of the anguish he had caused. The grave of one was where the ocean looked in fury, the grave of the other in quiet, watered by the tears of grateful millions of freemen.

Absorbed with thoughts like these, for the first time my inflexible nature gave way to its *feelings*. I could not help it.

I am sorry that they do not keep it better. It should be a marble castle in which the angel of light might watch his dust till the morn of the resurrection.

I turned from the tomb, and on the tree there sat a moaning dove. It seemed to be conscious that we came there to weep. Warble on, little bird! When we are blest with a home in paradise, I will feed thee with fruits immortal.

The sun is sinking in a blaze of glory. The skies are of a crimson hue, and the foliage of the tree throws its shadow upon our path. The tame deer are sporting around us, and with many pleasures and regrets we leave.

It is now nearly 7 o'clock, P.M., and we have 18 miles to go; so for the present, farewell.

Kah-ge-ga-gah-bowh.

### LETTER 4

*Norfolk, Va., May 29, 1849.*

Dear Sir:

From the date of my letter you will learn that I am still going south, instead of north or west.

Norfolk is now full of alarming rumors. The cholera is here, and people are more religiously inclined than usual. A revival is now in progress in one of the churches, the result of which, will I trust remain longer than the epidemic; though, doubtless, in some cases it will pass away with the alarm that gave it birth.

This place is favorably situated for commerce, having a good harbor, the best I have ever seen. The land in its vicinity is very good for agricultural purposes, and the principal products are corn, tobacco and sweet potatoes. Ships are here from all ports. In view are vessels just arrived, others just departing. Hark! you can hear the sailor's song and the rattling of the cordage. Up, up go the sails, one toss of the sailor's hat, one adieu to the landsmen and they are off. These white sails on the ocean are like lilies on the pond, dotting it wherever commerce has travelled.

There is something sublimely grand in the idea of a frail bark struggling across from continent to continent. Storm raging, winds howling and waves moaning, and thus to be upon the deep, hemmed in by the mighty walls of the ocean!—but I must stop writing about it, for a sensation of sea sickness already creeps over me at the bare thought of it.

It is near 10 o'clock A.M., and curiosity leads me to go over the ferry to the place where that ship of ships, the 'Pennsylvania,' is anchored. Her masts tower above all others, a hundred feet higher than the highest. When I inquired whether I could be conveyed on board, I was told that the cholera was on board, and that one of the four persons who had been attacked by it was dead, So, instead of going on board the ship, I strolled about the navy yard, which exceeds any place of the kind I have ever seen; the row of houses, work-shops and ship houses. What a noisy place. Go it, ye hammer and tongs and saw-mills! There are at present a thousand men at work in this yard. Spike-makers cable and anchor-makers, groups here and groups there making extensive preparations for war! and nothing is done for peace. I think the day is not far distant when the good reputation of our nation will not be based on the number of its guns or the size of its naval fleet.

Cannons and balls! This is a part of civilization which I hope my people will never learn. Some time ago the famous warrior Black Hawk was brought from Washington to this yard to see the preparations which the government was making for war; more particularly, however, to see the great ship. I am told that he was conducted all over the yard, and no sign of emotion did he manifest until he was led to the great ship. He gazed in wonder at the tall masts, the strong rigging, the steam engine and the boilers, and asked 'Who made this great canoe?' He was told, and with a shake of the head, said, 'I should like to see the man that made this big canoe; he must be a great warrior.' He inquired who it was that guided it. When he was shown, he could hardly believe that the person had power in his arms to steer such a canoe in a storm.

Strawberries are plenty here, but few persons eat them, supposing them to contain too much cholera. I devoured a pretty good portion of them the other day, and am certain there was none in those I ate. In Portsmouth, I found the streets well limed and *white-washed*. I think the prevailing epidemic will rage here as the ground is very low, flat, and there is much stagnant water.

The famous Cypress Swamp is not far from here, where the staves are obtained, and in which snakes and alligators abound.

Many runaway slaves are housed in this swamp and live like bears in the woods, seldom seeing any white people. Some have lived thus for twenty years. They raise their grain in patches, and the region is very large.

The Virginians are a very hospitable people. About a year ago while in Richmond, a request was sent to me to visit Charles City. In about a week afterwards I made arrangements to go.

When I arrived in the city I did not know it. I alighted and found about one thousand people who had met to hear the Indian. A church was open. Tall oaks and pines shadowed us, that had 'maintained their position,' for at least a hundred years. There was not another house at a less distance than three miles—and such was Charles City! I thought if that was a city, we could boast of many cities in the wild woods.

Though the people here are very hospitable, there are two classes of Yankees against whom they hold an inveterable dislike, namely, fanatical abolitionists and clock-pedlers.

Would to God slavery was abolished; but there is too much fire and brimstone in the denunciations of men of misguided zeal. What! crush the Constitution of the United States? It seems like a mole beneath the earth, crying out, 'take down the sun, for it does me no good. If you ask, what shall be done to abolish slavery? I reply, use those means which are in the hands of the people; diffuse sound education, let the ministry of north and south *preach and practise a pure Christianity*; then will the slaves be set free.

The Virginians are not a stubborn people. Many of them have spoken freely to me and expressed their convictions of the evils of slavery, but they are much like the *Indian* in one particular; they *will not be driven to do a good act.* You may drive an Indian to the very gate of heaven, but he will not enter to enjoy its pleasures; but entwine the thread of love and gentleness with the hand of kindness and you can lead him. Yea, a nation too. That spirit which is thus diffused in the act, disarms the savage breast of its fires, and thus it is with all men.

I had expected to have been on my way west before this, but the Indian department having no funds at its disposal, I shall be obliged to endeavor to interest the American people during this summer. Having received assurances of kindness from the various departments of government I am led to hope that at the next session of Congress I shall secure its aid.

My next will be a notice of the nobel deeds of Pocahontas, the daughter of the renowned Powhatan, the pride and glory of the American Indians.

I am, sir,

Yours, &c.

Kah-ge-ga-gah-bowh.

## LETTER 5

*Chesapeake Bay, July 15, 1849.*

### James River—Smith and Pocahontas.

Dear Sir:

The noble river which has its name from the first adventurer in that part of our country now known as Virginia, flows amid scenes of picturesque beauty. It is swollen by a number of smaller streams that empty into it. I never gazed on any object in my life more attentively than I did on that river when for the first time I passed over its surface. I gazed thoughtfully on either side, and fancied a bold, untutored Indian bounding among its shaded coverts before the pale face came among his tribe with those elements of sin which have caused the downfall and almost entire extinction of his race.

About noon quite a stir was seen among the passengers of the 'Curtis Peck,' as we passed down the river. Many eyes were directed towards a point on our left, and some one said, 'We shall soon see old Jamestown.' It was at this place that the first settlement was made by Smith and his comrades in the year 1607. Virginia can boast of the many sons she has produced to fill the presidential chair of our nation, and of many daughters who signalized themselves by acts of bravery in the struggle for freedom. Of these last, none exceeds in point of disinterested benevolence, Pocahontas, the daughter of Powhatan, the then ruling chief of that vast area of country. Smith was taken by a party of the warriors of Powhatan some distance from his own residence, and after being led about from village to village as an object of wonder, escorted by a party of warriors dressed in skins of wild beasts, and their heads decorated very fantastically with feathers, was led to Werowocomoco, on the north side of the Fork River, at that time the residence of Powhatan.

Word had previously been sent to the chief that the pale stranger had been taken, and no doubt his pleasure was asked respecting the disposal of him. Smith was taken by a guard to the door of Powhatan's lodge, and he was not mistaken in his suppostion that he was to be presented to that renowned prince. Around were the wigwams of the warriors, and he was abliged to withstand the inquisitive gaze of the people. He says, in his narrative, that when he entered the lodge, Powhatan sat on his throne at the upper part of the enclosure, with a majesty he had never before seen in Christian or pagan lands. The lofty and bold demeanor of the prince gave Smith a very favorable opinion of him. His family and friends were around him, and his couch was hung with rich furs.

A consultation was held to decide as to what should be done. Meanwhile, he was treated as a distinguished warrior of their nation. The queen herself brought the water that he used in washing. She placed food before him and desired him to eat, but the anxiety he felt as to his fate prevented him from partaking. It was at length decided that he should die at their hands, as he was at the head of the band of strangers that had come among them, and they knew not but that his intentions were evil.

Preparations for his execution were quickly made—the song and the dance begun. All gazed at the victim with wild intensity. The woman brought their young to look at the pale stranger. Young and old pitied his fate, but, according to the custom of the people, remained silent, and looked on the fulfillment of the decrees of the aged.

The warriors were commanded by Powhatan to bring a stone from the side of the river. All being arranged, the victim was seized by two warriors, and led to the place of execution. Smith showed not the least sign of fear, but calmly laid himself down as if to sleep, upon the spot from which he never expected to rise. The warriors stood with their heavy clubs raised, which, at the beck of Powhatan, would fall upon the bold adventurer. Men, women and children surrounded the spot, and it was at this time that they sympathized with the ill-fated man.

A little girl was now seen whispering in the ears of Powhatan. Her simple and childlike actions betrayed the feelings of a heart which pitied Smith. She spake earnestly, and held on his arms, as if she would not be denied her request. The chief advanced. One motion from him, and all would be over. A shout pierced the air, and Powhatan gave the word. As soon as given, Pocahontas flew from beside her father, and flung herself between Smith and the uplifted club of the warrior, and gazed with imploring look and eyes bathed in tears, upon her father. O what a lovely picture!—how godlike! how noble! Hard-hearted must that man be who could not be moved by such an exhibition. The warrior's arms hung down; the fiery flash of Powhatan's eye disappeared, as he bade his warriors desist. Pocahontas having done her work, ran among the crowd, to escape the gaze of the people. Smith was liberated, and by special favor became an inmate of the chief's lodge.

Pocahontas was but ten or eleven years old when this occurred, and how romantic must have been the scene! Heroic was the deed which has immortalized her name! Reader, she was a savage! And it has been said of her race, that they are without tears, unfeeling, cold, cruel, revengeful; but show me, if you can, in American history a parallel.

A few words more. First, historians have disagreed as to the motive that influenced her in the matter. Some say that Pocahontas loved Smith. I cannot find anything in the history of those times that leads me to suppose that the love she had for him was any greater than that she had for all her fellow-creatures. Smith has been charged with ingratitude on account of his not reciprocating the love which some have supposed the Indian girl bestowed upon him. I, for one, admire the deed of Pocahontas, and have have always regarded Smith as a worthy man in every particular. As a warrior, bold—in his schemes, fearless—in danger, calm—and in misfortune, never despairing. Notwithstanding all these traits of character, I still must censure his after conduct. When Pocahontas was in England, he did not notice her, nor even acknowledge her as a benefactor, although by periling her life she had saved his own. Such conduct on his part stamps his character with a foul blot, which his deeds of bravery can never conceal.

Second, her name which must have been given her after her rescue of Smith—indicates that her nation looked on her with some suspicion—*Pah-ka-on-tis*. In this, she suffered wrongfully. Partially disowned by her nation, the neglect she received in England at the hands of Smith while in England, was more than her spirit could bear, and after receiving Christian baptism, she died at Gravesend, England in the year 1617.

Pocahontas! No marble would long enough endure, to hand down the record of her noble deeds to all who should listen to the story of her heroism. you will not wonder that I admire her character, or think her name merits a place among the great of earth.

I am yours, etc.,

Kah-ge-ga-gah-bowh.

P.S. I leave soon for the West. You will next hear from me at Niagara; then from the Falls of St. Marie—Lake Superior—Falls of St Anthony, and the Rocky Mountains.

# (*For the Chicago Tribune.*)
# The Pleasures of Summer Travel in the West

"He sucks intelligence in every clime,
And spreads the honey of his deep research,
At his return—a rich repast for me."

The many sources of recreation and amusement which a traveller finds along his way in the West, are varied and interesting, and seem to me a world of successive glowing scenes. My memory still burns with the heat of excitement, caused by the animating objects of interest with which I have often been surrounded. The wide spread Prairies—the gardens of Nature—the streams of crystal waters which roll their tides over the pebbled course of vales, singing their music to the skies—the bluffs towering on each side of the 'Father of the Waters,' as it seeks its level in the Ocean, far off the sunny South—the mounds which often, one after the other, in chains, skirt their way through woodlands and then on the Prairies—the relics, or rather the tomb-stones of bygone generations now resting in their silence—the waving grass over the rolling Prairie by gentle winds, and the thousand wild flowers which often makes the very air sweet with their fragrance. O, the West, the West, the mighty West for me!—where groves wave their tops to the sweet air, wholesome, fresh and pure; and where game roams with the child of the forest, from brook to brook, and quaffs wholesome waters as they gush from the side of hills.

During the past season, wandering over the great West, I found much pleasure, perhaps more, where few would feel interested. The same things may not excite in the minds of many, while, from my own nature, and the early associations of childhood, they seem natural.

In ascending the waters of the Mississippi, I found many things

203

which gave me pleasure. The towering naked bluffs on the banks are imposingly grand at times. They appear like giant sentinels watching with vigilence the silent waters of the river below. In the morning they appear to blaze forth in the air, when the sun arose with an unclouded sky.

It was just evening, when the boat, which carried a full freight of merchandise and passengers, neared the "mountain in the water," about 90 miles above the town of Prairie du Chien. We had been puffing and puffing all the day long, and our boat was still heading up stream. On our right, was a vast wilderness, and on our left was to be seen the naked peaks of the bluffs, as though in the act of falling on the waters, as they dimly appeared, while the rays of the sun rapidly disappeared from the waters of the great river. Between these is the noted mountains called the 'mountain in the water,' because it is surrounded at its base with the waters of the river. When we were nearly ten miles from it we could discover the woods which skirted the edge—the lone pine and cedar trees which deck its brow. The sun no longer reflected on the waters, nor its rays lighted the lillies of the vale, but, the mountain in the water assumed one of the grandest scenes I ever beheld. There it was in full view, clothed in all the princely array of nature. The shadows of the bluffs from the western banks began to creep up to its heights, slowly ascending to its top. All around in nature's own garb and in nature's own fires glowed with its splendor. The wild water fowl in flocks ascended, and in descending lit on the surface of the water, and the surrounding shore was echoing with our boat's hoarse puff, which seemed animated with the pleasing view. The top of the mountain was in a blaze—the red sky of the west reflected in the waters, and the sun's rays began to disrobe the mountain; "five minutes more," said I, as I held the watch in my hand, "and then the sun will sink," and as the last rays of the sun disappeared, the shades of night began to creep from the waters below, until they covered the whole from view. The mountain and light reminded me of the death of the virtuous, dying in full hope of immortality disrobed of their cares; and to slumber in submission to the will of a propitious God.

The next morning, at sunrise, we were just entering the lake called 'Lake Pepin.' The river here widens, and the bluffs can be seen unobscured on each shore. The pebbly beach is full of cornelians, which are found along its shore. One of those bluffs is noted for being the place where a Sioux damsel, some eighty years ago, made a fatal leap on account of disappointed love.

The numerous things of interest which I found in the Upper Mississippi, I cannot now speak of; but my visit to the Government offices of the Territory, and to the American Fur Co., having been satisfactory, as well as to the Indians, whom I had seen, in pursuance of the great object of concentrating the North-West Indian tribes, which every where met with favor.

I had two days of hunting to my satisfaction, which will last me until next summer. One was to hunt with the gun; and having secured a brace of pigeons and about a dozen of wild ducks, I returned that day satisfied; but the following, at the crystal waters of St. Croix, was worth all the shooting, when with my angling rod I caught over three dozen of the very best of speckled trout. My hands twitch at the recollection of that day's sport, I cannot write intelligibly, and will finish in my next the ramble I made in the valley.

I remain, Yours, &c.

Kah-ge-ga-gah-bowh.

or, G. Copway, Ojibway Nation.

*Chicago, Ill, Oct.* 16th, 1849.

# Notices of the Press.

LECTURE OF KAH-GE-GA-GAH-BOWH

On the subject of Concentrating the Indians of the North-West, upon Territory, to be set apart by the General Government.

Last evening the celebrated Ojibway Chief, Kah-ge-ga-gah-bowh, or Geo. Copway, lectured in the City Saloon, upon the above subject, to a large and highly gratified audience. The lecturer commenced by refering to the present condition of the Indians—the calamitous effects of the policy pursued towards them by the U. S. Government—the causes which have heretofore operated to check their progress in civilization, and to thwart the efforts constantly being made by philanthropists who have gone among them for that purpose—all going to show that the inevitable destiny of the Indian race, is a yet deeper condition of degredation, of ignorance of, barbarism, and final extirpation, unless some scheme be devised for the amelioration of their condition.

Mr. Copway, after having obtained his education, at the hands of some benevolent gentlemen of this State, during the years 1838–9, returned to his nation, fired with the noble impulse of expending his energies in labors for the elevation of his people. For years he toiled and planned in this behalf, established schools and missions—instructed his people in the art of Agriculture—endeavored to teach them the true principles of government, and all other things calculated to advance them in civilization and individual happiness. These labors gave evidence of abundant fruit; but it was only for a day. A stroke of policy on the part of the General Government—the purchase of lands owned by the tribe—their removal to another territory—the influences under which this removal was affected—the duplicity of agents—the cupidity of contractors and traders—the malign influences and corrupting examples daily around and before them—these obliterated all traces of past labors—destroyed in a day the work of years and laid prostrate the hopes that had animated the hearts of the laborers.

Mr. Copway had thus become fully convinced that under existing circumstances the cause of his brethren must ever remain hopeless, unless something be done to place them in a position entirely removed from the causes which have heretofore barred their progress in civilization. Impressed with this belief he had devoted much serious reflection to the subject, the result of which is embodied in the following scheme:

The Indians of the North-west consisting of about 100,000 souls, to be concentrated upon Territory to be set apart to their use in perpetuity, by the Government of the U.S. one hundred miles north of Council Bluffs, on the east bank of the Missouri river. The territory thus given to be one hundred and fifty miles square. A government to be at once organized, by the appointment of a Governor (who shall be a white man) Lieut. Governor and Secretary of State, by the President of the U.S. A Territorial Council to be elected by the different tribes, in proportion to their population, which council shall pass all laws needful for the government of the whole people, subject to the veto of the Governor. The lands to be distributed, free of cost, to the people, subject to such regulations of transfer and limitation as the council shall establish. One of which, however, must be that it shall never be transferred to white men. Common schools and higher seminaries of learning to be established throughout the territory, a leading branch in all of which shall be the science and practice of Agriculture. White residents to be excluded except such as shall be employed by the U. S. and Territorial Governments. For the present the Territory to be represented at Washington by Commisioners to be appointed by the Council. Enjoying these facilities for civilization—from the necessity of things becoming confirmed in local habits, and compelled to the pursuits which elevate and refine—having become familiarized with our institutions and prepared to appreciate, love and live under them—in process of time the Indian Territory to apply for admission into the Union as a State, and become an integral part of the great confederacy.

Such is a meagre outline of Mr. Copway's plan. The arguments by which he supported it were plausible and forcible. His audience were carried along with him, and by loud and repeated applause testified to the reasonableness and justice of his arguments and conclusions. We regret that our limits prevent us from giving a more complete synopsis of the address, which occupied near two hours in the delivery. Mr. Copway is a forcible speaker—at times witty, convulsing his audience with laughter, and now thrilling them with bursts of lofty eloquence, and now convincing them by cogent logic. The peroration of Mr. C.'s speech was touching and impressive in the highest degree. No one that heard it will readily forget it, or easily loose the impressions made by it.

We may add in conclusion, that whatever may be said in regard to the plausibility of Mr. Copway's scheme, all must admit that this much and more he may in all justice claim from us for his people. He, as representative of those who once owned the entire continent from sea to sea, without a rival to dispute their claims, may well *demand* of us who by the law of might have forcibly taken posession of their fair heritage, so small a boon as the one he now craves from the American people.

### AN IMPRESSIVE SERMON.

Yesterday afternoon, amidst the celebration of the solemnities of religion that took place in this City of Churches, few perhaps could have produced more interest than the sermon of the Rev. Mr. Copway, otherwise known as the Indian Chief, Kak-ge-ga-gah-bowh. It was delivered before a large congregation in the church at the corner of Tillory and Lawrence Sts. The subject of the lecture was principally confined to the influence of Christianity with all its sublime influences among the untutored children of the West—the remnants of those who were once possessors of this soil. The advance of the pioneer white man, as he bore his fire-water and the worst passions of the white man, with tribes whose habits taught them to be contented with that which nature in all its abundance had produced, were the subjects upon which he dilated. If the people of this country would send such men as William Penn among them, they would be able to reciprocate the kindness of their white brethern. But alas! on account of the want of schools amidst the Indians, may be caused that subserviency to their customs, that makes them resort again to the blanket and the wigwam. Their training not being attended to according to the persuasion of the Christian religion he must go back instead of going forward. The things which are best adapted to advance the natives of the West, are not those that have been the best adapted to their customs. Education in a different form is necessary. The doctrine to love one another by binding the good fellowship of all nations, is the one that should be inculcated to them.

Human nature is the same everywhere, and the same feelings actuate the hearts of the Christian.

The Rev. Gentleman attributed to these as well as other causes, the interception of the advance of civilization amongst the children of the West. There are other reasons that he said might be given, that retarded their improvement. This was the introduction of the disease called the small pox, and others that were disposed among them, which their knowledge of medicine was unable to control.

The second is the introduction of fire-arms from the bands of the French, Spanish and English, which has thinned their ranks. The bravery of the Indian has caused him to be placed in the front ranks; and soon his tribe became depopulated. The happiness that reigned around the fire-side of the Indian's domestic circle, has been dashed to the ground before these influences; and the introduction of intoxicating liquors, that deprave the moral pulsations of the heart, and send him to an untimely grave.

It was this that destroyed the brightest virtues of a noble people. The tide of avarice and thirst of gold runs on and brings to the trader profit, at the expense of demoralization and death. It causes them to covet an enormous territory that is not cultivated, because it is so good—that roads and farms and house should spring up within it, and cities become populated. The natural consequence that will ensue, is that resistance will follow, and the boom of the cannon, and the roll of the warriors gun, will sound the last requiem of a departed race.

The Rev. Gentleman then concluded by stating that such horrors would be averted by selecting a home that would afford them a resting place, in the Minesotta territory, on the banks of the Mississippi, until in the course of time, they would learn the arts and sciences, and become attached to the place of their concentration.

The above is but a slight sketch of the remarks that were delivered; remarks which lead many to hope that the time may yet come when the aborigines of a new world—which has afforded a resting place to the tribes that were persecuted by the old, when new ideas had dawned upon them, and made them seek these shores to acquire a liberty that was denied them at home—will finally become a portion of civilized humanity, and worthy associates with their pale brethren, both in this world and the next.

This celebrated chief of the Ojibways, after a laborious tour South, has returned to our city. He is engaged to deliver lectures in Boston and vicinity the coming two weeks. His lectures on the Manners and Customs of his people are very interesting. The one delivered not long since in this City upon the "Romance of Poetry of the Indians" was an interesting and beautiful production.

We purpose in this notice, however, to mention only his lectures on Temperance, hoping to answer the many queries made to us on this subject by friends from various parts of New England. To this end we extract from the *Charleston Courier*, a notice of one of his lectures in that City, which comes so near the point, that we give it preference to any thing we can write.

"A crowded house assembled to listen to Mr. Copway, the Indian Chief and orator. He argued the cause of Temperance in every variety of manner, insisting mainly, as was to be expected, on its profound and even awful relations to the Red nations of the West. Shouting aloud in clear tones, he exclaimed with true Indian enthusiasm, in reference to that cause, "*I love it!*" Then, with manner more subdued, he dwelt, on the reasons why he loved it. He demonstrated successively that it was favorable to humanity, favorable to morality, and favorable to religion. With burning indignation he depicted the wrongs that had been inflicted on his brethren by unprincipled traders, who were themselves often, but the scum and refuse of civilization, and the only medium of communication between the Indians and the better class of whites. What, he asked, could be expected from the members of his nation, when goaded, insulted, corrupted, and maddened by these agents of hell? He showed how much these disastrous influences had been mitigated by the missionaries of Christianity and the Temperance Reform. He then applied the subject to the state and prospects of the cause among the whites. Here he seemed as much at home as the most experienced Temperance Lecturer of a paler hue.

A keen observer must he have been of our institutions, our social structure, and our prevailing character, whether for good or evil. Much even of his English was singularly idiomatic. Biting satire—pungent anecdote, set off with most expressive Indian gesticulation—strokes of wit and humor—touches of pathos—bursts of vehement declamation after the manner now of a Forest, or a Cooper, and now of a zealous Western preacher—slip shod conversational talk—most poetical descriptions of nature, fearless statement, off hand, calm, Indian independance, all together, formed a compound of a rather rare and inimitable nature. And although there might have been a few things for a very fastidious taste to object against, yet on the whole, *he* must have been a querulous man indeed who came away dissatisfied with his evening's treat, or unimpressed afresh with the inherent beauty, excellence and necessity of the Total Abstinence Cause.

Dr. Menderhall was the President, and Rev. Mr. Kendrick, the Chaplain of the evening.

# Notes to Text

Unless otherwise indicated, biographical information has been taken from the *Dictionary of American Biography, Dictionary of Canadian Biography,* and *Dictionary of National Biography.* All references to Copway's *Traditional History* are to the 1850 edition.

The editors have compared the 1850 edition of Copway's *Life,* which is reprinted in this volume, with Weed and Parsons's 1847 edition, Harmstead's first and second 1847 editions (Harmstead issued at least six), and the 1851 British edition. Important differences among the texts of the various editions are included in these notes. Harmstead's second 1847 edition includes hymns in English and Ojibwe at the beginning and end of the book. The British edition contains literary quotations at the beginning of each chapter. Because the publishers undoubtedly added the hymns and quotations, these are not included in these notes. The British edition uses the spelling *Ojibway* rather than *Ojebwa* and combines chapters 7 and 8 into a single chapter. It also includes Copway's "Address before the Legislature of Pennsylvania" and "Letters of the Author and Notices of the Public Press" in separate chapters, listed in the table of contents.

DEDICATION. The first phrase reads, "To Christians of all denominations," in the British edition.

65 Indian race. This paragraph is omitted in the British edition.

65 blessed above. The British edition replaces the last two paragraphs with:

> My book goes to the firesides of the thousand happy homes of the white man! As much as I may desire to see them in person, my short stay in this country will not allow me this pleasure. Tell your own story of my gratitude to the white man,—my joy and pleasures. Whisper in the ears of your children to pray for the red man.
>
> Yes! go, where I never shall be, and you will still be speaking, long, long after my tears will have ceased to flow, and I be numbered with the past.
>
> Visit the gaudy palaces of the great, and whisper in their ears what rivers are in store for doing good.
>
> Visit the humble homes of the poor, and let the cares, hopes, and joys of the one you speak of comfort and console the care-worn pilgrims of earth; for I love them because they are my brethren in affliction!
>
> *September,* 1850.

69    called the Indians. The British edition inserts the following passage
before the first paragraph:

> From a land of wildness and desolate solitude I come, and at the feet
> of noble Britons drop the tears of pleasure, and pay a humble homage,
> not to man, but to the greatness of the Palefaces,—or that which makes
> them great,—science and religion; in presenting myself before them as
> I do. None of my race have, perhaps, seen the different phases of one
> man's varied history as I have. The path I have trodden has been here
> and there rugged, steep, and intricate. Flowers and thorns have clus-
> tered in my bosom at the same time, and have left the aching heart to
> bleed. Sunshine has also succeeded the darkest hours of sorrow and
> the bereavements of the past. I have shouted to-day in the ecstacies of
> delight, and to-morrow I have sobbed in agony for departed joys! Yet,
> after all, I could wish to live a life over again, which, of itself, has some
> bright spots, which the future itself cannot afface with its glory.
> Thought recurs to the innocency of childhood, when no care ap-
> peared, as foreboding clouds in the distant sky; but when, half-naked, I
> sent my shout of merry laughter into the distant woods, or mocked the
> birds which sang over me. A nature as free as the deer, a heart as light
> as the dawn of day.
>
> Fancy's pictures are not needed in my life to represent the past. The
> realities stare at me, and the days which I have spent in the forest yet
> cause a momentary joy, and give life's wheel smoothness in their pas-
> sage to the grave. Lakes, rivers, wild woods, and mountain peaks, fre-
> quented in youth, arise, and still can I feel the glowing of youth's fires,
> which then were fanned by the breath of heaven. I drank from the
> hand of Nature. Her cup, ever running over, gave its delight, which
> nothing could supply, but that which runs in a stream from the skies.
> The earth then was covered with new-born beauties and blossoms.
>
> Among the many considerations which have induced me to consent
> to the publication of this work, is that the Christian public may do more
> good to my poor brethren, in sending them the means of education
> and Christian instruction.

69    *Mon-e-doos*. In the Ojibwe world-view, all elements are animate and
potentially hostile to humankind. However, they must be appeased through
governing spirits. There are numerous eternal spirits, or manitos, who appear as spirit protectors of plants, birds, beasts, elemental forces, and life circumstances. See Landes 22–31. Johnston describes them as "the unseen realities of individual beings and places and events that are beyond human
understanding but are still clearly real" (*The Manitous* xii).

70    "port of peace." Copway includes four stanzas from this poem,

which he attributes to "that poet of Scotland" in *Copway's American Indian* 10 July 1851: 2. We are unable to identify the author and the poem.

70 "all the earth." 1 Kings 2.2.

71 Rice Lake. Founded in 1798, Cobourg was originally called Amherst but renamed Cobourg in 1819; it is located on the north shore of Lake Ontario, about seventy miles east of Toronto. The Ojibwe call Rice Lake (named for its abundant wild rice) *Pamadusgodayong*, meaning "lake of plains." In 1904 Chief Robert Paudash explained that the lake was so named because "when the Mississagas first came down to the mouth of the river, the southern shore of Rice Lake opposite appeared to be flat since it had been cleared of forest, being the corn-fields of the Mohawks" (Guillet 12).

71 river Trent. Copway writes the name of this important river as the *Sah-ge-dah-we-ge-woh-ong*, which Augustus Jones, the early surveyor, translated as "strong Waters Rapids." The Trent River and the connective rivers and lakes were a major traffic artery between Georgian Bay on Lake Huron and the eastern end of Lake Ontario.

71 Anderson farm. About 1700 the Ojibwe pushed the Iroquois out of southern Ontario. See D. Smith, *Sacred Feathers* 19. This village was located near the eastern mouth of the Otonabee River, where it flows into Rice Lake.

71 *Crane tribe.* According to Warren, each Ojibwe clan is identified with a symbol or totem taken from nature, usually an animal, bird, fish, or reptile. Among the Ojibwe, clan membership descends through the male line. An individual is considered a close blood relation to all other Indians of the same clan, regardless of the band to which they belong. Consequently, intermarriage among clan members was formerly strictly forbidden. The original five clans were expanded. Warren lists twenty-one and Johnston, twenty-seven. One of the original five clans, the most important bird clan, was the Crane. Warren notes that members of the Crane clan were numerous and that they resided mostly on the south shores of Lake Superior and toward the east in Canada. Warren translates the name for this clan, *Bus-in-as-see*, as "Echomaker," which alludes to the loud, clear, far-reaching cry of the crane. Johnston describes the crane as a symbol of leadership. According to Warren, members of this clan were noted for possessing naturally a loud, ringing voice and are the acknowledged orators of the tribe; in former times, when different tribes met in councils, they acted as interpreters of the wishes of their tribe. "They claim, with some apparent justice, the chieftainship over the other clans of the Ojibways" (Warren 41–47, quote on 46–47; Johnston, *Ojibway Heritage* 53).

72 *Eagle tribe.* According to Johnston, the Eagle clan was identified with foresight and courage (*Ojibway Heritage* 53). Warren describes this group, *Me-gizzee*, as a branch of the Crane clan (44, 48).

75 in the interior. In the British edition, this sentence is preceded by,

"The change of seasons changed also our mode of living, as well as the place where we then had our wigwam."

76  Bay Quinty. The Bay of Quinte is an arm of Lake Ontario at its northeastern end; Belleville and Trenton are on its north shore. The Trent River empties into Lake Ontario at what is now Trenton.

79  "at home." A common hymn, found especially in Baptist and Mennonite hymnals.

81  Ke-sha-mon-e-doo. In the British edition, this sentence opens with, "However absurd may have been our notions of the multiplied deities of the earth, yet as a general thing, the Ojibways, . . ."

81  in the *Sun*. According to Johnston, *Kitche Manitou* made rock, water, fire, and wind out of nothing and from these created the physical world of sun, stars, moon, and earth. Father Sun superseded all the aspects of the physical world (*Ojibway Heritage* 12, 22).

81  "when we wake." Milton, *Paradise Lost* 4.677.

81  Ma-je-mah-ne-doo. Evil manitos are the cannibalistic windigos and underwater creatures (Landes 31). According to Vecsey, the Matchi Manito or evil manito reflects Christian influence. Missionaries taught the Ojibwes about the Christian Devil, sometimes associating it with the Underwater Manito or the windigo (82). See also T. Smith 104.

82  ceremonies every spring. Johnston notes that each spring when the sap flowed, the Ojibwe celebrated thanksgiving in ceremony for surviving the winter. This public ceremony coincided with their return to community living after spending the winter in family groups (*Ojibway Heritage* 144; see also Vecsey 110).

82  Grand Medicine Lodge. In *Traditional History*, Copway gives a much more detailed description of this religion and recounts the myth of its origin (165–75; cf. Warren 67–68).

82  Masonic institution. The British edition adds, after this sentence,

A medicine man is the most important personage in the worship of the Indians. He is the high priest of the ceremony, and keeps all the records of traditions and emblems. He is also the keeper of the great bag of herbs, which is opened only when lectures are given to illustrate them.

He is supposed to possess a great power over man and beast, and, therefore, to court his favour was an object worthy the consideration of young men.

86  "we'll end." See McKenney 189–90. Copway and McKenney quote the war song of Wa-ba-jick, a great war chief of La Pointe, on Lake Superior. The song was translated by his daughter, O-shau-guscoday-way-gua, called Susan by her husband, John Johnston (1762–1828). Their daughter, Jane, married Henry Rowe Schoolcraft.

86    in omens. The British edition adds, before this sentence, "Superstition raises and nurses children from the cradle—through the wide world. Laugh as we may at another's simplicity and folly, the civilised and uncivilised have always had their notions of ghost-spirits."

89    "our sins forgiven." Hymn 13, stanza 2, *Collection of Hymns* 46.

89    this country. The British edition inserts the following note: "This tradition[al] history of the Ojibways will soon be given to the public, and each may judge for himself with reference to the former history of our Indians."

90    "lost tribes of Israel." Copway alludes to the theory that Native Americans were descended from one of the "Ten Lost Tribes" of Israel, which was popular in the first half of the nineteenth century. Boudinot argues that because Indians differed from all the "savages" ever known to the people of the Old World, they were one of the lost tribes. He analyzed their cultures and religions to demonstrate his point. For a Jewish perspective, see Noah. Apess alludes to the theory in *A Son of the Forest*, asserting that Indians are the only people who "retain the original complexion of our father Adam" (in O'Connell 10).

90    they have conquered. Copway may be alluding to Ojibwe victories over the Iroquois and Dakotas.

90    massacred by hundreds. After the fall of Huronia in 1649/50, the warfare between the Iroquois and Ojibwe became more intense. In the 1660s, the Iroquois established villages along Lake Ontario. By 1687, the Mississaugas and their allies forced the Iroquois from the north shore of Lake Ontario. The Mississaugas occupied these lakeshore sites by 1696. The wars ended in 1701 (Tanner 10, maps 6 and 7 on 33, 34).

90    down the St. Lawrence. According to Ojibwe tradition, their people once lived near the salt ocean, probably at the mouth of the St. Lawrence. In the late sixteenth or early seventeenth centuries, the Ojibwes, the Potawatomis, and the Ottawas journeyed west to Lake Huron. When they reached Mackinac Straits, they separated but maintained a loose association called "the three fires." The Ojibwes settled around Sault Ste. Marie and later inhabited both shores of Lake Superior (Danziger 7).

91    between the Hurons and the Ojebwas. There is no record of such a council.

91    whites at Quebec. Samuel de Champlain established a fur trading post at Quebec in 1608. The French set up a settlement at Ville Marie (now Montreal) in 1642. Shortly thereafter, the Great Lakes Algonquins came to trade with the French.

92    "thirsts for gold." Alexander Pope, *An Essay on Man*, lines 98–108.

93    "life, and health, and peace." Hymn 1, stanzas 1–3, *Collection of Hymns* 37. The lyrics are by Charles Wesley (1739) and frequently appeared

in Protestant hymnals. Information provided by Gregory Singleton, Northeastern University.

93 "welcome in heaven." This hymn, with anonymous authorship and tune, is included in most late-eighteenth and early-nineteenth-century hymnals. Information provided by Gregory Singleton, Northeastern University.

94 abused, deceived, and cheated. By the treaty made with the Ojibwe at Smith's Creek (Port Hope) on 5 November 1818, the British government gained title to parts of present-day Ontario: Victoria, Peterborough, Durham, and Northumberland Counties. In return, the Crown promised the Ojibwe an annual payment of £740, not £750, as Copway states. See treaty no. 20 in *Indian Treaties and Surrenders* 1: 48–49. Today several of the islands still belong to the Rice Lake band. In chapter 17, under "7. Chippewas at Rice Lake," Copway includes the correct figure, "an annuity of £740," which is cited directly from the Bagot Commission Report of 1844.

94 Rev. James Evans. James Evans (1801–46), teacher, Methodist missionary, and linguist.

95 Methodist Missionary Society. See "Report on the Affairs of the Indians in Canada," *Journals of the Legislative Assembly of Canada*, 1844–45, appendix EEE; 1847, appendix T.

95 under the following circumstances. The British edition adds, before this sentence, "Several years we have been with the English people after the war, and learned to drink the fire-water of the Paleface. The day at last arrived when we were to learn something from them."

95 Port Hope. Originally called Smith's Creek, the town was renamed by the local inhabitants in 1817. It is situated approximately fifty-five miles east of Toronto on the north shore of Lake Ontario.

95 Credit River, and Grape Island. In the 1830s Mississauga villages were located at the confluence of the Credit River and Lake Ontario, west of present-day Toronto, and on Grape Island, in the Bay of Quinte, west of present-day Kingston (Tanner map 23 on 127).

96 "to heaven is gone." Hymn 3, stanza 1, line 1, *Collection of Hymns* 38.

98 Methinks, . . . blessed me. The British edition replaces this passage with: "The people were all around me kneeling, and most of them praying."

99 "a rebel as me." Hymn 8, stanza 4, *Collection of Hymns* 42.

99 Poutash Island. A small island in Rice Lake, immediately east of Hiawatha (Rice Lake) Indian Reserve.

101 *I was converted*. In the British edition, this chapter opens with: "Here comes the sunshine of my life. The first ray of light flashed in my soul, and, strange as it may appear, it remained."

101 *in my heart*. In the British edition this sentence reads: "I now began to feel as if I was a sinner before God."

101 I was so agitated . . . *"Glory to Jesus."* In the British edition this pas-

sage reads: "I was so agitated and alarmed that I knew not which way to turn in order to get relief, and while kneeling down with the rest I found relief, as though a stream had been let loose from the skies to my heart. Joy succeeded this knowledge, and, were I to live long, I never can forget the feelings with which I rose and spoke the following first English words—'*Glory to Jesus.*'

102 "charms our fears." Hymn 1, stanza 3, *Collection of Hymns* 37.

102 John Sunday. John Sunday (c. 1795–1875), or Shawundais, meaning "Sultry Heat," Mississauga veteran of the War of 1812, chief, and later a Methodist missionary. John Clark commented that the change Sunday produced in the conduct of "many of the Indians, was matter of astonishment to all" [sic] (qtd. in Hall 99; Hall also includes a long excerpt from one of Sunday's fiery missionary speeches [100–104]).

103 Daniel McMullen. McMullen (1799–1874) was a Methodist missionary at Rice Lake. See his letters of February 1830, 1 June 1833, 18 November 1833, and 4 June 1834 in the Methodist newspaper *The Christian Guardian* (Toronto) 13 March 1830, 8 July 1833, 4 December 1833, and 11 June 1834; and "Ministerial Obituary. The Rev. Daniel McMullen," *Canadian Methodist Magazine* 2 [1875]: 188–92.

103 Rev. Wm. Case. William Case (1780–1855), Methodist missionary, served in the district of the Bay of Quinte, Upper Canada. In 1809 Case was stationed in Detroit, and from 1809 to 1827 he was presiding elder of the Methodist Church in Canada and northwestern New York. In 1828, after the Canadian Methodists separated from those in the United States, Case became superintendent of Indian missions and schools in Upper Canada. He was general superintendent of the Methodist Episcopal Church in Canada from 1828 to 1833.

103 Rev. John Clark. John Clark (1797–1854), American Methodist missionary. Admitted on trial in 1820 to the New York Conference, he served the Indians of Michigan and Wisconsin from 1832 to 1836. In 1836 he was transferred as presiding elder to Chicago, Illinois Conference. Clark then moved to become a pastor in Texas and New York, returning to Chicago and the Illinois Rock River Conference in 1852. He subsequently persuaded Ms. Eliza Garrett to give one hundred thousand dollars to found what is now Garrett Evangelical Theological Seminary in Evanston. Hall provides considerable information about Clark and the missionary movement in the Upper Midwest.

103 John Johnson. John Johnson (c. 1810–92), or Enmegahbowh ("One Who Stands Before His People"), belonged to the Rice Lake Ojibwe, or Mississauga Indian band, in Upper Canada. Copway described him as his cousin. For over a half century, he served first with the Methodists and then the Episcopalians in Wisconsin and Minnesota. See Jackson.

103 Caubage. John Caubage (b. ca. 1805), Cahbeach or Kah-beege, an

Ojibwe interpreter and Methodist preacher, also belonged to the Rice Lake Ojibwe. He spent approximately twenty years in Methodist mission work on Lake Superior before returning to Rice Lake, where he was the resident Methodist missionary. Copway described him as his uncle in *Traditional History* (133).

104 Mr. William Lyon McKenzie. William Lyon Mackenzie (1795–1861), journalist and politician. Elected the first mayor of Toronto in 1834, he led the Rebellion of 1837 in Upper Canada (now Ontario). After he fled to New York, Mackenzie was convicted of violating U.S. neutrality laws. Imprisoned for a year, he remained in the United States for ten years before returning to Canada.

104 Pane-ta-wa-go-shene. Penetanguishene is a town located at the head of the Penetanguishene Bay on the Southern Georgian Bay of Lake Huron, approximately ninety miles north of Toronto. The Narrows, or the present-day city of Orillia, is at the narrows between Lake Simcoe and Lake Couchiching, north of Toronto. The Methodists had a mission here in the 1830s. Coldwater was a model Indian village north of the Narrows, established in the 1830s by the government of Upper Canada. By the early 1840s, it had been disbanded. Holland Landing is immediately south of Lake Simcoe. Navigation was possible from this point of the Holland River north to Lake Simcoe. In the 1830s the Methodists had a school on Snake Island, located in Lake Simcoe.

104 Chandler and Bourne. Daniel Meeker Chandler (1810–42). Born at Oronville, New York, Chandler became a Methodist preacher in 1834 as a member of the Troy (New York) Conference. With Milton Bourne, he left that year to become a missionary to the Indians. From 1834 to 1836, Chandler served at Kewawenon Mission on Lake Superior before moving on to Sault Ste. Marie. Chandler gives a vivid account of life as a missionary in his letters and journals, from which Prindle quotes copiously.

In 1834 Milton Bourne (1810–65) was employed at the Sault Ste. Marie Mission. He was made a deacon in the Illinois Conference in 1839, ordained as an elder in the Illinois Rock River Conference in 1841, and was admitted on trial in Wisconsin in 1843. He served churches in Wisconsin and Illinois until superannuated in 1863. He died two years later in Macomb, Illinois (Field 193–96; transcript, "Minutes of the Rock River Conference, Plattville, Wisconsin, 30 August 1841," 38; *Minutes of the Annual Conferences of the Methodist Episcopal Church, . . . 1839–1845* [hereafter *Minutes*], 3: 6, 8; both at Union Library, Seabury-Western Theological Seminary and Garrett-Evangelical Theological Seminary, Evanston IL; Blake 294).

104 H. P. Chase. Henry Pahtahguahong Chase (1818–1900), an Ojibwe interpreter, Methodist minister, and later an Anglican clergyman.

105 for his friends. This paragraph is omitted from the British edition.

105   "sufficient for you." Copway paraphrases 2 Cor. 12.9.

105   Pictured Rocks. These consist of a layer of soft sandstone, topped with hard dolomite forms. Mineral seepage has colorfully painted the rocks: iron shows up red; copper, blue and green; and limestone, white. The cliffs rise to considerable height. According to Copway, the marks on the pictured rocks are thought to be the footsteps of the Great Spirit (*Traditional History* 156n.).

105   Grand Island. It lies off shore, west of Munising, Michigan.

105   Aunce Bay. The French named the south shore of Keweenaw Bay *L'Anse*, meaning "cove." The site was a campground for French explorers, fur traders, and missionaries.

106   *"Holy Ghost."* Acts 2.4.

108   William Herkimer. William Herkimer, or Herchmer (1801–75), a Mississauga Indian of mixed ancestry, became a Methodist church worker and later a minister.

110   Charles Holiday. Probably a member of the Holiday family at Aunce Bay. John Holiday had been a trader there since 1802. William was a trader at Aunce Bay as well (Warren 392; Neill 467 n. 2).

110   Marksman. Peter Marksman (Gah-go-dah-ah-quah) (c. 1815–92), an Ojibwe Methodist preacher, was born at Fond du Lac on Lake Superior but raised in the Sault Ste. Marie area. Converted by John Clark in 1833 and baptized by Peter Jones, he served at various missions with Clark before accompanying the missionary, Copway, and John Johnson to Lac Court Oreilles. From 1837 to 1839 he attended Ebenezer College in Jacksonville, Illinois. He subsequently became a Methodist missionary, serving primarily in Michigan. See Pitezel.

110   La Pointe. An early Jesuit mission on Madeline Island, on the southwestern end of Lake Superior. It later became a fur trade post and then a fishing center. A Protestant mission was established there in the early 1830s.

111   Porcupine Mountains. Ontonagon and the Ontonagon ("Ah-too-nah-kun") River are located in the upper peninsula of Michigan, on the southern shore of Lake Superior east of the Porcupine Mountains. The Porcupine Range is the highest mountain range in the U.S. Midwest.

111   land of *Nod*. This sentence is omitted from the British edition.

112   Mr. Warren. Lyman Marcus Warren (1794–1847) was an American fur trader at La Pointe. In 1821 he married Marie, or Mary, Cadotte, daughter of the trader Michel Cadotte. The eldest of their eight children was William Whipple Warren, author of *History of the Ojibways*. See Williams 9–12.

112   Rev. Mr. Hall. Sherman Hall (d. 1879), a Presbyterian minister. The American Board of Commissioners for Foreign Missions in Boston sent him to establish a mission at La Pointe. He directed the mission there from 1831 to 1853.

112 "in Christ Jesus?" Eph. 2.6.

112 Ottawa Lake. Also known as Lac Court Oreilles, which flows into the Chippewa River, south of La Pointe.

113 *Moose tail.* Warren gives the name as Mo-so-ne, a member of the Catfish clan. He was resident chief at Lac Court Oreilles, formerly known as Lake Ottaway (318). In his *Traditional History,* Copway describes how the chief showed him the sites of numerous Ojibwe-Sioux battles (57).

113 Me-no-me-nee Mills. Probably the area near the confluence of the Chippewa and Menominee Rivers (the latter was also known as the Red Cedar River) in what is now west-central Wisconsin. Lyman Warren, father of William Whipple Warren, and several others operated mills there. See Brunson, *A Western Pioneer* 2: 146.

116 "everlasting life." John 3.16.

116 school near Jacksonville, Illinois. Rev. Peter Akers opened the Ebenezer Manual Labor School in the summer of 1837.

117 Rev. Jno. Mitchell. John T. Mitchell (1810–63), a Methodist preacher renowned for his impressive delivery. Accepted into the Illinois Conference in 1831, he served at Jacksonville that year and again from 1836 to 1838, subsequently moving to Springfield, Chicago, and Mt. Morris. In 1848 he moved to Ohio, becoming secretary in the Cincinnati Conference (1851–63) and serving as chairman of the book committee of the Western Book Concern (Field 240–46; Kalb 8).

117 *Brown Co., Ill.* Mt. Sterling, Lynville, Manchester, Rushville, and Versailles are towns in west-central Illinois. Lynnville and Manchester (both in Scott County) are approximately fifteen miles west and fourteen miles southwest, respectively, of Jacksonville; Versailles and Mt. Sterling (both in Brown County) are approximately twenty-four and thirty-three miles northwest of Jacksonville; Rushville (Schuyler County) is around sixty-five miles northwest of Jacksonville.

117 Brother Troy. Rev. Edward Troy (1819–45) was born in Hamilton County, Ohio, and licensed in 1838 to preach on the Jacksonville circuit. Admitted on trial at the next Illinois conference, he was appointed to a series of circuits in central Illinois ("Edward Troy," "Illinois Conference [1845]," 3: 662, in *Minutes*).

117 Brother Wm. Piper W. G. Piper is listed as the preacher on the Mt. Sterling circuit in 1845 (*Combined History* 217).

117 Dr. Akers. Rev. Peter Akers (1790–1886), teacher, lawyer, and later a Methodist clergyman, founded and was first superintendent of the Ebenezer Manual Labor School near Jacksonville in southern Illinois. He was also president of McKendree College at various times ("Akers, [Rev.] Peter" 753).

118 Brother Berryman. N. G. Berryman was a presiding elder on the Mt. Sterling circuit in 1843 (*Combined History* 217).

118 *Huddlestun.* A Methodist minister, Allen Huddleston studied at Ebenezer Manual Labor School; he and Samuel Spates attended the school with Copway, Johnson, and Marksman in order to learn Indian languages. Copway reports Huddleston's death from dysentery on 30 December 1840 in chapter 13. This death is confirmed in the *Western Christian Advocate* 1 March 1841 (rpt. in the *Christian Guardian* [Toronto] 14 April 1841: 1.3). See also Pitezel 70.

118 Benson, Otwell, Corey, Edmunson, and Hale. Born in Boston, John Henry Benson (1797–1843) came west at age twenty-three and was licensed to preach in 1826. In 1828 he was admitted on trial and appointed to the Sangamon circuit, where he served until his death. Stith Mead Otwell (1805–43) was born in Georgia and, at eleven, moved with his family to Illinois. In 1826, he was both licensed to preach and admitted on trial by the Illinois Conference. Because of continuing ill health, he was superannuated, serving as treasurer of the Conference Missionary Society ("John Henry Benson" and "Stith Mead Otwell," "Illinois Conference [1843]," 3: 456–57, in *Minutes*).

Originally a Quaker, Joseph Edmonson (1798–1844) was born in Virginia and became a traveling preacher in Missouri in 1823. He later transferred to the Illinois Conference, serving circuits in central and southwestern Illinois ("Joseph Edmonson," "Illinois Conference Obituary [1844]," 3: 586–87, in *Minutes*). There is little information about David Corey, who was superannuated from 1839 through 1842 (see *Minutes* 3: 192, 194).

Jesse Haile (d. 1845) was admitted on trial in 1813 by the Tennessee Conference. He subsequently served on circuits in Missouri and central and southern Illinois ("Jesse Haile," "Illinois Conference [1845]," 3: 661–62, in *Minutes*).

118 Moses C. This may be Moses Clampet, or Clampitt (spelling varies), who attended the Illinois Conferences from 1836 through 1838 but was superannuated from 1839 through 1843 (Typescript, "Journal of the Illinois Annual Conferences of the Methodist Episcopal Church," in Union Library, Seabury-Western Theological Seminary and Garrett-Evangelical Theological Seminary, Evanston, IL).

119 *"cleanseth from all sin."* 1 John 1.7.

119 Pitner is there now. William Pitner (1806–80). Leaton calls Pitner "the most eccentric" in the Illinois Conference. According to Leaton, Pitner was dropped from his first preaching assignment because many of his parishioners felt his "unlettered mind, his peculiar and awkward deportment, his impulsive and erratic mode of speech, and his very singular illustrations in the pulpit" were unbecoming (314). After spending six months at Illinois College at Jackson, he was appointed to a series of circuits in Illinois and Missouri, moving almost yearly. In 1851 he moved to California and by the 1860s settled in Washington Territory, where he died.

119   William J. Rutledge. Rutledge was the preacher on the Mt. Sterling circuit in 1842 and 1844. In 1856 he was second pastor of the West Charge Methodist Church in Bloomington, Illinois. Rev. James Shaw, who replaced him, described Rutledge as "eloquent as a preacher and one of the most genial men." The presiding elder of the circuit in 1858, Rutledge returned to Bloomington twenty years later (Shaw 225–26; *Combined History* 217).

120   Dr. Vandevanter. Dr. Saul Vandeventer (b. 1818) of Versailles was among the earliest physicians of Brown County, Illinois (*Combined History* 302–3).

120   Brother Bond. Rev. Granville Bond (1805–63), one of the leading Methodist pioneers of Brown County, Illinois. Settling in the county in 1828, he became an indefatigable preacher and founder of churches (*Combined History* 73, 215–16).

120   Bloomfield, in 1839. The Illinois Conference for 1839 was held in Bloomington, Illinois (formerly called "Bloomfield"), in east-central Illinois.

120   Brothers Spates. Rev. Samuel Spates (1815–87) was selected in 1837 to attend Ebenezer Manual Labor School, spending two years there while Copway was also a student. Admitted in 1839 on trial in the Illinois Conference, he was sent first to the Chippewa Mission on the upper Mississippi and then to Sandy Lake, serving at both places with John Johnson. After brief sojourns in Illinois and at Sault Ste. Marie, he returned to Sandy Lake in 1846, remaining until 1855, when antagonism against the missionaries became so great that they fled for their lives. Thereafter he served the Minnesota Conference (Hobart 18–19).

120   Brother Kavanaugh. Benjamin T. Kavanaugh, a Methodist minister, was continued on trial at the 1836 Conference, Rushville, Illinois (Typescript, "Journal of the Illinois Annual Conferences of the Methodist Episcopal Church"). At the first Rock River Conference, held in Mt. Morris, Illinois, in 1840, Kavanaugh served as secretary and was appointed superintendent of the Indian missions (Beggs 315; Pennewell 87). He is listed as an elder at the Rock River Annual Conferences held in Chicago in 1842 and in Dubuque, Iowa, in 1843 (Typescript, "Minutes of the Rock River Annual Conference of the Methodist Episcopal Church, 1840–1852." Both the "Journal" and the "Minutes" are in the Union Library, Seabury-Western Seminary and Garrett-Evangelical Theological Seminary, Evanston IL). From 1841 through 1844 he was presiding elder of the Platteville, Wisconsin, District; he was removed in 1844 from the Rock River Conference (Bennett 73, 79, 474).

120   *the place of skunks.* Many explanations of this name have been given. Vogel concludes that there is overwhelming evidence that *chicago* means wild garlic, leek, or onions. The garlic or wild onion was "stinking weed" or

"skunk weed." He suggests that the similarity in terms is the source for interpreting it as "skunk place" (24–25).

120    James Madison. Madison's name was William. *A Directory for the City of Buffalo* (Buffalo: Charles Faxon, 1837) lists Madison as living on Jackson Street (97); the *Commercial Advertiser Directory for the City of Buffalo* (Buffalo: Jewett, Thomas and Co., and Cutting, 1847), lists his temperance boardinghouse at 92 Main Street (100).

120    Brother Copeland. Rev. John Copeland was a Methodist minister in Rochester (Ward 124).

121    Sister Luckey's. Dorcas Luckey, widow of James, ran a boardinghouse at 347 Broom Street. (*Longworth's American Almanac, New-York Register and City Directory* [New York: Thomas Longworth, 1839] 417).

121    Dr. Bangs. Nathan Bangs (1778–1862), Methodist minister, publisher, and historian. Licensed in 1801, he served in Upper Canada, returning to the United States as the War of 1812 drew near. He began a series of official church journals, founded the Methodist Missionary Society, and became in 1841 acting president of Wesleyan University in Connecticut. For an account of the development of the Methodist Church in the early nineteenth century, see his four-volume *History of the Methodist Episcopal Church: From the Year 1829 to the Year 1840* (New York: Carleton and Porter, 1857). Copway alludes to Bangs's *Centenary Sermon*.

122    brother Abraham Hedenburg. In the *Directory of the City of Newark* (Newark: Aaron Guest, 1840), B. T. Pierson lists "Abram" Hedenberg as a harness maker at 1512 Market, house at 78 Halsey (75); the 1847 *Directory* lists him as operating a fruit, confectionery, and toy store at 254 Broad Street (113). There were numerous Hedenbergs in Newark during this period.

122    Brother Bartine. Pierson's *Directory of the City of Newark* (1840) lists Rev. David W. Bartine as pastor at 12 Franklin Street and resident at 17 Franklin Street (44).

122    Brother Ayers. Rev. James Ayers, pastor of the Methodist Church at 54 Halsey; residence at 98 Plane Street (Pierson, *Directory of the City of Newark* [1840] 38, 41).

122    especially to Brother Hedenburg. The following note was added in the British edition: "My English friends will, I hope, excuse me for calling the good people I have met 'Brother' (though this apology may not be required by many, yet it is necessary with some), for God is my father and every man a brother."

122    Brother H. Merrell's family. Possibly Haram Merrill, who resided at Chambers Street Court. No "Merrell" is listed in *Stimpson's Boston Directory* (Boston: Charles Stimpson, 1840) (297, 380).

123    Rev. E. Taylor. Edward Thompson Taylor (1793–1871), Boston

chaplain of seamen. Father Taylor, as he was affectionately called, walked the "quarter deck" of his Seaman's Bethel Methodist Church for forty years. He was regarded as one of the greatest American preachers of his generation. Harriet Martineau, Dickens, Emerson, and Whitman all left tributes to him. The sermon of Father Mapple in Melville's *Moby Dick* portrays Taylor's manner of preaching.

124 Rev. Mr. Seymour. Rev. Truman Seymour, pastor of the First Methodist Church, resided at 58 Division (L.G. Hoffman, *Hoffman's Albany Directory* [Albany: Author, 1840] 216).

124 Brother Page. Rev. F. D. Page, pastor of the Third Methodist Church at 90 South Place (*Hoffman's Albany Directory* [1840] 190).

124 Mr. McCaulay. John Macaulay (1792–1857) served as inspector general of Upper Canada from 1839 to 1841.

125 Alderville. Located immediately south of Rice Lake, near Roseneath.

126 "firmly on a rock." Ps. 40.2

127 President of the Council. Joseph Sawyer or Nawahjegezhegwabe (1786–1863), a Mississauga war veteran of the War of 1812, Methodist convert, and head chief of the Mississauga of the Credit River. The Grand Council met at the Credit River Mission at the end of January 1840. Several hundred chiefs and warriors from across Upper Canada attended.

127 Lord Sydenham. Charles Poulett Thomson, first Baron Sydenham (1799–1841), governor general of Canada (1839–41). Sydenham contended that the Indians could not be "civilized," that Indian hunters and fishers could not adjust to agriculture. See D. Smith, *Sacred Feathers* 182–83.

127 Lord John Russell. British statesman and prime minister (1846–52). In 1841 he served as the colonial secretary in the British cabinet.

127 Captain Howell's family. Henry Howell (1790–1869). Born in Knaresborough, Yorkshire, he moved with his family to a farm near Toronto.

127 Elizabeth. Elizabeth Howell (1817–1904) was born in England and emigrated to Canada with her family around 1820.

129 *mother* and *sister* have gone. See chapter 8 for Copway's description of their deaths.

130 Black Rock. A small U.S. settlement on the Niagara River, beside Buffalo and opposite Fort Erie, on the Canadian side. It is now part of Buffalo, New York.

131 Whig Convention at Fort Meigs. General William Henry Harrison attended a huge Whig rally, which opened on 11 June 1840 at Fort Meigs, Ohio. Attended by forty thousand people, the convention included a sham attack on the fort by a band of Indians (Holt 464–65; "Harrison's Great Speech").

131    Mr. and Mrs. Peet. In 1826 Samuel Peet (1797–1855), minister and fund-raiser, became pastor of the Presbyterian Church in Euclid, Ohio, and married Mrs. Martha Dennison Sherman, a widow. From 1833 to 1837 he was the agent of the American Seaman's Friend Society. In 1837 he moved to Wisconsin as pastor of the Green Bay Presbyterian Church. From 1839 to 1852 he served the Milwaukee Presbyterian Church and other Presbyterian and Congregational churches in Wisconsin, was the salaried agent for the American Home Missionary Society, and served as the financial agent for Beloit College. Peet then moved to Illinois as pastor of the Congregational Church in Batavia, west of Chicago, resigning in 1854 to become financial agent and president of the Board of Directors of the proposed Chicago Theological Seminary. See Murphy.

131    Rev. Mr. Colclazier. Henry Colclazer (1809–84) was born in Alexandria, Virginia, and admitted on trial to the Ohio Conference of the Methodist Episcopal Church in 1828. While serving in Ohio, he was pastor of the church attended by Rutherford B. Hayes, who later became president. In 1835 he helped obtain a charter for the seminary that became Albion College. That year he became presiding elder of the New Ann Arbor District and the first librarian of the University of Michigan, serving from 1837 to 1845. Noted for his eloquent preaching and logical sermons, Colclazer subsequently moved east, serving churches in New Jersey, Pennsylvania, and Delaware. He was elected twice as a delegate to the General Conference: 1840 from Michigan and 1860 from Pennsylvania (Brunger; Pitezel 88).

131    Amherstburg. The town is located near Bar Point in southwestern Ontario, south of Windsor.

132    Winnebago Lake. Located in southeastern Wisconsin. During this period, the only non-Native inhabitants were in what was then known as Winnebago, present-day Oshkosh.

132    Brother White. By appointment from the New York Oneida Conference in 1834, Rev. George White was made the officiating clergyman in Green Bay; he transferred to the Illinois Conference in 1836. In Green Bay he kept a boardinghouse. White later became a clerk for the government at Washington. H. A. Gallup, an early settler of Oshkosh, called him "one of Natures noblemen" (qtd. in *Biographical and Statistical History of the City of Oshkosh* [Oshkosh: Finney and Davis, 1867] 19; see also Bennett 26, 29, 473, 474).

132    St. Peters. A Sioux Indian agency located at the confluence of the Mississippi and a branch of the Minnesota River in southern Minnesota, near present-day Minneapolis.

132    Brothers Garvin, Pond, Denton, and their wives. Rev. Daniel Gavin married Miss Lucy Cornelia Stevens in the spring of 1839. According to Riggs, Gavin and his wife resided at Red Wing for a while and then "re-

moved to East Canada, where they labored for the French population" ("The Dakota Mission" 118).

With his older brother, Samuel, Rev. Gideon Hollister Pond (1810–78) came in 1834 to the land of the Dakotas, later Minnesota Territory, to work with the tribal members of Lake Calhoun Village. In 1837 he married Sarah Poage and was ordained by the Dakota Presbytery in 1848. Pond was noted for his mastery of the Dakota language. After the Dakotas were removed to upper Minnesota under the terms of the 1851 treaties, Pond stayed among the settlers, who immediately took possession of Indian lands. With Rev. Stephen R. Riggs, he wrote *The Dakota First Reading Book* (1839); he and his brother translated parts of the Bible into Dakota as well. See "Memorial Notices of Rev. Gideon H. Pond by Messrs. Riggs, Williamson, and Sibley," *Collections of the Minnesota Historical Society* 3 (1870–80): 356–71; Riggs, "The Dakota Mission" 115–28.

Denton may be Persis Dentan, a Swiss missionary preaching among the Dakotas in 1837. His wife was formerly Miss Skinner of the Mackinaw mission (Riggs, "The Dakota Mission" 117).

133   been concealed there. The Elk and Rice Rivers branch off the Mississippi near Gull Lake, north of Minneapolis and west of Fond du Lac. The Rum River branches off north of Minneapolis and runs into Mille Lacs Lake. By the 1830s Ojibwe expansion into former Dakota territory was virtually complete (Tanner 149, map 28 on 149).

134   Chief Hole-in-the-sky. Puk-o-nay-keshig, Pug-o-na-ghe-zhisk, or Bug-on-a-keshig (c.1800–1847), more commonly known as Hole-in-the-Day. Born near La Pointe, Wisconsin, this Ojibwe chief was a fierce adversary of both the Sioux and the federal government. Though not a hereditary chief, he was selected to lead by force of his personality, eloquence, and bravery. Hole-in-the-Day and his brother, Song-uk-um-ig (Strong Ground), inherited the chieftainship of Ba-be-sig-aun-dib-ay (Curly Head), civil and war chief of the Lower Mississippi, or Gull Lake, Ojibwes. This was the last request of the old chief, who died in 1825 on the way home from the treaty conference in Prairie du Chien. Hole-in-the-Day's village was near Gull Lake, where he occupied part of the territory between the Ojibwes and the Sioux. He died in 1847 from injuries received when he was thrown from a cart while intoxicated. See Clark, "Reminiscences"; Diedrich 2–11.

In *Traditional History*, Copway says that Hole-in-the-Day often confidently affirmed that had it not been for the federal government's partition of lands among the Indians, "he would have made his village at St. Peters, and hunting grounds of his young men would have extended far into the western plains of the Sioux" (64–65).

136   "Lord J. Russell." In the British edition, the following passage is after the signature:

The above is a fair specimen of the treatment we have received, in many cases, from those who ought to have done all they could to raise us to a position of respectability.

The natives are now doing well. They have farms of their own, upon which many of them raise from ten to fifteen hundred bushels of wheat for their families. By their own means they have kept up their schools. Churches, erected by themselves, are everywhere to be seen. We have ministers and school-teachers belonging to our own nation. And yet we have not improved.

I would ask, how much encouragement and assistance in education have we received from our former fathers? Again and again we have asked to be aided in education; if we had asked for whiskey, we could have got it; but anything to raise and benefit us we could not get.

136   "has afflicted us." Copway paraphrases Ps. 90.15.

136   "for nought." Copway paraphrases Isa. 49.4.

137   chief Little Crow's village. Mdewakanton Santee Dakota leader and father of the Little Crow. By the 1830s, the Mdewakanton, the leading eastern division of the Dakota Sioux, retained villages on the Mississippi and lower Minnesota Rivers (Tanner 149).

137   Fort Snelling. Fort Snelling was built in 1819 on a commanding bluff above the Mississippi and Minnesota Rivers. Now part of Minneapolis, the fort was, for nearly three decades, the U.S. government's administrative center in the upper Mississippi country.

138   "freeze with horror." The phrase "made my seated heart knock at my ribs against the use of nature" is from Shakespeare's *Macbeth* 1.3.136.

139   Sandy Lake Mission. Sandy Lake is immediately west of Fond du Lac on Lake Superior. See Tanner map 28 on 148.

139   "past finding out." Rom. 11.33.

139   "against me." Gen. 42.36.

139   head of Lake Superior. Platteville is located in southwestern Wisconsin, south of Prairie du Chien. In 1830, the Fond du Lac Ojibwe village was at the southwestern mouth of Lake Superior, near present-day Duluth.

139   James Simpson. James W. Simpson (1818–70) came to Minnesota in 1841, serving at the Sandy Lake Mission about a year. In 1843 he settled in St. Paul and engaged in commission business ("Simpson, James W." 706).

139   Saint Croix River. The Saint Croix, which forms the boundary between Wisconsin and Minnesota, flows into the Mississippi River.

139   Burnt-wood River. The Bois Brule River branches off the St. Croix River in northwestern Wisconsin; it runs north between the towns of Maple and Iron River into Lake Superior. This was a common canoe route.

140   Rev. Mr. Ely. Edmund Franklin Ely (1809–82) arrived in Minnesota in 1833, serving as schoolteacher and missionary at Sandy Lake. In 1834 he

moved to Fond du Lac, where he was that mission's first schoolteacher and missionary. Ely transferred to Pokegama in 1839 and served at La Pointe in the late 1840s. See Nute; Castle 666–67.

141 "weary are at rest." Job 3.17.

142 Rev. Messrs. Hall and Wheeler. In 1831 Leonard H. Wheeler (d. 1872) and Sherman Hall arrived at the La Pointe Mission. In the early 1850s Wheeler staunchly opposed efforts to remove the Ojibwes. He removed the mission to Odanah in 1845, where he remained until 1866. His missionary work was supported by the American Board of Commissioners for Foreign Missions, a Congregationalist and New School Presbyterian organization, which also supported Hall, William T. Boutwell, and Edmund T. Ely. For an account of Wheeler's missionary work, see Davidson 447–51, and Sproat 201 n. 2.

Hall (d. 1879) remained at La Pointe until 1853. He subsequently moved to Crow Wing on the Mississippi (Davidson 442, 444, 445, 446, 447).

142 Rev. Mr. Boutwell. William T. Boutwell (ca. 1802–90), a Dartmouth graduate from New Hampshire, arrived at La Pointe in June 1832. See Hickerson; Davidson 444, 445; Boutwell's papers are in the Minnesota Historical Society.

142 Council of the Ojebwa nation. On 4 October 1842, at La Pointe, the Ojibwe chiefs made a treaty with the U.S. government. See Kappler 2: 542–44.

142 R. Stewart. Robert Stuart of Detroit, a former trader in charge of American Fur Trade operations headquartered on Mackinac Island, Michigan. He attended the La Pointe Treaty council.

143 Rev. Messrs. Stinson, Green, and Jones. Joseph Stinson (1802–62) was a Methodist minister who served from 1833 to 1840 as superintendent of missions in Upper Canada. Anson Green (1801–79), a Methodist minister, was elected in 1842 as president of the Wesleyan Methodist Church in Canada. Peter Jones (1802–56) was the leading Native Methodist minister in Upper Canada, or Canada West, from the mid-1820s to his death.

143 Rev. J. R. Goodrich. James R. Goodrich (1805–86), Methodist minister, was admitted to the New York Conference in 1828; in 1837 he and Milton Bourne transferred to the Illinois Conference. From 1841 to 1844 he was presiding elder of the Green Bay District. In 1844 he became presiding elder of the Chicago District, resigning at the end of that year to become a merchandiser in Dubuque, Iowa (Field 203–4).

143 sent to Credit River. The oldest and most important Methodist mission station in Upper Canada, the Credit River Mission was established in 1826, about fifteen miles west of Toronto.

144 Rev. Wm. Ryerson. William Ryerson (1797–1872) was one of Canadian Methodism's best-known preachers.

144   Governor Metcalf. Charles Theophilus Metcalfe (1785–1846), governor of the Canadas (now Ontario and Quebec), 1843–46.

145   was held at Saugeeng. The council of Ojibwes and Ottawas was held in early July 1845.

146   Chief John Jones. He was one of the chiefs of the Ojibwes of Owen Sound. He was not related to Peter Jones of the Credit Mission. Peter Jones's brother, John Jones, was secretary of the Council.

147   kind offer of the lands. The section from the beginning of chapter 16 through this phrase is repeated verbatim, with changes in paragraphing, in Copway's *Traditional History* (146–50).

148   David Wa-wa-nosh. David Wawanosh was the son of the Ojibwe chief Joshua Wawanosh, of the Lake St. Clair band in Upper Canada.

149   Rev. Mr. Wilkinson. Henry Wilkinson, a Methodist minister.

150   Canada Methodists. This paragraph is omitted from the British edition.

150   McCue, D. Sawyer, J. Youngs. McCue may be the individual identified as one of the three chiefs of the Mud Lake Ojibwa in chapter 17, "8. Chippewas at Mud Lake." James Young (1804–48) was a Mississauga from the Credit Mission.

151   "thy blush." Shakespeare, *Hamlet* 3.41.

151   "be most miserable." Copway paraphrases 1 Cor. 15.19.

151   would be "past." 1 Sam. 15.32.

152   Sketch of the Ojebwa, or Chippeway, Nation. With slight variations in phrasing, Copway repeats this material (through the end of the paragraph under the subhead "15. Chippewas and Others, in the Township of Bedford") in his *Traditional History*, chapter 13, "The Ojebway or Chippewa Residents of Canada East," 176–95. The names of the chiefs, given at the end of the account of each group here, are placed in the subtitles in *Traditional History*, which omits the numbers of the sections.

152   was thirty thousand. Copway quotes from Samuel Gardiner Drake, "Chronicles of the Indians," *The Old Indian Chronicle*, in the entry for 1496: "Out of 100,000 Indians but about 30,000 remain upon Hispaniola." Copway cites the same figure from Drake's book, in *Traditional History* (176).

152   Col. McKinney. Copway alludes to Thomas McKenney's *History of the Indian Tribes of North America* (3 vols., 1836–44), coauthored with James Hall. He consistently spells the author's name as "McKinney." Copway praises McKenney in almost the same words in *Traditional History*: "The best work upon the Indians of North America, is that deservedly popular book written by Colonel McKinney, of New York, a gentleman of extensive information, and undoubted friend of the red man" (176).

154   Report of the Commissioners, in 1842. Copway has made selected extracts from the "Report on the Affairs of the Indians in Canada," *Journals*

*of the Legislative Assembly of Canada*, 1844–45, appendix EEE. Copway has added, at the end of each description of the respective Ojibwa communities, the names of their chiefs. The report, also known as the Bagot Commission Report, was completed in 1844 and was presented to the Legislative Assembly of Canada on 20 March 1845.

155    Sir John Colborne. Sir John Colborne, first Baron Seaton (1778–1863), lieutenant governor of Upper Canada (1828–36). In 1839 he was appointed governor-in-chief of British North America.

156    Col. M'Kie. Alexander McKee (ca. 1735–99), Indian agent and fur trader.

158    General Darling. Major-General Henry Charles Darling was in charge of the Indian Department for several years.

158    Mr. Anderson. Thomas Gummersall Anderson (1779–1875), usually referred to as "T. G. Anderson," was Indian agent on Manitoulin Island from 1837 to 1845.

159    Sir Francis Head. Sir Francis Bond Head (1793–1875), lieutenant governor of Upper Canada (1835–38).

161    Pocahontas. See note to letter 5.

161    Massasoit. Massasoit (1580–1661) was chief of the Wampanoag Indians. In 1621 he signed a peace treaty with the settlers that remained in force for fifty-four years (Drake, *Biography and History* 2: 15–17, 19–26; Hodge 2: 817).

161    Skenandoah. As a chief of the Oneidas, Skenandoa (d. 1816) became a devout Christian convert and staunch friend of the colonists. During the Revolutionary War, he supported the colonies and aided in repelling Canadian invasions. As a result of his efforts, the Oneidas declared in 1775 that they would remain neutral during the Revolutionary War (Cyrus Thomas and William Beauchamp, "Skenandoa," Hodge 2: 588).

161    Logan. Tahgahjute or John Logan (c. 1725–80), a Cayuga, was the son of an Indian woman and a white captive who was reared among the Cayugas and became a chief. Tahgahjute married into the Shawnees, gaining great influence among them. He was on good terms with the settlers until marauders murdered several Indians, including Logan's relatives. The conflict became known as Lord Dunsmore's War. Logan is most famous for his eloquent refusal to meet with Governor Dunsmore in a peace council (Drake, *Biography and History* 5: 25–28; Cyrus Thomas, "John Logan," Hodge 1: 772).

161    Kusic. Nicholas Cusick (Tuscarora, ca. 1751–1841), also known as Kayhanatso, Kagnatshon, and Kanaghtoh, a resident of the Tuscarora Village near Lewiston, New York. Cusick was commissioned as a lieutenant on 1 June 1779 and was one of the few Native American lieutenants in the Revolutionary War. He served as the personal bodyguard for the Marquis de la

Lafayette. His sabotage missions and information on British troop movement helped forestall a major campaign in central New York (*Buffalo Courier Express* 8 October 1861: 30 [information provided by Daniel F. Littlefield Jr.]; Hatcher 1: 227; White 1: 856; Graymont 197).

161   Pushmataha. This Choctaw leader (1764–1824) became *mingo*, or leader, of the Oklahannali, or Six Towns, district of the Choctaws. He successfully opposed Tecumseh's attempts to rally his people. Pushmataha converted his warriors into efficient soldiers who served under General Andrew Jackson and General Claiborne, fighting Creeks and Seminoles. He became known to the settlers as "the Indian General." General Jackson frequently said that he was the greatest and bravest Indian he ever knew (Drake, *Biography and History* 4: 57–58; "Pushmataha," Hodge 2: 236).

161   Philip. Philip (Wampanoag, c. 1640–76), Metacom or Metacomet, was the son of Massasoit. He was given the name Philip by the English. Spurious accusations of murder against Metacom provided the Wampanoags and the Puritans with grounds for attacking each other by mid-1675. Though Metacom tried to rally other New England nations, the Indian cause began to fail by spring of 1676. In August Puritan forces captured his wife and son and killed Metacom. For the next twenty-five years, they displayed his severed head on a pole in Plymouth (Drake, *Biography and History* 3: 13–40; Daniel R. Mandell, "Metacom [King Philip]," in Hoxie 373–75).

William Apess described Philip as a "noted warrior, whose natural abilities shone like those of the great and mighty Philip of Greece, or of Alexander the Great, or like those of Washington" (qtd. in O'Connell 277).

161   Tecumseh. Known also as Tecumthe or Tecumtha, Tecumseh (c. 1768–1813), a Shawnee chief, and his brother Tenskwatawa (known as "the Prophet") organized a village called the Prophet's Town on the White and Tippecanoe Rivers in Indiana. Their goal was to combine all the Indians from Canada to Florida in a confederacy to resist white encroachment. After the outbreak of the War of 1812, Tecumseh led his troops in support of the British. In 1813 he was killed in a battle with Governor William Henry Harrison on the Thames, near modern Moraviantown, Ontario. Copway published a description entitled "Scenes in the West. Death of Tecumseh" in *Copway's American Indian*, 9 August 1851, 3.1; Drake, *Biography and History* 5: 99–107; R. David Edmunds, "Tecumseh," in Hoxie 620–21.

161   Osceola. Leader of his people in the Second Seminole War, Osceola (c. 1804–38) was the son of an Englishman named William Powell and Polly Copinger, an Upper Muscogee Creek. During the First Seminole War in 1817–18, he and other Indians were captured by Andrew Jackson's soldiers. He subsequently settled among the Tallahassees, winning great fame for his patriotic actions and anti-American stance. In 1835 he led a party that killed Charley Emathla, an advocate of removal; he also killed Wiley Thompson,

the Indian agent who had emprisoned him earlier that year. These actions precipitated the Second Seminole War (1835–42). During this period he led various bands and influenced others to oppose the U.S. Army. Though outnumbered, Osceola and his warriors achieved their greatest victory in December 1835 at Withlacoochee River. U.S. troops then pursued the Seminoles from northern Florida into the swamps to the south. In 1837, exhausted and ill from malaria, Osceola was arrested at Fort Peyton, Florida, where he had gone to talk peace (Donald Fixico, "Osceola," in Hoxie 450–52).

161   Petalesharro. Petalsharo, or Pitareshru (b. 1797), was a Skidi Pawnee chief and a courageous warrior. Noted for his chivalry, he once rescued a captive Comanche woman whom the Pawnee were about to sacrifice (Drake, *Biography and History* 5: 116–18; "Petalesharo," Hodge 2: 236).

162   Edward Everett, Esq. By 1850 Edward Everett (1794–1865), a Unitarian clergyman, had served as congressman from and governor of Massachusetts, U.S. ambassador to Britain, and president of Harvard University. He was one of America's most famous orators.

167   *Legislature of South Carolina.* The text of this address is the same as it appears in the *Charleston Courier* 22 December 1848. The speech was given on 15 December 1848.

175   in its reading. The headnote is omitted in the British edition. The address, chapter 17 in that edition, is introduced with this note: "The following address before the Legislature of Pennsylvania will give some idea of the great object I have been endeavouring to bring before the different legislative bodies of the United States. At the close of the address I insert a copy of the resolution which has been passed in the North Carolina Legislature, as a specimen of the desire entertained by many for the success of my cause in America. Many others have passed similar resolutions. I have received letters of commendation from Government and from the mayors of the largest cities, and it is for this great object that I desire the kind aid of the Christian public."

178   Mr. Albert Gallatin. Albert Gallatin (1761–1849), American statesman. In 1836 he published *Synopsis of the Indian Tribes within the United States East of the Rocky Mountains and in the British and Russian Possessions in North America.* He founded the American Ethnological Society of New York in 1842.

179   sold it to the United States. In the British edition, this note is added: "That is, living on their annuities for the time being."

181   John Quincy. John W. Quinney (the Dish; 1797–1855), a Mahican Baptist preacher and Stockbridge Indian political leader.

185   that part of Canada. Copway errs here. The Six Nations only came into existence after the Tuscaroras joined the Five Nation Iroquois Confed-

eracy in the early 1720s. Further, the French only sold firearms to Christian Indian converts.

185 against the French. Contrary to Copway's assertion, the French and Spanish were allies during the Seven Years War. Spain joined the war against England in 1762.

188 before their God. In the British edition the following passage is inserted after this paragraph:

A few days after I had delivered the foregoing address, a very appropriate resolution was passed by the Pennsylvanian Legislature, approving of my plan for saving my poor brethren.

I laid a petition before the Congress of the United States at their last meeting, which will be acted on during the coming session, and I shall never cease to petition the Government until something is done in furtherance of the object I have proposed.

I subjoin a copy of the resolution passed by the Legislature of North Carolina, after I had delivered an address before that body:—

"Whereas, the condition of the various Indian tribes upon the western frontier of the United States appeals to the humanity and justice of the General Government, to devise some plan by which a permanent home may be secured to them; by which their existence as a people may be secured and perpetuated; by which their moral, intellectual, and social condition may be improved, and the blessings of civilisation and civil liberty at length secured to them:

"Be it therefore resolved, &c., that we recommend this subject to the serious consideration of the Congress of the United States, that in the exercise of their wisdom they may mature a plan by which the *Indian Tribes* inhabiting our western frontier territory may be placed more directly under the paternal care of the General Government; by which a specific region of country may be set apart for their permanent abode, secured to them for ever against further encroachment, and undisturbed by the great current of westward emigration; by which their moral, intellectual, and social condition may be improved and elevated; by which the blessings of education, civilisation, and Christianity may be imparted to them; by which they may all be brought together and united in one grand confederation, and thus prepared for the enjoyment of civil and religious liberty; and, if found practicable, they may be ultimately admitted into out Federal Union."

Governor Ch. Manly, of this State, transmitted the above resolution to the Congress of the United States.

189 Letter 1. This letter is chapter 17 in the British edition. The chapter opens with: "The following letters were originally addressed to the news-

papers in Boston. I have been requested to give them in this work, with a few of the notices from the editors of the American papers, to whom I owe a great debt of gratitude for aiding me in all that I have done for my brethren."

190   "of my heart." "To the River Charles," lines 33–36.

193   Mayor Seaton. William Winston Seaton (1785–1866), a Whig, Freemason, and Unitarian, was an associate editor of the *National Intelligencer* of Washington. He and Joseph Gales, his brother-in-law, became the exclusive reporters on Congress from 1789–1824. Seaton was the mayor of Washington DC from 1849 to 1850.

193   Mr. Washington. Probably John Augustine Washington. The president bequeathed the estate to his wife, Mary Custis Washington, for her lifetime. After she died in 1802, Bushrod Washington, the president's nephew, inherited. When he died in 1829, it was then inherited by John Augustine Washington Jr., the son of Bushrod's brother Corbin. After John Augustine's death in 1832, his widow held title to the property until her death in 1855, when it became the property of John Augustine Washington, a nephew. See Lossing 336–37, 340.

193   John S. Adams. John Stowell Adams (1823–93), son of Isaac Adams and Mary Stowell, was an editor and writer. He wrote *Town and Country* (1855) and *Half-Hour Stories* (1858), collections of inspirational short stories, and other narratives. Among the poetry anthologies he edited are: *Flora's Album* (1847), *The Floral Wreath* (1851), and *The Seasons* (1853); he also compiled *The Boston Temperance Glee Book* (1851) and *The Psalms of Life* (1857). His *5000 Musical Terms* (1851) later appeared as *Adams' New Musical Dictionary of Fifteen Thousand Technical Words, Phrases . . . Signs* (1865, 1893). Copway published several of Adams's poems, written for *Copway's American Indian*, such as "Thoughts That Come from Long Ago" (10 July 1851, 4.2), "The Love That Wanes Not" (19 July 1851, 2.1), and "The Battle of the Red Men" (4 October 1851, 3.1). See Stowell 157.

195   millions of freemen. This was a popular comparison in the Romantic period. Byron praises Washington and castigates Napoleon in *Don Juan*, canto 9, st. 8–9. The poet's "Ode to Napoleon" and *Childe Harold* (canto 3, st. 36–45) contain some of his harshest attacks on the emperor.

196   Black Hawk. For an account of Black Hawk's (Mesquakie, 1767–1838) visit to Norfolk on 5 June 1833, his visit to the Navy Yard in Gosport and the *Delaware*, and his speech delivered in Norfolk, see Drake, *Life and Adventures of Black Hawk* 205–6.

198   in the year 1607. Pocahontas or Matoaka (ca. 1596–1617), daughter of Chief Powhatan, befriended the colonists and taught Captain John Smith her language. According to the legend, first recounted by Smith in his *Generall Historie of Virginia, New England, and the Summer Isles* (1624), he was taken

236

prisoner in 1607 and was about to be killed by Powhatan when Pocahontas (then eleven or twelve) seized his head in her arms and saved his life. J. Frederick Fausz suggests that if she did interpose herself between the captain and his possible executioners and "prevailed upon her father" to free him, she was "probably performing a symbolic and highly orchestrated ceremony—a public acknowledgement that Powhatan, through his biological daughter, was adopting Smith as his 'son' and making him an honorary—but subordinate—chieftain, or 'werowance.'" ("Pocahontos (Matoaka)," in Hoxie 490–92).

After the incident she became even more attached to the colonists. Abducted by the English in 1613, she became a Christian convert, took the name Rebecca, married John Rolfe in 1614, and bore a son in 1615. The next year she accompanied Rolfe to England, where she died in 1617, just before they were to sail back to the New World. The myth of Pocohantas became the stereotype for the Indian princess who rejected her own people to protect non-Indians (Drake, *Biography and History* 4: 16–20).

In *Copway's American Indian* (1 July 1851, 3.3), Copway quoted Lydia Howard Huntley Sigourney's romanticized depiction of the rescue, which he refers to as her *Sketches of Virginia* (probably her "First Church at Jamestown, Virginia," in *Scenes in My Native Land* 21–31, which includes her poem and commentary). Pocohantas was the name of the Copways' daughter, who died in 1850 at age three.

203   *For the Chicago Tribune.* We have been unable to find an October or later issue that includes this letter. Few issues from the fall of 1849 are extant.

204   Lake Pepin. Lake Pepin is an expansion of the Mississippi River between Minnesota and Wisconsin, sixty miles below St. Anthony Falls. It is nearly twenty-two miles long and two and a half miles wide at its greatest widith. Limestone cliffs, some four hundred feet high, line Lake Pepin's shores. Red Wing, Minnesota, is at its head and Wabasha, Minnesota, at its foot ("Pepin, Lake," *Encyclopedia Americana* 1994 ed.).

211   a Forest. Edwin Forrest (1806–72), an American actor noted for his Shakespearean roles.

# Bibliography

Archival sources and city directories are cited in full on first appearance in the notes.

"Akers, (Rev.) Peter." *History of Morgan County.* Ed. William F. Short. *Historical Encyclopedia of Illinois.* Ed. Newton Bateman and Paul Selby. Chicago: Munsell, 1906. 753.

Andrews, William L. "The 1850s: The First Afro-American Literary Renaissance." *Literary Romanticism in America.* Ed. William L. Andrews. Baton Rouge: Louisiana State Univ. Press, 1981. 38–60.

Apess, William. *Eulogy on King Philip, as Pronounced at the Odeon, in Federal Street, Boston, by the Rev. William Apes, an Indian.* Boston: Author, 1836.

———. *The Experiences of Five Christian Indians of the Pequod Tribe; or, The Indian's Looking-Glass for the White Man.* Boston: Dow, 1833. Repub. as *Experience of Five Christian Indians, of the Pequod Tribe.* 2nd ed. Boston: Printed for the Publisher, 1837.

———. *A Son of the Forest. The Experience of William Apes, a Native of the Forest, Comprising a Notice of the Pequod Tribe of Indians. Written by Himself.* New York: Author, 1829. Repub. as *A Son of the Forest. The Experience of William Apes, a Native of the Forest. Written by Himself.* 2nd ed. rev. and cor. New York: Author, 1831.

Armstrong, William H. *Warrior in Two Camps: Ely S. Parker, Union General and Seneca Chief.* Buffalo NY: Buffalo Historical Society, 1978.

Aupaumut, Hendrick. "A Narrative of an Embassy to the Western Indians, from the Original Manuscript of Hendrick Aupaumut, with Prefatory Remarks by Dr. B. H. Coates." *Pennsylvania Historical Society Memoirs* 2.1 (1827): 61–131.

Bangs, Nathan. *Centenary Sermon, Preached in the Vestry-Street Church, in the City of New York, October 25, 1839, on the One Hundredth Year of Methodism.* New York: n.p., 1839.

Barclay, Wade C. *Missionary Motivation and Expansion.* New York: Board of Missions and Church Extension of the Methodist Church, 1949. Vol 1 of *Early American Methodism, 1769–1844.* 2 vols.

Beggs, Rev. S. R. *Pages from the Early History of the West and Northwest, Embracing Reminiscence and Incidents of Settlement and Growth, and Sketches of the Material and Religious Progress of the States of Ohio, Indiana, Illinois, and Missouri, with Especial Reference to the History of Methodism.* Cincinnati: Methodist Book Concern, 1868.

Bibliography

Bennett, Rev. P. S. *History of Methodism in Wisconsin. In Four Parts.* Part 3 written by Rev. James Lawson. Cincinnati: Cranston and Stowe, 1890.

Berkhofer, Robert F., Jr. *The White Man's Indian: Images of the American Indian from Columbus to the Present.* 1978. New York: Vintage, 1979.

Bieder, Robert E. *Science Encounters the Indian, 1820–1880: The Early Years of American Ethnology.* Norman: Univ. of Oklahoma Press, 1986.

Black, Mary P. "Ojibwa Power Belief System." *Anthropology of Power.* Ed. R. D. Fogelson and R. N. Adams. New York: Academic, 1977. 141–51.

Black Hawk. *Black Hawk: An Autobiography.* Trans. Antoine Le Claire, revised for publication by John B. Patterson. Orig. pub. as *Life of Ma-ka-tai-me-she-kia-kiak, or Black Hawk.* 1833. Introd. Donald Jackson. Urbana: Univ. of Illinois Press, 1955.

Blake, William. *Cross and Flame in Wisconsin: The Story of United Methodism in the Badger State.* Sun Prairie: Commission on Archives and History, Wisconsin Conference, United Methodist Church, 1973.

Boudinot, Elias. *A Star in the West; or, A Humble Attempt to Discover the Long Lost Ten Tribes of Israel,* . . . Trenton NJ: Fenton, Hutchinson, Dunham, 1816.

Boyle, Don Harrison. *The Social Order of a Frontier Community: Jacksonville, Illinois, 1825–70.* Urbana: Univ. of Illinois Press, 1978.

Brown, Jennifer S. H. "Northern Algonquins from Lake Superior and Hudson Bay to Manitoba in the Historical Period." *Native Peoples: The Canadian Experience.* Ed. R. Bruce Morrison and C. Roderick Wilson. Toronto: McClelland and Stewart, 1986, 203–36.

Brumble, H. David, III. *American Indian Autobiography.* Berkeley: Univ. of California Press, 1988.

———. *An Annotated Bibliography of American Indian and Eskimo Autobiographies.* Lincoln: Univ. of Nebraska Press, 1981.

Brunger, Ronald A. "Colclazer, Henry." *The Encyclopedia of World Methodism.* 1974. 1:535–36.

Brunson, Rev. Alfred. "A Sketch of Hole-in-the-Day." *Collections of the State Historical Society of Wisconsin* 5 (1867–69): 387–401.

———. *A Western Pioneer; or, Incidents in the Life and Times of Rev. Alfred Brunson,* . . . 2 vols. Cincinnati: Hitchcock and Walden, 1879.

Butterfield, Stephen. *Black Autobiography in America.* Amherst: Univ. of Massachusetts Press, 1974.

Careless, J. M. S., *The Union of the Canadas: The Growth of Canadian Institutions, 1841–1857.* Toronto: McClelland and Stewart, 1967.

Carroll, John. *Case and His Contemporaries.* 5 vols. Toronto: Methodist Conference Office, 1867–77.

Castle, Henry A. *Minnesota, Its Story and Biography.* 3 vols. Chicago: Lewis, 1915.

## Bibliography

Clark, Rev. Julius T. *The Ojibue Conquest: An Indian Episode*. Souvenir ed. N.p.: n.p., 1898. (Rpt. in *The Valley of the Trent*. Ed. Edwin C. Guillet. Toronto: Champlain Society, 1957. 442–62).

———. "Reminiscences of the Chippewa Chief, Hole-in-the-Day." *Collections of the State Historical Society of Wisconsin* 5 (1867–69): 378–409.

Clifton, James. "Wisconsin Death March: Explaining the Extremes in Old Northwest Indian Removal." *Transactions of the Wisconsin Academy of Sciences, Arts and Letters* 75 (1987): 1–39.

———. "The Tribal History—An Obsolete Paradigm." *American Indian Culture and Research Journal* 3.4 (1979): 81–100.

Colombo, John Robert, comp. *Writer's Map of Ontario*. Toronto: Colombo and Company, n.d. [early 1990s].

*Collection of Hymns for the Use of Native Christians or the Iroquois, to Which Are Added a Few Hymns in the Chippeway Tongue*. Trans. Peter Jones. New York: A. Hoyt, 1827.

*Combined History of Schuyler and Brown Counties, Illinois*. Philadelphia: W. R. Brink, 1882.

Cooley, Thomas. *Educated Lives: The Rise of Modern Autobiography in America*. Columbus: Ohio State Univ. Press, 1976.

Copway, George (Kahgegagahbowh). *Copway's American Indian*. 10 July–4 October 1851. British Library, Colindale.

———. "The End of the Trail." *The Saturday Evening Post* 30 March 1850. Rpt. in *The Best of the Post 1728 to 1976*. Spec. Bicentennial Issue July/August 1976: 25.

———. *The Life, History and Travels of Kah-ge-ga-gah-bowh (George Copway), a Young Indian Chief of the Ojebwa Nation, . . . with a Sketch of the Present State of the Ojebwa Nation, in Regard to Christianity and Their Future Prospects*. Albany NY: Weed and Parsons, 1847; Philadelphia: Harmstead, 1847. Repub. as *The Life, Letters and Speeches of Kah-ge-ga-gah-bowh or, G. Copway, Chief Ojibway Nation*. 2nd ed. rev. New York: Benedict, 1850; and as *Recollections of a Forest Life; or, The Life and Travels of Kah-ge-ga-gah-bowh, or George Copway, Chief of the Ojibwey Nation*. London: Gilpin, 1850; 2nd ed. 1851.

———. *The Ojibway Conquest: A Tale of the Northwest. By Kah-ge-ga-gah-bowh, or G. Copway, Chief of the Ojibway Nation*. New York: G. P. Putnam, 1850.

———. *Organization of a New Indian Territory, East of the Missouri River. Arguments and Reasons Submitted to the Honorable Members of the Senate and House of Representatives of the 31st Congress of the United States; by the Indian Chief Kah-ge-ga-gah-bouh* [sic], *or Geo. Copway*. New York: Benedict, 1850.

———. *Running Sketches of Men and Places, in England, France, Germany, Belgium, and Scotland*. New York: Riker, 1851.

———. *The Traditional History and Characteristic Sketches of the Ojibwey Nation*. London: Gilpin, 1850; Boston: Mussey, 1851. Repub. as *Indian Life and In-*

*dian History, by an Indian Author, Embracing the Traditions of the North American Indian Tribes Regarding Themselves, Particularly of That Most Important of All the Tribes, the Ojibweys.* 1858. New York: AMS, 1977.

Corkery, John. "The Irish Immigrations." *Kawartha Heritage.* Ed. A. O. C. Cole and Jean Murray Cole. Peterborough ON: Peterborough Atlas Foundation, 1981. 149–56.

Craig, G. M. *Upper Canada: The Formative Years, 1784–1841.* Toronto: McClelland and Stewart, 1963.

Cruikshank, Julie, Angela Sidney, Kitty Smith, and Annie Ned. *Life Lived Like a Story: Life Stories of Three Yukon Elders.* American Indian Lives. Lincoln: Univ. of Nebraska Press, 1990.

Cumming, John. "A Puritan among the Chippewas." *Michigan History* 51.3 (1967): 213–25.

Danziger, Edmund Jefferson, Jr. *The Chippewas of Lake Superior.* Civilization of the American Indian 148. Norman: Univ. of Oklahoma Press, 1979.

Davidson, John N. "Missions on Chequamegon Bay." *Collections of the State Historical Society of Wisconsin* 12 (1892): 434–52.

Diedrich, Mark. *The Chiefs Hole-in-the-Day of the Mississippi Chippewa.* Minneapolis: Coyote Books, 1986.

Dippie, Brian W. *Catlin and His Contemporaries.* Lincoln: Univ. of Nebraska Press, 1990.

Drake, Samuel G. *Biography and History of Indians of North America, Comprising a General Account of Them, and Details in the Lives of All the Most Distinguished Chiefs,* . . . 3rd. ed., rev. Boston: O. L. Perkins, 1834. (First edition published as *Indian Biography*).

———. *The Life and Adventures of Black Hawk: With Sketches of Keokuk, the Sac and Fox Indians, and the Late Black Hawk War.* Cincinnati: George Conclin, 1849.

———. *The Old Indian Chronicle,* . . . *and Chronicles of the Indians from the Discovery of America to the Present Time.* Boston: Antiquarian Institute, 1836.

"Ebenezer Manual Labor School." *History of Morgan County.* Ed. William F. Short. *Historical Encyclopedia of Illinois.* Ed. Newton Bateman and Paul Selby. Chicago: Munsell, 1906. 707.

Equiano, Olaudah (Gustavas Vassa). *The Interesting Narrative of the Life of Olaudah Equiano or Gustavus Vassa, the African.* 1789. Ed. and introd. Robert J. Allison. Bedford Series in History and Culture. New York: St. Martins, 1995.

Evers, Joseph C. *The History of the Southern Illinois Conference, the Methodist Church.* Nashville: Parthenon, 1964.

Field, Rev. Alvaro D. *Worthies and Workers, Both Ministers and Laymen, of the Rock River Conference.* Cincinnati: Cranston and Curtis, 1896.

## Bibliography

"First Settler in Oshkosh." *Biographical and Statistical History of the City of Oshkosh, Winnebago Co., Wisconsin, . . .* Oshkosh: Finney and Davis, 1867.

Foster, Francis Smith. *Witnessing Slavery: The Development of the Ante-bellum Slave Narratives.* Contributions in Afro-American and African Studies 46. Westport, CT: Greenwood, 1979.

Foster, Frank Hugh. "The Oberlin Ojibway Mission." *Ohio Church History Society Papers* 2 (1892): 1–25.

French, Goldwin. *Parsons and Politics: The Role of Wesleyan Methodists in Upper Canada and the Maritimes from 1780 to 1855.* Toronto: Ryerson, 1962.

Genzmer, George Harvey. "George Copway." *Dictionary of American Biography.* 1930 ed.

Graham, Elizabeth. *Medicine Man to Missionary.* Toronto: Peter Martin, 1975.

Grant, John Webster. *Moon of Wintertime: Missionaries and the Indians of Canada in Encounter since 1534.* Toronto: Univ. of Toronto Press, 1984.

Graymont, Barbara. *The Iroquois in the American Revolution.* Syracuse NY: Syracuse Univ. Press, 1972.

Guillet, Edwin C., ed. *The Valley of the Trent.* Ontario Series 1. Toronto: Champlain Society, 1957.

Hall, Rev. B. M. *The Life of Rev. John Clark.* Introd. Bishop Morris. New York: Carlton and Porter, 1857.

Harris, J. W. "Brunson, Alfred." *The Encyclopedia of World Methodism.* 1974

"Harrison's Great Speech at the Wonderful 'Log Cabin' Campaign Meeting at Ft. Meigs, in 1840." *Toledo Blade* 8 May 1890. Rpt. in *Ohio Archaeological and Historical Quarterly* 17.1 (1908): 197–207.

Hatcher, Patricia Law. *Abstract of Graves of Revolutionary Patriots.* 4 vols. Dallas: Pioneer Heritage Press, 1987.

Hickerson, Harold. "William T. Boutwell of the American Board and the Pillager Chippewa: The History of a Failure." *Ethnohistory* 12.1 (1965): 1–29.

Hobart, Chauncey. *History of Methodism in Minnesota.* Red Wing MN: Red Wing, 1887.

Hodder, F. H. "Some Phases of the Dred Scott Case." *Mississippi Valley Historical Review* 16.1 (June 1929): 3–22.

Hodge, Frederick W., ed. *Handbook of American Indians North of Mexico. Bulletin of the Bureau of American Ethnology 30.* 2 parts. Washington DC: Government Printing Office, 1907–10. Rpt. 2 vols. New York: Pageant Books, 1959.

Holt, Edgar Allan. "Party Politics in Ohio, 1840–1850." *Ohio Archaeological and Historical Publications* 37 (1928): 439–591; 38 (1929): 47–182.

Hoxie, Frederick E., ed. *Encyclopedia of North American Indians.* Boston: Houghton Mifflin, 1996.

*Indian Treaties and Surrenders.* 2 vols. Ottawa: Queen's Printer, 1891.

Jackson, Leroy. "Enmegahbowh—A Chippewa Missionary." *Collections of the State Historical Society of North Dakota* 2 (1908): 473–92.

Jennings, Francis. "Francis Parkman: A Brahmin among Untouchables." *William and Mary Quarterly.* 3rd ser. 42 (1985): 305–28.

Johnston, Basil. *The Manitous: The Spiritual World of the Ojibway.* New York: HarperCollins, 1995.

———. *Ojibway Heritage.* New York: Columbia Univ. Press, 1976.

Jones, D. William. "Canada, Geographic Board." *Handbook of the Indians of Canada.* 1913. Toronto: Coles, 1971.

Jones, Peter (Kahkewaquonaby). *History of the Ojebway Indians, with Especial Reference to Their Conversion to Christianity.* 1861. Freeport NY: Books for Libraries, 1970.

———. *Life and Journals of Kah-ke-wa-quo-na-by (Rev. Peter Jones), Wesleyan Missionary.* Published under the direction of the Missionary Committee, Canada Conference. Toronto: Anson Green at the Wesleyan Printing Establishment, 1860.

Kalb, D. G. *A Synoptic History of the First Methodist Episcopal Church in Springfield, Ill., 1820–1884.* Springfield: State Journal, 1884.

Kappler, Charles J., comp. and ed. *Indian Affairs: Laws and Treaties.* Foreword by Brantley Blue. 2 vols. New York: Interland Publishing, 1979. Rpt. of vol. 2 of *Indian Affairs: Laws and Treaties.* 2 vols. Washington DC: Government Printing Office, 1904.

Keiser, Albert. *The Indian in American Literature.* 1933. New York: Octagon, 1970.

Kelly, M. T. "Native Biographies. Beaten but Unbowed." *Saturday Night* (May 1988): 82–83, 85.

Keyes, Elisha Williams. "Julius Taylor Clark." *Proceedings of the State Historical Society of Wisconsin at Its 56th Annual Meeting.* Madison: State Historical Society of Wisconsin, 1909. 140–45.

Knobel, Dale T. "Know-Nothings and Indians: Strange Bedfellows?" *Western Historical Quarterly* 15 (1984): 175–98.

———. *Paddy and the Republic: Ethnicity and Nationality in Ante-bellum America.* Middletown CT: Wesleyan Univ. Press, 1986.

Krupat, Arnold. *For Those Who Come After: A Study of Native American Autobiography.* Berkeley: Univ. of California Press, 1985.

———. *The Voice in the Margin: Native American Literature and the Canon.* Berkeley: Univ. of California Press, 1989.

Landes, Ruth. *Ojibwe Religion and the Midéwiwin.* Madison: Univ. of Wisconsin Press, 1968.

Leaton, Rev. James. *The History of Methodism in Illinois, from 1803–1832.* Cincinnati: Walden and Stowe, 1883.

Longfellow, Henry Wadsworth. *The Letters of Henry Wadsworth Longfellow.* Ed. Andrew Hilen. 6 vols. Cambridge: Belknap-Harvard Univ. Press, 1966.

Longfellow, Samuel. *Life of Henry Wadsworth Longfellow with Extracts from His Journals and Correspondence.* 2 vols. Boston: Ticknor, 1886.

Lossing, Benson J. *The Home of Washington and Its Associations, Historical, Biographical, and Pictorial.* Rev. ed. New York: Townsend, 1866.

Martin, Norma, et al. *Gore's Landing and the Rice Lake Plains.* Cobourg ON: Heritage Gore's Landing, 1986.

McKenney, Thomas L. *Sketches of a Tour to the Lakes, of the Character and Customs of the Chippeway Indians, and Incidents Connected with the Treaty of Fond Du Lac.* 1827. Minneapolis: Ross and Haines, 1959.

Melton, J. Gordon. *Log Cabins to Steeples: The Complete Story of the United Methodist Church in Illinois, Including All Constituent Elements of the United Methodist Church.* N.p. [Chicago?]: Commissions on Archives and History, Northern, Central, and Southern Illinois Conferences, 1974.

Murphy, Lawrence. *Religion and Education on the Frontier: A Life of Stephen Peet.* Dubuque IA: *Telegraph Herald,* 1942.

Murray, David. *Forked Tongues: Speech, Writing and Representation in North American Indian Texts.* Bloomington: Indiana Univ. Press, 1991.

Neill, Rev. Edward D. "History of the Ojibways, and Their Connection with Fur Traders, Based upon Official and Other Records." *History of the Ojibway Nation.* By William Warren. Minneapolis: Ross and Haines, 1957, 1970, 1974. 395–510.

Noah, M. M. *Discourse on the Evidences of the American Indians Being the Descendants of the Lost Tribes of Israel.* New York: James Van Norden, 1837.

Nute, Grace Lee. "The Edmund Franklin Ely Papers." *Minnesota History* 6.4 (1925): 343–54.

Occom, Samson. *A Sermon Preached by Samsom Occom, . . . at the Execution of Moses Paul, an Indian, Who Was Executed at New Haven, September 1, 1772, for the Murder of Moses Cook, . . .* 10th ed. Bennington VT: William Watson, 1772. *Heath Anthology of American Literature.* Ed. Paul Lauter. 2nd ed. Lexington MA: Heath, 1994. 1:947–62.

———. "A Short Narrative of My Life." *Heath Anthology of American Literature.* Ed. Paul Lauter. 2nd ed. Lexington MA: Heath, 1994. 1:942–47. [Note: not published in Occom's lifetime.]

O'Connell, Barry, ed. *On Our Own Ground: The Complete Writings of William Apess, a Pequot.* Native Americans of the North East: Culture, History, and the Contemporary. Amherst: Univ. of Massachusetts Press, 1992.

Parker, Arthur C. *The Life of General Ely S. Parker.* Buffalo NY: Buffalo Historical Society, 1919.

Parkman, Francis. *Letters of Francis Parkman.* Ed. and introd. Wilbur R. Jacobs. 2 vols. Norman: Univ. of Oklahoma Press, 1960.

Pascal, Roy. *Design and Truth in Autobiography.* Cambridge: Harvard Univ. Press, 1960.

Pearce, Roy Harvey. *Savagism and Civilization: A Study of the Indian and the American Mind.* 1953. Introd. Arnold Krupat. Afterword Roy Harvey Pearce. Berkeley: Univ. of California Press, 1988.

Pennewell, Almer. *The Methodist Movement in Northern Illinois.* Sycamore IL: *Sycamore Tribune*, 1942.

Pilling, James Constantine. *Bibliography of the Algonquian Languages.* Washington DC: Government Printing Office, 1891.

Pitezel, John H. *Life of Rev. Peter Marksman, an Ojibwa Missionary, Illustrating the Triumphs of the Gospel among the Ojibwa Indians.* Cincinnati: Western Methodist Book Concern, 1891.

Prindle, Rev. Cyrus. *Memoir of the Rev. Daniel Meeker Chandler; for Several Years Missionary among the Indians, at Ke-wa-we-non, and Sault De. St. Marie, Lake Superior.* Middlebury VT: Ephraim Maxham, 1842.

"The Rev. Daniel McMullen. Ministerial Obituary." *Canadian Methodist Magazine* 2 (1875): 188–92.

Riggs, Rev. S. R. "The Dakota Mission." *Collections of the Minnesota Historical Society* 3 (1870–80): 115–28.

———. "Sketch of Mr. Pond's Life." *The IAPI OAYE (Word Carrier)* April 1878. Rpt. in "Memorial Notices of Rev. Gideon H. Pond by Messrs. [Rev. Stephen R.] Riggs, [Rev. Thomas S.] Williamson, and [General H.] Sibley." *Collections of the Minnesota Historical Society* 3 (1870–80): 358–71.

Ruoff, A. LaVonne Brown. "Three Nineteenth-Century American Indian Autobiographers." *Redefining American Literary History.* Ed. A. LaVonne Brown Ruoff and Jerry W. Ward Jr. New York: Modern Language Association, 1990. 251–69.

Schmalz, Peter S. *The Ojibwa of Southern Ontario.* Toronto: Univ. of Toronto Press, 1991.

Schoolcraft, Henry Rowe. *Algic Researches, Comprising Inquiries Respecting the Mental Characteristics of the North American Indians.* 2 vols. New York: Harper, 1839.

———. *Narrative of an Expedition through the Upper Mississippi to Itasca Lake. . . .*New York: Harper, 1834.

Seyersted, Per. "The Indian in Knickerbocker's New Amsterdam." *The Indian Historian* 7.3 (1974): 14–28.

Shaw, Rev. James. *Twelve Years in America: Being Observations on the Country, the People, Institutions and Religion; with Notices of Slavery and the Late War. . . .* Chicago: Poe and Hitchcock, 1867.

Shea, Daniel B., Jr. *Spiritual Autobiography in Early America*. Princeton: Princeton Univ. Press, 1968.

Shulman, Robert. "Parkman's Indians and American Violence." *The Massachusetts Review* 12 (1971): 221–39.

Sigourney, Mrs. L. H. *Scenes in My Native Land*. Boston: James Monroe, 1845.

"Simpson, James W." *Minnesota Biographies, 1655–1912. Collections of the Minnesota Historical Society* 14 (1912): 706.

Smith, Alice Elizabeth. *James Duane Doty, Frontier Promoter*. Madison: State Historical Society of Wisconsin, 1954.

Smith, Donald B. "The Dispossession of the Mississauga Indians: A Missing Chapter in the Early History of Upper Canada." *Ontario History* 73 (1981): 67–87.

———. "Kahgegahgahbowh." *Dictionary of Canadian Biography, 1861–70*. 1976 ed.

———. "The Life of George Copway or Kah-ge-ga-gah-bowh (1818–1869)—And a Review of His Writings." *Journal of Canadian Studies* 23.3 (fall 1988): 5–38.

———. *Sacred Feathers: The Reverend Peter Jones (Kahkewaquonaby) and the Mississauga Indians*. American Indian Lives. Lincoln: Univ. of Nebraska Press, 1987.

———. "Who Are the Mississauga?" *Ontario History* 67 (1975): 211–22.

Smith, Theresa S. *The Island of the Anishnaabeg: Thunders and Water Monsters in the Traditional Ojibwe Life-World*. Moscow: Univ. of Idaho Press, 1995.

Spindler, Timothy J. "George Copway: Cultural Broker and Communicator." Master's thesis. Univ. of Wisconsin–Eau Claire, 1990.

Sproat, Florantha Thompson. "La Pointe Letters." *Wisconsin Magazine of History* 16.1 (1932): 85–95, 199–210.

Squier, E. G. "Historical and Mythological Traditions of the Algonquins." *The American Whig Review* February 1849. Rpt. in *The Indian Miscellany*. Ed. W. W. Beach. Albany NY: J. Munsell, 1877. 9–42.

Starr, G. A. *Defoe and Spiritual Autobiography*. Princeton: Princeton Univ. Press, 1965.

Stepto, Robert B. *From Behind the Veil: A Study of Afro-American Narratives*. Urbana: Univ. of Illinois Press, 1979.

Stowell, William H. H. *Stowell Genealogy: A Record of the Descendants of Samuel Stowell of Hingham, Mass*. Rutland VT: Tuttle, 1922.

Sturtevant, William. "Creek into Seminole." *North American Indians in Historical Perspective*. Ed. Eleanor Burke Leacock and Nancy Oestreich Lurie. New York: Random, 1971. 92–128.

Swann, Brian, and Arnold Krupat. Introduction. *I Tell You Now: Auto-*

*biographical Essays.* Ed. Brian Swann and Arnold Krupat. American Indian Lives. Lincoln: Univ. of Nebraska Press, 1987. ix–xv.

Tanner, Helen Hornbeck, ed. *Atlas of Great Lakes Indian History.* Civilization of the American Indian 174. Norman: Univ. of Oklahoma Press and Newberry Library, 1987.

Toelken, Barre. "Cultural Bilingualism and Composition: Native American Education at the University of Oregon." *English for American Indians* (1971): 19–32.

Trennert, Robert A. *Alternative to Extinction. Federal Indian Policy and the Beginnings of the Reservation System, 1846–51.* Philadelphia: Temple Univ. Press, 1975.

Vecsey, Christopher. *Traditional Ojibwa Religion and Its Historical Changes.* Philadelphia: American Philosophical Society, 1983.

Vernon, Walter N., and Ruth M. Vernon. "Indian Missions of North America." *The Encyclopedia of World Methodism.* 1974 ed.

Vogel, Virgil J. *Indian Place Names in Illinois.* Pamphlet Series 4. Springfield: Illinois State Historical Society, 1963.

Wallace, Anthony F. C. *The Long, Bitter Trail: Andrew Jackson and the Indians.* New York: Hill and Wang, 1993.

Ward, Rev. F. DeW. *Churches of Rochester. Ecclesiastical History of Rochester, N.Y. . . .* Rochester: Erastus Darrow, 1871.

Warren, William W. *History of the Ojibway Nation, Based upon Traditions and Oral Statements. Collections of the Minnesota Historical Society* 5 (1885). Minneapolis: Ross and Haines, 1957, 1970, 1974. Intro. by W. Roger Buffalohead. Minneapolis: Minnesota Historical Society, 1984.

White, Virgil D., ed. *Genealogical Abstracts of Revolutionary War Pension Files.* 4 vols. Waynesboro TN: National Historical, 1990.

Williams, J. Fletcher. "Memoir of William W. Warren." *History of the Ojibway Nation.* William W. Warren. Minneapolis: Ross and Haines, 1957, 1970, 1974. Minneapolis: Minnesota Historical Scoiety, 1984.

Zolla, Elemire. *The Writer and the Shaman.* New York: Harcourt, 1973.

# Index

In the American Indian Lives series

*Singing an Indian Song*
*A Biography of D'Arcy McNickle*
By Dorothy R. Parker

*Crashing Thunder*
*The Autobiography of an American Indian*
Edited by Paul Radin

*Turtle Lung Woman's Granddaughter*
By Delphine Red Shirt and Lone Woman

*Telling a Good One*
*The Process of a Native American Collaborative Biography*
By Theodore Rios and Kathleen Mullen Sands

*Sacred Feathers*
*The Reverend Peter Jones (Kahkewaquonaby) and the Mississauga Indians*
By Donald B. Smith

*Grandmother's Grandchild*
*My Crow Indian Life*
By Alma Hogan Snell
Edited by Becky Matthews
Foreword by Peter Nabokov

*No One Ever Asked Me*
*The World War II Memoirs of an Omaha Indian Soldier*
By Hollis D. Stabler
Edited by Victoria Smith

*Blue Jacket*
*Warrior of the Shawnees*
By John Sugden

*I Tell You Now*
*Autobiographical Essays by Native American Writers*
Edited by Brian Swann and Arnold Krupat

*Postindian Conversations*
By Gerald Vizenor and A. Robert Lee

*Chainbreaker*
*The Revolutionary War Memoirs of Governor Blacksnake*
As told to Benjamin Williams
Edited by Thomas S. Abler

*Standing in the Light*
*A Lakota Way of Seeing*
By Severt Young Bear and R. D. Theisz

*Sarah Winnemucca*
By Sally Zanjani

CPSIA information can be obtained at www.ICGtesting.com
Printed in the USA
BVOW021507150712

295194BV00002B/4/A